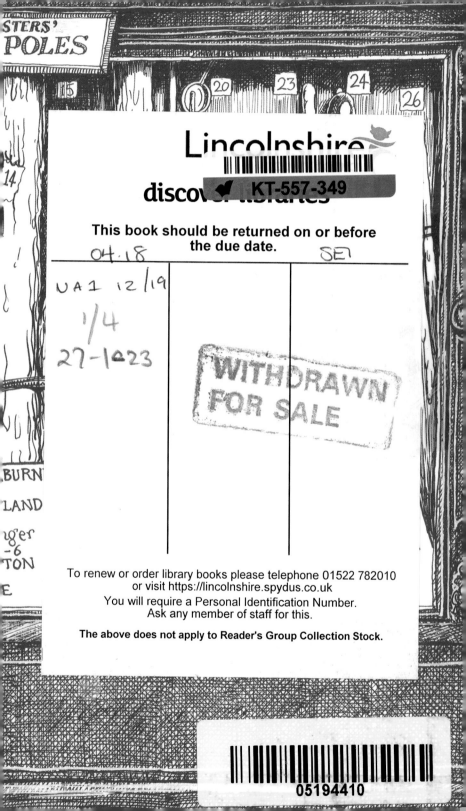

Gimson's
PRIME
MINISTERS

By the same author

The Desired Effect
Boris: The Adventures of Boris Johnson
Gimson's Kings & Queens: Brief Lives of the Monarchs since 1066

Gimson's PRIME MINISTERS

BRIEF LIVES *from* WALPOLE *to* MAY

BY ANDREW GIMSON

illustrated by

Martin Rowson

◨ SQUARE PEG

1 3 5 7 9 10 8 6 4 2

Square Peg, an imprint of Vintage,
20 Vauxhall Bridge Road,
London SW1V 2SA

Square Peg is part of the Penguin Random House group of companies
whose addresses can be found at global.penguinrandomhouse.com

Penguin
Random House
UK

Text copyright © Andrew Gimson 2018
Illustrations copyright © Martin Rowson 2018

First published by Square Peg in 2018

Penguin.co.uk/vintage

A CIP catalogue record for this book is available from the British Library

ISBN 9781910931431

Typeset in India by Integra Software Services Pvt. Ltd, Pondicherry

Printed and bound in Great Britain by Clays Ltd, St Ives plc

Penguin Random House is committed to a sustainable future for our
business, our readers and our planet. This book is made from Forest
Stewardship Council® certified paper.

For Sally

Never was man more flattered nor more abused; and his long power was probably the chief cause of both.

LORD CHESTERFIELD ON
SIR ROBERT WALPOLE, PRIME MINISTER 1721–42

Yes, I have climbed to the top of the greasy pole.

BENJAMIN DISRAELI
ON BECOMING PRIME MINISTER IN 1868

Never forget, Arthur, the garden belongs to Number 10, and has nothing to do with Number 11.

LORD ROSEBERY, WHO HAD RESIGNED FROM
THE PRIME MINISTERSHIP SEVEN YEARS
EARLIER, ADVISING ARTHUR BALFOUR ON
BECOMING PRIME MINISTER IN 1902

There is one thing about politics that I think cannot be disputed: if a man stays in them long enough, they nearly always reveal him for what he is, and he tends to get not only what he deserves, but to find in his fate the reflection of his own strength and weakness.

CLEMENT ATTLEE, PRIME MINISTER 1945–51

Gladstone and Disraeli never had to put up with this.

HAROLD MACMILLAN AS PRIME MINISTER, WHILE WALKING DOWN A LITTER-FILLED CORRIDOR IN A HOTEL IN LLANDUDNO DURING THE CONSERVATIVE PARTY CONFERENCE IN 1962

CONTENTS

INTRODUCTION

To become prime minister, and play the role with some slight degree of success, you will need the following qualities:

1. Courage.
2. Luck.
3. Hunger for power.
4. Eloquence, including the ability to think on your feet in the Commons.
5. The ability to distribute patronage in such a way as to gratify to a sufficient degree the appetites of your followers. Contenders for the prime ministership who have thought themselves too grand to do this have failed.
6. A different style to your predecessor, of whom people have grown sick. Soon they will be sick of you.
7. An acute feel for public opinion, and, in the earlier part of this book, an equally acute sense of how to manage the monarch. The longer you are in Downing Street, the harder it becomes to see things as others see them, or even to remember this is necessary.
8. The capacity to rise to a crisis, and give the nation its idea of itself.
9. An understanding of the money, which is the most important thing controlled by the Commons.
10. Respectability, or at least the absence of embarrassing eccentricities.

11. The energy and stamina to do (and to want to do) very heavy work. Overwork has shortened the lives of many of the people in this book.

12. The willingness and skill to perform that most humiliating manoeuvre, the U-turn. A free people cannot be ordered about: you are there to persuade MPs, and the wider nation, to follow your lead, which cannot be in a direction they do not want to take. You are not a tyrant, and must sometimes have the common prudence to change course. So although you need to know when to stick to your guns, you must also convey a tactful awareness of your own vulnerability.

The prime minister requires, in fact, a bizarre combination of qualities. He or she must be at once ordinary and extraordinary, conventional and innovative, safe and audacious, banal and brilliant, a follower and a leader, sensitive to every change in the political weather but tough enough to endure terrible disasters, on the side of the people but able to build a Cabinet from members of the elite.

For a short time, a certain individual may manage to do this better than anyone else. But it is not something anyone is likely to be able to do for very long. The average length of time each of the prime ministers in this book has spent in office, not always in a single stint, is five and a half years. At the top end of the scale is Sir Robert Walpole, who was in power for twenty years and 309 days. At the bottom we find George Canning, a brilliant and amusing figure, but prime minister for only 119 days.

The secret of the prime ministers is that they are weak. We give them an impossible job and blame them when they fail to perform it. The prime minister serves as a kind of glorified scapegoat. It is notable how many of them are remembered, if at all, for a single failure: Lord North for losing the American colonies, Neville Chamberlain for the fruitless appeasement of Hitler, Sir

Anthony Eden for the Suez debacle, Tony Blair for the Iraq War, David Cameron for losing the EU referendum. Throughout the twentieth century, British prime ministers strove to cope with the decline and fall of the British Empire, something even Winston Churchill could not avert.

In the eighteenth century, the prime minister's function was to take the blame on behalf of the monarch. Nowadays, he or she is there to take the blame on behalf of the people, and often on behalf of colleagues too. The Conservatives treated one of their most remarkable leaders, Sir Robert Peel, as a renegade, while Labour MPs came to regard Ramsay MacDonald, who had done so much to create their party, as the worst traitor of all. The role of prime minister is essentially a sacrificial one.

Not that those who compete against each other for it are inclined to see it in this light. They believe they will be powerful, and they assure us they have the solutions we seek, however disappointing their predecessors may have proved. And it is true that most of them have a honeymoon period during which we allow ourselves to share in their optimism, for as voters we are torn between conflicting impulses. We long to believe we have found a saviour, but are determined to throw overboard whoever fails to save us. We allow the stage to be dominated for a time by a successful prime minister, but then restore equality (for which all democracies have a deep yearning) by dragging that individual back down to our own level, often with brutal abruptness.

Previous writers have sought to define the office of prime minister in terms of its fluctuating powers: an approach that can lead to arid constitutional theorising. In this book, temperament is restored to the central place it always in practice occupies.

The greatest prime ministers have tended to be fighters and gamblers. But after a warrior PM the country often wants a calmer, more consensual figure, who may have a touch of greatness too. Clement Attlee, who succeeded Churchill, was the greatest master of understatement in British history, but also, by conducting a team of strong ministers, one of the greatest reformers.

There are very few complete duds in this book, for the Commons can detect a dud as soon as he or she begins to speak. For the same reason, it is virtually impossible for a criminal, or a demagogue, to become prime minister. Someone like Donald Trump could not get to 10 Downing Street. The Commons sees through, and will not tolerate, that kind of person. This check on the abuse of power is highly effective, but generally overlooked. Three of the greatest failures in this book – Lord Bute, Lord Aberdeen and Lord Rosebery – failed because they had never sat in the Commons.

All but four prime ministers (Spencer Compton, Pitt the Younger, A. J. Balfour and Edward Heath) have been married, though some were widowed either before or during their time in office. In many cases a devoted and intelligent spouse has been of the greatest help to a prime minister.

I have met every prime minister since Margaret Thatcher, but although most of them have remarkable qualities, none has displayed her force of personality. In the 1980s, I went to lunch in 10 Downing Street with her, along with about six other journalists, all of them older and more distinguished than myself. She astonished me by delivering an economics lecture in tones which might have been designed to impress a few simple truths on a class of 7-year-olds. In the weeks after this event, my fellow guests astonished me by reproducing, in their columns, much of what she had said. She was, after all, prime minister, and journalists like to be able to retail inside dope to their readers.

Tony Blair laughed very charmingly when I inadvertently insulted him while lunching with him at the Gay Hussar, a few years before he seized control of the Labour Party. I gained more of my political education from the Sunday lunches given by Shirley and Bill Letwin in their house off Regent's Park, where the politics of the day were discussed with bohemian irreverence by about a dozen guests, sometimes including the philosopher Michael Oakeshott or the politician Sir Keith Joseph. In 1983, Shirley and Bill's son, Oliver, suggested I come and work in the Conservative Research Department in Smith Square. I protested that I had until that point had nothing to do with the Conservative Party, but he said this did not matter, as they just needed someone who could write.

Having taken the job, I began to immerse myself in political history, for to write about the politics of the present day without discovering what went before is to suffer from a kind of self-inflicted short-sightedness. In particular, I began reading the biographies of such giants as Disraeli and Gladstone, which tend to be extremely long. I wished there was a single, relatively short book where I could begin by acquainting myself with the whole sweep of British political history over the last three centuries, told in the form of brief lives. This book is my attempt, after thirty-five years of reading and writing about politics, to fill that gap.

When one is young, giants seem to walk the earth, and I profited from the talk and work of many illustrious figures, including Peter Utley, Alistair Cooke (now Lord Lexden), Alan Watkins, Ferdinand Mount, Frank Johnson, Peregrine Worsthorne and Charles Moore. In 1984, the latter offered me my first job in journalism, as deputy editor of *The Spectator*. I have since contributed to most parts of what used to be called Fleet Street, have lived in Germany for six years to see if they do things better there, and spent seven years as the *Daily Telegraph*'s parliamentary sketch-writer.

Little is said here about the eleven monarchs who occupied the throne in this period, for their characters have already been drawn in *Gimson's Kings and Queens*. And for full details of the political transactions touched on in these pages, the reader will have to look elsewhere. If these had been included, the book would have become intolerably long.

There is no bibliography, because in the age of Google, it is seldom difficult to trace a book or a quotation. The most enjoyable books I have read include Bagehot's essay on *The Character of Sir Robert Peel*, Disraeli's *Sybil* and *Coningsby*, Maynard Keynes's few pages entitled *Mr Lloyd George: A Fragment*, Winston Churchill's essays on Rosebery, Asquith and Balfour in *Great Contemporaries*, Chips Channon on Chamberlain in his *Diaries*, Roy Jenkins's essays on various prime ministers in *The Chancellors*, and *Attlee's Great Contemporaries*, a collection of Attlee's journalism edited by Frank Field. *The Oxford Dictionary of National Biography*, available online for anyone with a public library card, is a good first port of call for almost any subject. Of long and admirable books about prime ministers there is no end, but two which might be overlooked are Lord Rosebery's *Chatham: His Early Life and Connections*, and Robert Blake's first book, *The Unknown Prime Minister: the Life and Times of Andrew Bonar Law*, in which the author observes that 'such a book, if it is to have any real value, cannot be short'.

I cannot end without thanking Martin Rowson for his beautiful drawings, my agent, Andrew Gordon, for his invariably astute guidance, Michael Crick and William Franklin for advice about obscure and useful books, my publishers at Square Peg, Rowan Yapp, Harriet Dobson, Sophie Harris and Jo Whitford, for creating such a handsome volume, and above all my wife, Sally Gimson, who greets so much of what I say with a bracing incredulity.

Andrew Gimson, Gospel Oak, October 2017

A SHORT NOTE ON THE BRITISH CONSTITUTION

Before the Great Reform Bill of 1832, the monarch decided who to send for to be prime minister, and even after that landmark he or she enjoyed a degree of discretion. But there was never any point in sending for someone who could not command a majority in the Commons, so parliamentary ability was from the first indispensable.

The first two Hanoverian kings, George I (1714–27) and George II (1727–60), had been brought over from Germany by Parliament because they were Protestants, so were reckoned to favour liberty rather than absolutism. But as foreigners, who longed to spend time in Hanover, they needed someone who could run the British government for them, and obtain for them a handsome income voted by Parliament: a circumstance which greatly favoured the development of the office of prime minister.

In order to control the Commons, it was necessary to have a band of followers. In the eighteenth century, the Whigs and the Tories contended against each other for power, with the Whigs at first getting very much the better of it. General elections took place, but were not yet of decisive importance. As will be illustrated in the account of Sir Robert Walpole, patronage played a large role in securing and maintaining a parliamentary majority, but politics was an intensely competitive business, and the best players were brilliant. From the first, there was a battle between those who were In, so enjoying the fruits of office, and those who were Out, so resentful of their exclusion. Often the latter group gathered round the heir to the throne, hoping for better things in the next reign.

In the century after 1832, the vote was extended to more and more people, until in 1928 it became universal for women as well as men. General elections became decisive, and modern political parties were formed in order to fight them: the Conservatives from the 1830s, the Liberals from 1859 and Labour from 1900. Great men – Churchill leaps to mind – often chafed under the party system, but also shaped it to their and the country's needs.

A SHORT NOTE ON NAMES

In order to render the book easier to follow, I have disregarded the British aristocracy's habit of frequently changing their names. Each prime minister is referred to by whichever name he or she is best known. So Pitt the Elder remains 'Pitt', even after he has been ennobled as Earl of Chatham.

For some reason, this self-denying ordinance broke down while I was writing about Lord Salisbury, who in youth is Lord Robert Cecil, and becomes for a short time Lord Cranborne, before entering the House of Lords as Lord Salisbury.

The term 'prime minister' is used even for the long period when 'First Lord of the Treasury' – the title which still appears on the letter box at 10 Downing Street – would be more correct.

SIR ROBERT WALPOLE

Lived 1676–1745; prime minister 1721–42

Sir Robert Walpole invented the office of prime minister, and held it for longer than any of his successors. This fat, affable, shrewd, crude, fearless man had such a keen instinct for power, and for other men's weaknesses, that he dominated the House of Commons for almost twenty-one years. In his portraits, he looks as trenchant, grounded and confident as anyone in this book. His enemies accused him of buying votes and monopolising power, but what really annoyed them was that he worked the system better than they did, and kept them out.

He made himself indispensable to the first two Hanoverian kings and set, by his practice rather than by any theory, a constitutional pattern which has endured to this day.

Walpole was born in 1676 at Houghton in Norfolk, the son of a prosperous squire. He was educated at Eton and at King's College, Cambridge, and was intended for the Church, but the death of his two elder brothers enabled him to go into politics instead. He entered the Commons in 1701, and soon demonstrated his inestimable value to the Whig cause both as a debater and as a minister. In 1712, the Tories managed to get him confined to the Tower of London on trumped-up charges of corruption, but this pseudo-martyrdom increased his reputation.

With the arrival from Hanover in 1714 of George I, the Tories, some of whom sympathised with the rival House of Stuart, were swept from office and the Whigs, including Walpole, were back. He became First Lord of the Treasury and Chancellor of the Exchequer, where he demonstrated his acute grasp of financial affairs. In 1717, he followed his brother-in-law, Townshend, into Opposition, but three years later the South Sea Bubble – the maddest speculative fever ever to grip the country – burst, and Walpole seized his chance.

A large part of the ruling class was ruined. Walpole, who had made a huge personal profit by selling before the crash, used his gift of oratory and his financial acumen to restore confidence, and to defend both the Crown and his fellow Whigs against attack. His rivals fell away and his pre-eminence began.

George I did not speak English well, and Walpole did not speak either French or German, which were the King's preferred languages, so the two men conversed in dog Latin. The King's heart remained in Hanover, to which he made frequent visits: he needed someone to govern Britain, while the British needed a leader who would not allow Hanoverian interests to prevail. Walpole fulfilled both requirements.

In order to look like a normal country squire, he munched little red Norfolk apples during Commons debates, and let it be known that he opened letters from his gamekeeper before those to do with government business. He loved hunting, in Richmond Park if he could not get down to Norfolk, and said of himself that he was 'No Saint, no Spartan, no reformer'. He was at ease, in an eighteenth-century way, with sex and money and self-enrichment at public expense. He took a mistress twenty-five years younger than himself, the witty and beautiful Molly Skerret, whom he married after his first wife died.

Lord Chesterfield, a polished aristocrat, could not help feeling shocked by Walpole:

In private life he was good natured, Chearfull, social. Inelegant in his manners, loose in his morals. He had a coarse wit, which he was too free of for a Man in his Station, as it is always inconsistent with dignity. He was very able as a Minister, but without a certain Elevation of mind ... He was both the ablest Parliament man, and the ablest manager of a Parliament, that I believe ever lived. An artful rather than an eloquent speaker, he saw as by intuition, the disposition of the House, and pressed or receded accordingly. So clear in stating the most intricate matters, especially in the finances, that while he was speaking the most ignorant thought that they understood what they really did not.

Walpole refused the offer of a peerage. He knew the Commons was harder to control than the Lords, so demanded his personal attention. His language was as crude as any backwoodsman's: he said of Queen Caroline that he 'took the right sow by the ear', for it was through his friendship with her that he was able to control George II. Others supposed the way to the King's favour lay through his mistresses. They were mistaken. Caroline did not try to stand between her husband and his mistresses. She contented herself with ensuring that the mistresses had no power.

In 1727, George II had attempted, on ascending the throne, to get rid of Walpole. But within a few days it was clear that only Walpole could persuade the Commons to grant a handsome income to the royal couple. He was recalled to service, and the Civil List went through without a division. One mischief-maker tried to make trouble between Walpole and Caroline by telling her he had referred to her as 'the fat bitch'. She sent the chief minister the message that 'the fat bitch had forgiven him'.

Walpole described, to his successor Henry Pelham, the methods needed to steer George II:

Address and management are the weapons you must fight and defend with: plain truths will not be relished at first in opposition to prejudices, conceived and infused in favour of his own partialities; and you must dress up all you offer, with the appearance of no other view or tendency, but to promote his service in his own way, to the utmost of your power. And the more you can make anything appear to be his own, and agreeable to his declarations and orders, given to you before he went, the better you will be heard ...

We may smile at how tactfully the King had to be managed, but is it really much different to how an audience of voters, or of party activists, has to be managed today?

'All these men have their price,' Walpole once said, indicating some opposition Members of Parliament. He used patronage to entrench his power: he knew how to buy the support he needed by distributing offices of profit to MPs. He and his family carried off many of the plums, leading to bitter attacks on the 'Robinocracy', Robin being one of his nicknames; others were

Screenmaster-General, in reference to the way he shielded the Establishment, and Sir Bluestring, because of his membership of the Order of the Garter, whose sash he wore in the Commons. He took no interest in literature, and was assailed by the best writers of his time – Swift, Pope, Gay, Fielding – but this seems to have done him no harm. He was, however, so annoyed by the portrayal of himself as a thief in *The Beggar's Opera*, and by offensive allusions in the same work to his mistress, that he arranged for the passing in 1737 of the Licensing Act, under which, until 1968, all new plays had to be approved by the Lord Chamberlain. Gay, the offending author, had his next play banned.

Walpole used the spoils of office to build a Palladian masterpiece, Houghton Hall in Norfolk, which he filled with a stupendously expensive collection of paintings, later sold to Catherine the Great and today adorning the Hermitage in St Petersburg. Houghton is an intimate palace: it impresses you with its grandeur and classical statuary, but the rooms are small enough for the guests to be worked on by their genial host. His income was vast, but his debts were even larger, and were not paid off until many years after his death.

Unlike many notable leaders, Walpole hated the expense of war and wanted the country to grow rich in peace. This policy he managed to follow for many years, cutting taxes and promoting trade. Under his skilful management, the national debt was reduced by means of a sinking fund, and interest rates fell to only 3 per cent. In 1733, he introduced the Excise Bill, a reform of the customs duties on wine and tobacco which would have eliminated smuggling. This reasonable proposal was immensely unpopular and Walpole only saved himself by abandoning it.

The King yearned for a land war in Europe, in which he could demonstrate his martial prowess, while the City of London wanted a naval war to capture the trade of its competitors, but for many years Walpole managed to avert hostilities.

When the War of Jenkins' Ear against Spain broke out in 1739, his power was thrown into question, for he was not a war leader. His great ally, Queen Caroline, had died two years before, he had forced his most able rivals into Opposition and his own health was failing. The war started badly, as is usual in Britain, and Walpole took the blame, as is also usual. In 1741, he was accused in a Commons censure motion of making himself 'sole and prime minister'. The term 'prime minister' was at this time a gross insult, implying belligerent ambition and grasping self-interest.

Walpole met this attack with his usual intrepid self-confidence, and managed to hang on. In February 1742, he lost control of the Commons, resigned and was elevated to the House of Lords, where he remarked with wry amusement to another newly created peer: 'My Lord Bath, you and I are now as insignificant men as any in England.' That was an exaggeration: Walpole's enemies, who had spent years looking forward to his impeachment, narrowly failed to bring it about, and the King still valued his advice. In 1745, Walpole died of a lacerated bladder, caused by a remedy he had taken for kidney stones.

SIR SPENCER COMPTON

Lived 1673–1743; prime minister 1742–43

A capacity for rising to the level of events is a necessary qualification for success as a prime minister, and Sir Spencer Compton did not possess it. He was described by Lord Rosebery (prime minister in 1894–95) as 'the favourite nonentity of George II'. That king had previously employed him to run his household, and was attracted by Compton's punctilious subservience, which seemed to promise scope for royal assertion. So, on ascending the throne in 1727, George II told his father's first minister, Sir Robert Walpole, to go to Sir Spencer Compton and take instructions from him.

Compton was three years older than Walpole, and from a grander family. He served as Speaker of the House of Commons and also as Paymaster General, an office of colossal profit. But he was frightened out of his wits by the King's call to serve as first minister. His first task was to write the speech George II would deliver to the Privy Council. He asked Walpole to write it for him. Within a few days Compton made the humiliating admission that he felt unequal to the task of being first minister, and Walpole was reinstated. Compton, as a kind of consolation prize, was made Earl of Wilmington. Historians do not regard this episode as a prime ministership: it simply demonstrated Compton's inadequacy.

Yet when Walpole fell in 1742, George II's choice again fell on Compton, as we shall continue for the sake of simplicity to call him. He was a figurehead, but this suited his more able rivals, for the likelihood was that he would be a transient figure. Politics was dominated by foreign policy, and that was in the hands of the brilliant Lord Carteret.

In the summer of 1743, a few days after George II had led his troops into action against the French at Dettingen, the last British monarch to do so, Compton died in office. He is the only prime minister of whom no full-length biography has been written, and Lord Hervey's description of him explains why no ambitious young historian has felt tempted to fill the gap:

A plodding, heavy fellow, with great application, but no talents, and vast complaisance for a Court, without any address ... His only pleasures were money and eating; his only knowledge forms and precedents.

HENRY PELHAM

Lived 1694–1754; prime minister 1743–54

Other men were cleverer than Henry Pelham, but none was steadier. He possessed the judgement and tenacity needed to stay at the top for over a decade, a record of continuous service broken only (in ascending order) by Thatcher, North, Liverpool, Pitt the Younger and Walpole. His tolerance and good humour are caught in his reply to a proposal that the publication of (often largely invented) reports of Commons debates be punished with fines and imprisonment: 'Let them alone; they make better speeches for us than we can make for ourselves.'

He was born in 1694, and in 1715 commanded a troop of dragoons, raised in Sussex by him and his elder brother, which helped defeat the Jacobite rebellion. For this act of loyalty to the Hanoverian dynasty, which had only arrived on the British throne the previous year, the elder brother was created Duke of Newcastle and proceeded to help the younger to enter the Commons. Here, Pelham soon demonstrated his mastery of financial questions, his unremitting diligence and his gift for explaining things in clear, unshowy language. He became very close to Walpole, who was at once his friend and mentor, and under whom he served a ministerial apprenticeship of over twenty years. Pelham showed his gift as a conciliator by helping to keep his somewhat tricky elder brother, Newcastle, on side. During the Excise crisis of 1733, when Walpole was threatened outside the Commons by a well-dressed mob, Pelham pushed the prime minister into the passage leading to Alice's coffee house and, drawing his sword, barred the way with the words: 'Now, gentlemen, who will be the first to fall?'

When Walpole was at length driven from office, he wished Pelham to succeed him, and in 1743, after the brief interlude of Spencer Compton, this came to pass. The new prime minister's early years in office were precarious, for George II hoped to replace him with the altogether more brilliant figure of Carteret, who described Pelham as 'the chief clerk' and could not be bothered with the management of Parliament by the distribution of patronage: 'What is it to me who is a judge or who is a bishop? It is my business to make kings and emperors.'

Carteret was a specialist in foreign policy, for which he possessed exceptional qualifications. As Macaulay remarks, 'He spoke and wrote French, Italian, Spanish, Portuguese, German, even Swedish.' He thought Pelham's job was to pay the bills for

British participation in the War of the Austrian Succession, which lasted from 1740 to 1748. Pelham wanted to get a grip on the 'vast arrear' he had found at the Treasury, and doubted there was anything to be gained from the war, so wished as soon as possible to make peace.

In February 1746, Pelham forced the issue. He and his colleagues resigned. George II sent for Carteret (now known, rather confusingly, as Granville), who was unable to form a government, so in three days the King had to recall Pelham.

While Walpole had excluded dangerously gifted rivals, meaning the Opposition became stuffed with talented individuals, Pelham preferred to include them in a 'Broad Bottom' administration, and was now strong enough to bring even William Pitt – a brilliant orator very unpopular with the King for making slighting references to Hanover – into government.

Pelham consolidated the nation's finances. He sought tranquility, and attained it. In 1751, he tried to retire, but the King, who was by now fond of him, prevailed on him to carry on. In 1754, he died in office. Horace Walpole (son of Sir Robert Walpole) wrote of him: 'He lived without abusing his power and died poor.' The King lamented: 'Now I shall have no more peace.'

DUKE OF NEWCASTLE

Lived 1693–1768; prime minister 1754–56 and 1757–62

The Duke of Newcastle is the first and, so far, only prime minister in British history to take over from his brother. He was fourteen months older than Henry Pelham and, although deeply stricken by his death, within a few days recovered sufficiently to set about obtaining the vacant office. For this role, his qualifications and disqualifications were equally striking.

Newcastle was a flurried, flustered, anxious man, who would take hold of your lapels while he addressed you in a confused and rambling way. In most of the anecdotes about him, he appears absurd. On one occasion, he had to visit Pitt the Elder, who was confined to bed by gout. The room was freezing cold, for it was November and Pitt would have no fire, as this aggravated his symptoms. Newcastle, who was a great hypochondriac, asked if Pitt would mind if he climbed, cloak and all, into the other bed in the room, which belonged to Pitt's wife. Here the two statesmen were found, arguing from bed to bed about whether Admiral Hawke should put to sea in pursuit of the French. Newcastle thought it was too dangerous to risk the fleet at that stormy time of year, but Pitt carried the day and on 20 November 1759 Hawke won the decisive victory of Quiberon Bay.

Horace Walpole said of Newcastle, 'He was a Secretary of State without intelligence, a Duke without money, a man of infinite intrigue, without secrecy or policy, and a Minister despised and hated by his master, by all parties and Ministers, without being turned out by any.' Spencer Compton said of him, 'He always lost half an hour in the morning, which he was running after for the rest of the day without being able to overtake it.'

But Newcastle had greater abilities than his critics were prepared to admit. He held high office for almost fifty years because of his unflagging eagerness, diligence and ambition, and also because he was not too grand to disdain the arts of parliamentary management, on which gaining and holding power depended. At a young age, he inherited land in eleven counties, which gave him a controlling interest in at least a dozen seats in the House of Commons, with influence over many more. He made friends with George I, which was more than most Englishmen were able to do. He was obsessed by patronage, and gradually extended his reach into Scotland, the American colonies and the Church of England, where he appointed bishops who were not just orthodox, but who would vote the right way in the House of Lords. He entertained on a vast scale, ran up huge debts and ended his career much poorer than he had started it.

Walpole, to whom Newcastle early signified his allegiance, found in him a valuable subordinate, who served from 1724 as a Secretary of State, with a large measure of responsibility for foreign policy, though in 1739, swayed by popular pressure, Newcastle was far keener than Walpole on going to war with Spain.

For the decade from 1744 that Pelham, his beloved younger brother, served as prime minister, Newcastle continued to act as a valued subordinate, though he was also jealous and craved an equal share in power: 'everything, as far as possible, should first be talked over by you and me'. When Newcastle became prime minister, everything went wrong, for although he had by now accumulated great experience, he was frightened of taking decisions. He had never served in the Commons, and was worried about bringing into the government anyone with the ability to control that chamber, who might soon outshine him. Britain drifted into an undeclared war with France and, as usual, things started badly. Pitt, whose gifts as a war leader were desperately needed but whom George II could not abide, resigned from the Cabinet and launched a series of devastating attacks on Newcastle from the backbenches. Amid humiliations in America and India, the fall of Minorca to the French was the most embarrassing defeat of all, for a relief expedition sent under Admiral Byng had sailed back to Gibraltar without fully engaging the enemy.

The public was dismayed and angry, and Newcastle knew he was in acute danger of being blamed for these defeats. So when a delegation from the City of London came to see the prime minister to complain about Byng's conduct, he replied: 'Oh! Indeed he shall be tried immediately – he shall be hanged directly.'

There was a considerable delay before Byng was shot on the quarterdeck of HMS *Monarch*, anchored off Portsmouth. The judges who tried him recommended clemency, and so did Pitt, but Newcastle made no attempt to persuade George II to show mercy. The way was open for Voltaire to explain, in *Candide*, that in England it is considered a good thing to kill an admiral from time to time '*pour encourager les autres*'.

Newcastle had by now been forced to resign, and that, one would have thought, was that. But his addiction to the game of politics and his ability to get along with George II meant he was soon back as prime minister, and so was Pitt, in an arrangement that for a time worked wonderfully well, with Newcastle providing the money while Pitt directed the war. In 1759, Britain celebrated a Year of Victories over the French.

In 1760, George II died and his 22-year-old grandson ascended the throne. For Newcastle, this was the beginning of the end. George III was very moral and very naïve. He disapproved intensely of the great Whig families who regarded themselves as the trustees of the Glorious Revolution of 1688, and had held a monopoly of power since the arrival in 1714 of George I from Hanover. George III wished Lord Bute to be his prime minister, and in 1762 he managed to get him.

There was now a 'purge of the Pelhamite innocents', with Newcastle's appointees cast out of their offices, and Newcastle himself stripped of the Lord Lieutenancies of Middlesex and Nottinghamshire. Yet even now, he could not renounce politics. He had one more minor comeback, as Privy Seal in 1765–66, and in 1768 he died at the age of seventy-five.

DUKE OF DEVONSHIRE

Lived 1720–64; prime minister 1756–57

The Duke of Devonshire had the attractive quality of quite genuinely not wishing to be prime minister, and held out for five days before yielding to the King's entreaties. This handsome and retiring nobleman took office at the age of thirty-six, and held it for only 225 days, the shortest span in the eighteenth century. He was from one of the great Whig families, and was chosen because he was a tactful and honest figure who knew how to mediate between different factions, as he had just shown while acting as Lord Lieutenant in Ireland. Dr Johnson said of him, 'If he promised you an acorn, and none had grown that year in his woods, he would have sent to Denmark for it.'

Pitt the Elder proposed Devonshire to fill the gap left by Newcastle's resignation, with Pitt himself as the most forceful minister. But Pitt spoiled this arrangement by resigning in protest against the execution of Admiral Byng (see above), which left the government rudderless.

Newcastle, who most definitely did want to be prime minister, was soon back, and so was Pitt, who definitely wanted to run the war. But Devonshire stayed in office as Lord Chamberlain, and in the words of Lord Waldegrave, 'lost no reputation, for great things had never been expected of him as a minister and in the ordinary business of his office he had shown great punctuality'.

When George III ascended the throne, he singled out Devonshire as a Whig aristocrat who deserved to be humiliated, which he did by refusing to see him when the duke arrived in October 1762 at court to say farewell. Devonshire at long last lost his temper, and tore off the gold key which was his badge of office as Chamberlain. In 1764, he died at the age of only forty-four at Spa, in what is now Belgium, where he had gone in search of a cure for dropsy. In the words of Amanda Foreman, 'He only participated in government out of a sense of duty and the effort it cost him ruined his health and destroyed his peace of mind.'

LORD BUTE

Lived 1713–92; prime minister 1762–63

L ord Bute was the most hated prime minister of all time. He was hissed and pelted by the London mob, which broke the windows of his house, and the upper classes loathed him too. His defenders point out that he was a distinguished botanist, but cannot deny he had little understanding of human nature. He possessed almost no parliamentary experience and reached the heights because he was a royal favourite. In the words of his contemporary, Bishop Warburton, 'Lord Bute is a very unfit man to be a Prime Minister of England. First, he is a Scotchman; secondly, he is the King's friend; and thirdly he is an honest man.'

His career turned on a chance meeting at Egham races in 1747. It started to rain, and Frederick, Prince of Wales, wished to play cards in a tent. A fourth player was needed, Bute was recruited and a friendship began between the prince and the Scottish peer.

Not that the prince had a high opinion of the newcomer's abilities: 'Bute, you are the very man to be envoy at some small proud German court where there is nothing to do.' But in 1751, the prince unexpectedly died, and his widow, Princess Augusta, who was from Gotha in Germany, grew deeply fond of Bute. Now he really was envoy to a small proud German court. The princess harboured the paranoid and quite unjustified fear that her late husband's brother, the Duke of Cumberland, intended to murder her eldest son, George, and make himself king instead. She entrusted the boy's education to Bute. The new Prince of Wales was shy and backward, kept by his mother in isolation from the temptations and depravities of English society, and he too became deeply fond of Bute, who was twenty-five years older than him. Bute was handsome – his legs were accounted remarkably fine – and took a serious interest in his pupil's education. The public assumed Bute had become Princess Augusta's lover. Why else did he keep visiting her? In English eyes, the idea that this could be for educational purposes was laughable.

In October 1760, the old king, George II, died and was succeeded by his 22-year-old grandson, who declared: 'Born and educated in this country I glory in the name of Briton.' The word 'Briton' had been inserted by Bute in the place of 'Englishman'. George III wished, with his former tutor's help, to be a patriot king, who would end party distinctions and drive out the corrupt Whig aristocracy that had held power since George I arrived from Hanover in 1714.

The aristocracy hated this, and so did the people. Bute was vilified as a Scotsman – the Scots being at this time cordially detested in England – and a favourite, who exercised a malign and secret influence behind the scenes. The jackboot – his symbol (for his first name was John and his last was pronounced 'Boot') – was burned by the mob, along with a petticoat representing Augusta. In response, he displayed his customary mixture of hauteur and naïvety. He had been a member of the House of Lords twenty years before, as a Scottish representative peer. But he had never spoken, and had annoyed the Whigs by voting with the Tories.

For a few months, Bute was the power behind the throne, and from March 1761 a Cabinet minister. But first Pitt and then Newcastle felt forced to resign, and in May 1762, he succeeded Newcastle as prime minister. Almost unbelievably, Bute had only delivered his maiden speech in January. To the disappointment of his listeners, it was not a total failure. But it was pompous and dull, so did nothing to lessen his unpopularity. He never discovered how to carry people with him.

The Seven Years War with France was drawing to a close. Bute was appalled by the cost of the war, drove forward the peace negotiations and defended the Treaty of Paris in February 1763, under which Britain made gains in Canada, India and the West Indies, and even regained Minorca.

It was a reasonable settlement, but Pitt denounced it and Bute became ever more hated. The libertine MP John Wilkes assailed, with scandalous freedom, Bute, the peace and even the King in the radical newspaper *The North Briton*, its very title a jibe at Bute's Scottishness. Bute worsened his position by imposing a deeply unpopular tax on cider. Eight days later, he resigned, unable to take any more vilification. He had served as prime minister for 344 days. For some years, he remained an influence on the King, though much less of one than his detractors supposed. He also remained deeply unpopular, until even the King became fed up with him and he faded into a long retirement where he pursued his botanical studies.

To Bute's credit, he persuaded George III to confer a pension on Dr Johnson. The great doctor said Bute was 'a very honourable man, a man who meant well', but 'a theoretical statesman, a book minister' who 'thought this country could be governed by the influence of the Crown alone', and 'showed an undue partiality to Scotchmen'.

GEORGE GRENVILLE

Lived 1712–70; prime minister 1763–65

George Grenville relished even the driest aspects of politics. According to a member of his family, 'An Act of Parliament was in itself entertaining to him, as was proved when he stole a turnpike bill out of somebody's pocket at a concert and read it in a corner in despite of all the efforts of the finest singers to attract his attention.' He was regarded as the ablest man of business in the House of Commons, but lacked charm; his career as prime minister was cut short by his tactless handling of George III, and he is remembered for his tactless treatment of the American colonists.

At the invitation of his uncle, Lord Cobham, he entered the Commons in 1741 as MP for Buckingham, a pocket borough with only thirteen voters. Grenville was one of the Patriot Boys who assailed Sir Robert Walpole. Soon he was in government himself, serving for many years as Treasurer of the Navy. He was shocked by the profligate spending of William Pitt, his brother-in-law, on the war with France, and aspired to sort out the public finances, by making rigorous economies and introducing new taxes.

In 1763, Grenville upheld the unpopular cider tax, which was the final act of Lord Bute's government, by asking where else the money was to come from. 'Tell me where,' he repeated, and on the Opposition benches, Pitt began to hum the tune of 'Gentle Shepherd, tell me where', a well-known song of the time.

The House laughed at Grenville, and from now on his nickname was 'Gentle Shepherd'. But George III turned to him to fill the gap left when Bute stepped down. Grenville drove a hard bargain: there was to be no 'secret influence' by Bute. He harassed the King, who said of him: 'When he has wearied me for two hours, he looks at his watch to see if he may not tire me for an hour more.' Grenville never knew when to stop. Now there was peace with France, he made drastic defence cuts, reducing the size of the army from 120,000 men to 30,000. Pitt deplored the sight of 'the bravest men the world ever saw, sent to starve in country villages'.

Grenville decided the American colonists must pay the cost of their own defence, by means of a new Stamp Act on legal transactions, passed in 1764. The colonists were affronted by this measure, and soon the cry of 'No taxation without representation' was heard. But Grenville did not have to deal with the problem, for George III contrived, in July 1765, to replace him and was determined never to have him back, stating that he 'would rather see the Devil in his closet than Mr Grenville'. In 1770, he died of a blood disorder at the age of fifty-eight. But his influence on British politics was not over. The Grenvilles and their cousins remained prominent for several generations, and one of his sons served as prime minister.

MARQUESS OF ROCKINGHAM

Lived 1730–82; prime minister 1765–66 and 1782

Some writers have mocked the Marquess of Rockingham for leading a government composed largely of his friends from the Jockey Club. It is true he had a passion for racing and gambling. He decided the name of one of England's classic races, the St Leger, built magnificent stables at his vast house, Wentworth Woodhouse, and was an enthusiastic patron of Stubbs, whose portrait of Whistlejacket, one of Rockingham's horses, today delights visitors to the National Gallery.

But the idea that love of the turf means political frivolity is simply wrong. Rockingham took his political responsibilities seriously. He was too shy to be a good public speaker, and is one of only four prime ministers who had not previously held ministerial office (the others being Ramsay MacDonald, Tony Blair and David Cameron). He understood the danger of alienating the American colonists far better than George III did, and his amiable disinterestedness commanded such respect among the Rockingham Whigs, as his followers became known, that he held them together through sixteen years in Opposition.

During the Jacobite uprising of 1745, Rockingham ran away at the age of fifteen and joined the Duke of Cumberland, who was about to pursue the rebels into Scotland. He was sent back home to Wentworth Woodhouse, and soon afterwards departed on a grand tour, during which, in Italy, he may have contracted a venereal disease, which accounted for the ill health from which he suffered for the rest of his life. In 1751, he took his seat in the House of Lords and became a regular attender, though he declined to speak. He had by now inherited vast estates, notably in Yorkshire, of which he took very good care, making use of the latest agricultural techniques.

In 1762, when George III dismissed the Duke of Devonshire, Rockingham resigned in sympathy from his place at court. Yet in 1765, the King was so anxious to get rid of Grenville as prime minister that he invited Rockingham to take over instead. The new prime minister decided the best thing to do with the Stamp Act, which had caused uproar in the American colonies, was to repeal it. He rendered this measure more acceptable at Westminster by putting through at the same time a Declaratory Act, which asserted the right of Parliament to tax the Americans. Rockingham intended, however, that this should be a 'sleeping sovereignty', with the colonies permitted to enjoy a 'salutary neglect'.

He also abolished the cider tax, which had caused uproar at home, and replaced it with a window tax. The Commons resolved, during his prime ministership, that 'general warrants', recently employed to get a grip on the troublesome John Wilkes by arresting no fewer than forty-nine people including Wilkes himself, were illegal. The generally disrespectful attitude of Wilkes is conveyed by his throwaway remark, in *An Essay on Woman*, that 'Life can little more supply / Than just a few good fucks, and then we die.'

From the beginning of his prime ministership, Rockingham employed as his private secretary an Irishman who was to emerge as one of the greatest writers on politics in the English language. It was Edmund Burke who asserted, in *Thoughts on the Cause of the Present Discontents*, the distinction between a faction, which is a temporary grouping intent on grasping power, and a political party, which is, or should be, united by 'some political principle in which they are all agreed'. Men of honour, Burke contended, are under an obligation not just to hold upright views, but to take part in politics: 'When bad men combine, the good must associate; else they will fall, one by one, an unpitied sacrifice in a contemptible struggle.'

George III soon became as fed up with Rockingham as he had been with Grenville, and contrived to bring in Pitt instead, before imagining that in the pliable Lord North he had found the very prime minister he needed. Rockingham could only watch, and protest, as the American colonies were lost under Lord North. But in 1782, Rockingham returned as prime minister. He set about making peace with the Americans, granting greater self-government to the Irish and reducing corruption at home. But after only three months back in office, he died at the age of fifty-two. Before doing so, he had the wit and generosity to change his will, in order to pay Edmund Burke's debts.

PITT THE ELDER

Lived 1708–78; prime minister 1766–68

Pitt the Elder was the most volcanic orator the House of Commons has ever known. No parliamentarian has been more feared. When he erupted, he could bury his opponents beneath a brilliant stream of ferocious, off-the-cuff abuse. For Pitt was not much given to understatement: 'I am sure I can save this country, and nobody else can,' as he told the Duke of Devonshire at the start of the Seven Years War.

Pitt believed in himself, and got the public to believe in him. Even Frederick the Great of Prussia believed in him, declaring:

'England has been a long time in labour, but she has, at last, brought forth a man.' Since 1940, Churchill has eclipsed Pitt's fame as a war leader. But the British Empire which fought its last great campaigns under Churchill sprang from the victories inspired by Pitt.

These were won before Pitt became prime minister. He was a very odd figure, who dominated the war ministry of which Newcastle was the titular head and abandoned the peacetime administration he himself was supposed to lead. The Pitts were a truculent family, much given to quarrelling among themselves. The future prime minister's grandfather, Diamond Pitt, had made his fortune in India and brought home an enormous diamond, which he at length managed to sell at a vast profit to the French royal family. He married his children into the peerage, and bought estates which gave him control of several parliamentary seats.

His grandson, William Pitt, was educated at Eton, which he detested, and Trinity College, Oxford, which he left without taking a degree. He suffered from lifelong ill health: gout quite often incapacitated him for months or years at a time, and bouts of crushing depression too. In 1731, he became, by purchase, a cornet in his uncle Lord Cobham's regiment. The £1,000 required (point-less to put this into modern money: just think of it as a very large sum, far beyond most people's means) was probably provided by the prime minister, Sir Robert Walpole, for Pitt was a younger son, without money of his own. But Pitt was soon staying for long periods at Stowe, Cobham's palatial mansion in Buckinghamshire, where the 'cousinhood' of Grenvilles and Lytteltons exchanged rebellious thoughts about Walpole. In 1735, at the age of twenty-seven, Pitt entered the Commons for the rotten borough of Old Sarum – which had five electors, and was owned by his elder brother – and emerged as a fierce critic of Walpole, who was so angered by this disloyalty that he had him deprived of his cornetcy.

Pitt was one of the Patriot Boys who harassed the prime minister, and enraged the King, by demanding a naval war and complaining that British interests were being sacrificed to the needs of Hanover. That was George II's native land, yet Pitt had the insufferable cheek to call it 'despicable'. After the fall of Walpole, in 1742, it took Pitt four years to attain, as Paymaster General, the ministerial office to which his talents plainly entitled him.

And there Pitt stuck for nine years. He ostentatiously declined to enrich himself at public expense, as other holders of that office were inclined to do, and this strengthened his reputation as a patriot. But his was not a meteoric rise, and he had formidable rivals, including Henry Fox, who said of him: 'He is a better speaker than I am, but thank God! I have more judgement.' Everyone, including his enemies, testified to the brilliance of Pitt's speeches, and we must take their word for it, as only fragments remain of what he said, and these are often unreliable, for parliamentary reporting lay a long way in the future.

Even if we had the words, we would not have the manner. He had a hooked nose, a hawk's eye, and it was said that Garrick himself had never acted better. Often Pitt heightened the drama by appearing as an invalid, who had to be helped to his place. He could not give set speeches: he had to be spontaneous. Pitt seldom knew what he was going to say, for his thoughts formed themselves as he spoke, which gave him the ability to respond with terrifying speed and directness. He was impetuous, imperious, indignant, swift to denounce any step towards 'national ignominy'. Horace Walpole, by no means a sycophantic observer, described in a letter to a friend a speech given by Pitt during an all-night debate: 'He spoke at past one, for an hour and thirty-five minutes: there was more humour, wit, vivacity, finer language, more boldness, in short, more astonishing perfections than even you, who are used to him, can conceive ...'

Pitt dominated the Commons. But in 1754, when the Duke of Newcastle became prime minister, he did not wish to use Pitt to lead in that house for the government. The King was determined not to have him, and Newcastle feared being outshone. So Newcastle tried using Fox in the Commons instead. Pitt went into Opposition, and forced first Fox's resignation, then Newcastle's.

In came the Duke of Devonshire as prime minister, with Pitt to run the war. Here was a statesman who revelled in conflict, and in the direction of forces. He took energetic steps to galvanise the war effort, which had so far been going very badly. But the unhappy affair of Admiral Byng intervened. In March 1757 Byng was executed, and a few weeks later George II sacked Pitt, who had pleaded for Byng's life.

Pitt's dismissal provoked a public outcry. He was presented with the freedom of the City of London, and of thirteen other cities. There was a popular clamour for the Great Commoner, as he was by now known, to be put in charge. While politicians squabbled, British forces were humiliated. At the end of June 1757, a new ministry was cobbled together, with Newcastle at its head and Pitt once more in charge of the war.

There followed the greatest series of victories in British history, so that 1759 became known as the Year of Victories. The capture the previous year of two French strongholds in North America, Louisbourg and Fort Duquesne (which was at once renamed Pittsburgh), was the prelude to General Wolfe's triumph at Quebec. The French also suffered heavy defeats in the Caribbean, West Africa, India, Germany and at sea: this last, at Quiberon Bay, was the most important of all, for it rendered impossible the invasion of Britain and the recapture of France's overseas possessions.

It would be absurd to give all the credit for these victories to Pitt. But his contemporaries were in no doubt that he inspired British commanders and their forces with an audacious confidence; a new spirit of attack to which the French had no answer. Admiral Rodney later described him as 'an illustrious example, how one great man, by his superior abilities, raised his drooping country, from the brink of despair, to the pinnacle of glory, and made her ... dreaded by the whole universe'. Pitt was now at the height of his fame, with a European reputation.

In 1760, George II died and was succeeded by his grandson, George III. The new king's mother and his favourite counsellor, Lord Bute, had between them persuaded him that Pitt was 'a true snake in the grass', who had deserted the heir to the throne and sided with George II. Pitt could not at once be sacked, because he was too popular, but his extravagant approach to grand strategy could at least be curbed, for his colleagues were alarmed by the enormous increase in the national debt. In 1761, Pitt demanded a pre-emptive war with Spain, which was about to come in on the French side. He saw a chance to capture the Spanish treasure fleet, but his colleagues were more interested in making peace than in widening the war. They refused his demand, and Pitt resigned, declaring in his most domineering tone that he 'would be responsible for nothing but what he directed'.

He was never quite the same again. He accepted a pension, and a peerage for his wife. Both were richly deserved. His wife, Hester, whom he married in 1754 when he was forty-six and she was thirty-four, was the sister of George Grenville. She had helped keep Pitt sane enough, and well enough, to sustain the rigours of leadership in time of war. Without her, he might have become impossibly eccentric. They were devoted to each other, and she gave birth to five children in seven years, including a boy, William, who from his earliest years displayed exceptional gifts and would himself go on to be prime minister.

Pitt, whose passions included landscape gardening, was reck-lessly extravagant, so he needed the pension, which was for £3,000 a year. But for a time, it impaired his popularity, which rested on the belief that he was different from other politicians. He remained, however, a formidable figure and from time to time he would issue terrible warnings to his country, in speeches which were still great parliamentary occasions. He condemned as too lenient the peace with France, which was signed in 1763. His country's victories, he knew, had created a thirst for revenge: 'France, like a vulture, is hovering over the British Empire, hungrily watching the prey that she is only waiting for the right moment to pounce upon.'

George III kept changing prime ministers, and in 1766 his choice fell on Pitt, who had denounced 'faction' in a manner pleasing to the royal mind. But Pitt's health was worse now, and he began by making the irreparable blunder of accepting a peerage. As the Earl of Chatham, he could no longer be the Great Commoner. It is true that life in the Lords was less strenuous, especially as he also declined the office of First Lord of the Treasury, which usually went with the prime ministership, opting instead to become Lord Privy Seal. But Pitt had a genius for dominating the Commons, and had thrown away his trump card before he started. The poet Thomas Gray said this was 'the weakest thing ever done by so great a man'.

At the start of 1767, his health broke down. He retired to Burton Pynsent, the estate in Somerset which he had been left some years before by an admirer he had never met. He had been peremptory with his colleagues, but now they did as they thought fit, without reference to Pitt. The Duke of Grafton, who as Chancellor of the Exchequer was the second man in the government, went down to see him, and found that 'his nerves and spirits were affected to a dreadful degree ... his great mind bowed down, and thus weakened by disorder'. Pitt signed over control of his affairs to his wife, and was attended by a doctor, Anthony Addington, who prescribed port and Madeira. After eighteen months of this absenteeism, the King at last accepted his resignation.

Pitt gradually recovered his health. He knew how intolerable the Americans would find any attempt to coerce them. 'You cannot conquer the Americans,' he declared. 'I might as well talk of driving them before me with this crutch.' And again: 'If I were an American, as I am an Englishman, while a foreign troop was landed in my country, I would never lay down my arms – never, never, never!' In these phrases one catches echoes of his overwhelming force as a speaker.

But the volcano was almost extinct now. At the last, he went to the Lords, supported by two of his sons and his son-in-law, to contest a motion proposed by the Duke of Richmond, who wanted the colonies to be allowed to go their own way. Pitt had changed his line, and told the House: 'If the Americans defend independence they will find me in their way.' Richmond replied to him, Pitt rose again to speak, and collapsed: a scene commemorated by John Singleton Copley in *The Death of the Earl of Chatham*, on display at the National Portrait Gallery.

Pitt lingered a month, and then he died. He was the greatest war leader of the period when Britain was acquiring a worldwide empire. But war and empire are not now celebrated as they once were, and his fame has dimmed.

On his monument in Westminster Abbey are found words that convey how a great number of his contemporaries (though not, it should be said, George III) wished to remember him:

Erected by the King and Parliament
As a Testimony to
The Virtues and Ability
Of
WILLIAM PITT EARL OF CHATHAM
During whose Administration
In the Reigns of George II and George III
Divine Providence
Exalted Great Britain
To an Height of Prosperity and Glory
Unknown to any Former Age

DUKE OF GRAFTON

Lived 1735–1811; prime minister 1768–70

The third Duke of Grafton was not power-hungry enough to make a lasting impression on national life. He was an agreeably laid-back nobleman, who as a young man reminded people of his great-great-grandfather, Charles II. That amusing and lascivious king had repopulated the aristocracy by conferring dukedoms on his illegitimate children.

Grafton loved racing, won the Derby three times and kept his own pack of hounds. He attracted a certain amount of adverse comment for putting his pleasures above his public duties. Horace

Walpole accused him of 'behaving like an apprentice, thinking the world should be postponed to a whore and a horse-race' – though this in a letter written in 1768 in which Walpole despaired of other politicians too.

When Grafton was only five, his father, a naval officer, died of fever in Jamaica. At the age of twenty, Grafton married an heiress, Anne Liddell, with whom he had several children, but with whom he was soon on bad terms. He spent a few months as an MP, before inheriting at the age of twenty-one the dukedom from his grandfather, with estates in Suffolk and Northamptonshire. Despite his grand position and excellent political connections, he was modest enough not to regard himself as a future prime minister and instead attempted to promote the claims of William Pitt, for whom he had conceived, as so many people did, an intense admiration.

In 1765, when he was still only twenty-nine, Grafton accepted with trepidation high ministerial office under his friend Lord Rockingham, but on condition that Pitt was brought in to lead the government as quickly as possible. When that did not happen, Grafton resigned. But within a few months, Rockingham was gone and Pitt became prime minister. He prevailed on the reluctant Grafton to serve as First Lord of the Treasury, and at first gave him detailed instructions on how to carry out his duties.

In the following year, 1767, Pitt became ill and stopped giving instructions to anyone. Grafton began living with Mrs Haughton, also known as Nancy Parsons. She was the lovely daughter of a Bond Street tailor (her beauty is attested by her portrait, painted by Reynolds, now in the Metropolitan Museum of Art), and had spent some time in the West Indies with a man called Haughton, who traded in slaves. In due course, Grafton took Mrs Haughton to the opera at the same time as Queen Charlotte, which even by the standards of an age that was relaxed about marital lapses was thought to be going a bit far, for the royal family was notoriously respectable.

But when George III at last accepted that Pitt was incapable of being prime minister, he turned to Grafton to replace him. Grafton, who was by now thirty-three, as usual protested his unfitness, and as usual allowed himself to be persuaded. Only Pitt the Younger reached the highest office at a younger age. A less happy distinction belongs to Grafton alone: at the time of writing, he is the only prime minister to have got divorced while in office, which he did by Act of Parliament in 1769. His wife had already had a son by another man, whom she proceeded to marry, while Grafton now got married, very happily, to Elizabeth Wrottesley, by whom he had many more children. Mrs Haughton was not alone for long: she found a new lover in the Duke of Dorset. Horace Walpole described her as 'the Duke of Grafton's Mrs Haughton, the Duke of Dorset's Mrs Haughton, everybody's Mrs Haughton'.

Two great questions faced Grafton as prime minister. One was what to do about John Wilkes, who at this time kept getting re-elected to Parliament as the MP for Middlesex, and kept getting debarred. Grafton, who was a man of tolerant inclinations, was generally sympathetic to Wilkes. The other question was how to calm down the American colonists. Grafton wanted to do away with all the taxes which were raising such a storm of protest on the far side of the Atlantic. He could not, however, prevail on his colleagues to get rid of the duty on tea. By a margin of five to four, the Cabinet voted in favour of maintaining that duty, with the prime minister in the minority.

In early 1770, Grafton found himself deserted by his two strongest supporters within the government. Even Pitt now attacked him, and he decided, after the apparent suicide of a new appointee, that he himself must resign. In his autobiography, written many years later, he described the prime ministership as 'an office which was peculiarly irksome to me'.

He continued to serve under the new prime minister, Lord North, but at length resigned in protest at the policy on America. Towards the end of his life, he became very interested in religion, published two books in which he called on the upper classes to lead more moral lives and worshipped as a Unitarian rather than an Anglican. But he was not convinced enough of his own rectitude to be a successful leader, for as he told the House of Lords in 1797: 'Wisdom is at no time more conspicuous, nor more amiable, than in the acknowledgment of error.'

LORD NORTH

Lived 1732–92; prime minister 1770–82

'The worst prime minister since Lord North.' For more than two centuries it has been customary to hurl this insult at any occupant of 10 Downing Street who has become unpopular. All most people can remember about North is that he lost the American colonies, which was one of the great reverses of British history.

To blame him for this disaster is, in a sense, entirely fair. He was prime minister, so he took the rap. That is how the British constitution works. But he was in a position to lose America because he was so popular, such a brilliant manager of men, and so willing to do what the king and parliament wanted, that he stayed in office for a dozen years. When one looks at his life, one finds to one's surprise that he was not just able (a frequent characteristic in senior politicians), but also loveable.

A few anecdotes will substantiate this astonishing claim. North was one night at Covent Garden when he was asked by a distant acquaintance to identify 'that plain-looking lady in the box opposite'. He replied in an amiable tone that she was his wife, whereupon the questioner tried to recover by saying, 'No, no, I meant the dreadful monster sitting next to her.'

'That, sir, is my daughter,' North replied. 'We are considered to be three of the ugliest people in London.'

Horace Walpole agreed that the prime minister was unprepossessing. He observed that North had 'two large prominent eyes that rolled about to no purpose, for he was utterly short-sighted, a wide mouth, thick lips and an inflated visage', which gave him 'the air of a blind trumpeter'.

In the Commons, North often slept, or seemed to sleep, in order to avoid getting drawn into argument. One day an opponent complained, in the middle of a violent attack, that 'the noble Lord is asleep', whereupon North, his eyes still shut, said, 'I wish to God I were.' On another occasion, he was nudged awake by a neighbour only to hear George Grenville talking about 1689, whereupon North delighted the house by complaining in a loud voice, 'You have wakened me nearly one hundred years too soon.' On yet another occasion, he raised 'a great and long laugh' by explaining to a supplicant for some office that 'when he only nodded, or squeezed the hand, or did not absolutely promise, he always meant No'.

North's father, who became the first Earl of Guilford (hence the son's courtesy title of 'Lord'), was a loyal courtier to Frederick, Prince of Wales, father of George III. Malicious voices whispered that the prince might be North's father too, for there was a marked resemblance between the two boys. This was untrue: Frederick, who died before he could become king, was merely North's godfather. One of North's great advantages, as prime minister, was that he knew the King well, but one of his weaknesses was that he deferred too often to royal urgings. He was himself too much of a courtier.

But he was by no means only a courtier. He entered the Commons in 1754, at the age of twenty-two. Soon he became a junior Treasury minister, and was good at that too. He was diligent, conciliatory and reliable. He spoke very frequently and very well, and this at a time when many backbenchers never spoke at all. When the government needed a loyalist who would move the motion to expel John Wilkes from the Commons, it turned to North. In 1767, he became Chancellor of the Exchequer, an office he was to keep throughout his prime ministership, which began in 1770, by which time George III had become fed up with five prime ministers in ten years.

The problem with understanding the nation's finances was that it made understanding the American colonists even more unlikely. North wanted to keep Britain solvent, which meant he was in favour of getting the colonists to contribute to the cost of their own defence. After all, the national debt had swollen by an alarming amount during the Seven Years War (1756–63), during which the French were thrown out of North America, a feat of arms for which the colonists ought to be duly grateful.

Men with greater minds – Pitt the Elder, Edmund Burke – saw the need to conciliate the Americans. Burke pointed out that the colonists were 'sprung from a nation in whose veins the blood of freedom circulates', and went on: 'An Englishman is the unfittest person on earth, to argue another Englishman into slavery.'

But most of the Commons was with North, who demanded the colonists pay their share. He voted in favour when the Cabinet decided in 1769 – so just before he became prime minister – to impose a duty on tea. In 1773, the colonists showed what they thought of this by tipping a cargo of tea into Boston Harbour: the Boston Tea Party. North responded with punitive measures, and asserted that 'four or five frigates' would be sufficient to deal with any resistance. In April 1775, the first shots were fired at Lexington and Concord.

One paradox of this war was that North did not want to fight it. Again and again he begged George III to replace him. The King refused, and within two years British redcoats suffered their first great humiliation, surrendering under General Burgoyne at Saratoga. Still the King would not let North go. Instead he paid his debts, which placed the minister under a yet greater obligation to the monarch.

France rushed to join the winning side, as did the other European powers. The American Revolution was France's chance to take revenge on Britain. But only the culminating disaster – the surrender under Lord Cornwallis at Yorktown in 1782 – secured for North his freedom. George III felt deserted by him.

North's daughter recalled that 'he would never allow us to call him prime minister', and that he said 'there was no such thing in the British constitution'. These attitudes were commendably modest, but also illustrate his unfitness to lead the nation through a great struggle.

He was only forty-nine years old when he stepped down, and still had a considerable parliamentary following. The next year he served as Home Secretary in the coalition government formed under the Duke of Portland. But after that North never again held office, for he was a critic of Pitt the Younger, who came in towards the end of that year.

Our last glimpse of North is at the end of his life, when he had become Earl of Guilford. He was by now totally blind, but still cheerful, still an amusing man to visit. His family cared for him devotedly, and he apologised for causing them so much trouble, and assured them he was in no pain. He died in 1792, having confided to his daughter that he feared his reputation would be wrecked by the loss of the colonies. As so often, he was correct.

EARL OF SHELBURNE

Lived 1737–1805; prime minister 1782–83

Lord Shelburne was a man of ability, but no one who worked with him ever wanted to work with him again. He was nicknamed Malagrida, after a Portuguese Jesuit who was put to death on trumped-up charges. The writer Oliver Goldsmith committed the famous faux pas of saying to Shelburne: 'I wonder they should call your Lordship Malagrida, for Malagrida was a very good man.' Shelburne was known too as 'the Jesuit of Berkeley Square', where he had purchased Lord Bute's house. For like the Jesuits, he had acquired an unmerited reputation as a treacherous intriguer. In the words of George Rose, a close colleague of Pitt the Younger, Shelburne sometimes harboured 'entirely groundless' suspicions of other people, and could also become 'offensively flattering'.

He is one of two British prime ministers born in Ireland, the other being Wellington. As a young man, he joined the army and performed with credit at the Battle of Minden in 1759. While still on active service, he was elected an MP, but he never sat in the Commons, for in 1761, at the age of twenty-five, he inherited his peerage, as well as large landed estates. His lack of experience in the Commons was a severe handicap. Shelburne never understood how to control that chamber, or even that it might be desirable to do so. He was a loner, who trusted to his own erratic judgement, and was an awkward colleague. When Lord Bute, who was a generation older but almost as inexperienced, offered him a ministerial post, Shelburne had the effrontery to try to set conditions. Such arrogance made a poor impression, which was never later effaced.

He became a great admirer of Pitt the Elder, in whose government he served, but regretted that despite a close political connection lasting ten years, he never so much as drank a glass of water with him. One suspects Pitt was not only guarding his privacy, but did not wish to have more than the bare minimum to do with Shelburne. Nor did Charles James Fox and Edmund Burke, two of the greatest parliamentarians of this period. Nor did Lord North, who in 1770 began twelve years as prime minister.

In 1780, Shelburne briefly became popular, by fighting a duel in Hyde Park with a Scotsman, Lieutenant Colonel Fullerton. Shelburne was slightly wounded in the groin, and reassured those present with the words: 'I don't think Lady Shelburne will be any the worse for it.'

He saw clearly the need to conciliate the Americans, and at the outbreak of hostilities in 1775, condemned 'the madness, injustice and infatuation' of coercing them 'into a blind and servile submission'. Only once the war was clearly lost did Shelburne have a chance of serving again in government. In 1782, he became Home Secretary under Lord Rockingham, and he took over as prime minister when Rockingham died.

Shelburne's main task was to make peace with the victorious Americans. This he achieved by giving them almost everything they wanted. He neglected, however, to prepare the Commons for these statesmanlike concessions, which MPs proceeded in February 1783 to vote down, whereupon Shelburne resigned. Peace was nevertheless concluded along the lines negotiated by Shelburne.

His head was full of progressive plans for economic and parliamentary reform, but he was never again to hold office, for a new star had begun to blaze with exceptional brightness: William Pitt, who served as Chancellor of the Exchequer under him.

Shelburne enjoyed entertaining men of letters at his house, Bowood, in Wiltshire. It appears he got on better with his social inferiors than with his equals. But they were not always kind about him. The philosopher Jeremy Bentham recalled: 'His manner was very imposing, very dignified, and he talked his vague generalities in the House of Lords in a very emphatic way, as if something good were at the bottom, when in fact there was nothing at all.'

Disraeli later confused matters by describing Shelburne, in the course of a fanciful account of English history at the start of one of his novels, *Sybil*, as 'the ablest and most accomplished minister of the eighteenth century'. That is absurd. In Dublin, however, a famous hotel, the Shelbourne, is named after this forgotten statesman.

DUKE OF PORTLAND

Lived 1738–1809; prime minister 1783 and 1807–09

The Duke of Portland was a Whig nobleman who 'possessed in an eminent degree the talent of dead silence'. He was shy, and found speaking in the House of Lords an almost unbearable ordeal. He was, however, an administrator of acknowledged firmness and integrity, who twice became prime minister because a compromise candidate was needed. The gap of twenty-four years between his two terms of office is a record.

In March 1783, George III implored William Pitt to become prime minister, but that cool-headed young man reckoned he

could not control a House of Commons where two great parliamentarians, Charles James Fox and Lord North, had just formed
a coalition with each other. Fox was unacceptable as prime
minister, for the King loathed him. But Fox proceeded to 'storm
the closet' – the closet being the king's study, where ministers
were received – and obliged George III to make Portland prime
minister.

As a young man, the duke had been elected to the Commons.
But he had never spoken there, and in 1762, at the age of
twenty-four, he inherited his dukedom. He had love affairs with
Maria, Countess of Waldegrave, and with the Duchess of Grafton,
before marrying Lady Dorothy Cavendish, daughter of the Duke
of Devonshire. Despite being no speaker, he showed an early and
intense devotion to politics, and was a loyal admirer of Lord
Rockingham. He served in Rockingham's government in 1765
and returned to office under Rockingham in 1782.

Portland meanwhile lost vast sums fighting elections in
Cumberland against the ghastly Sir James Lowther, who was very
rich and boasted: 'I would at any time spend £20,000 to make the
Duke of Portland spend fifteen, for I know I can hold out longer
than he can, and my meaning is to ruin the Duke of Portland.' In
this fight, which ended up in the law courts, Portland did come
close to ruining himself, but also came to be seen as a Whig martyr.

George III was from the first determined to get rid of Portland,
and with him of Fox. In December 1783, he managed to bring
this about, by getting the House of Lords to vote against the India
Bill: any peer who voted for the measure would, it was indicated,
be regarded as a 'personal enemy' by the King. This was entirely
improper, but out went Portland, who had signally failed to thwart
the manoeuvre, and in came Pitt. No blame was attached to
Portland, who was once again seen as a Whig martyr.

Pitt at length managed to woo Portland and other
conservative-minded Whigs away from Fox, who was disconcert-

ingly keen on the French Revolution. The duke served from 1794 to 1801 as Home Secretary, upholding public order with sternness at a time of great fear of revolution.

George III came to regard Portland as an admirable and reliable figure, and in 1807 invited him to take office again as prime minister. The duke was old, and had been operated on the year before for kidney stones. Although people had been impressed by the stoicism with which he bore that ordeal, he was in poor health. Against his better judgement, he agreed to serve, saying as he did so: 'My fears are not that the attempt to perform this duty will shorten my life, but that I shall neither bodily nor mentally perform it as I should.'

He proved unable to control the government, which contained a number of strong characters, including Spencer Perceval, Lord Hawkesbury (soon to become Lord Liverpool), George Canning and Lord Castlereagh. Portland was unable to act as peacemaker between these men, and the war against Napoleon was going badly. When Castlereagh discovered that Canning was trying to get him dismissed, he challenged him to a duel, fought in September 1809 on Putney Heath, in which Canning was slightly wounded. Portland, who had already suffered a stroke, resigned in October 1809, and at the end of that month died of a second stroke.

The name of this obscure but not contemptible prime minister is perpetuated in several London street names, and in the Portland Vase, a masterpiece of Roman glass which he lent to Josiah Wedgwood so it could be copied, after which the duke entrusted it to the care of the British Museum, where it can still be seen.

PITT THE YOUNGER

Lived 1759–1806; prime minister 1783–1801 and 1804–06

Pitt the Younger is the youngest prime minister in British history, and will surely remain so. He took office at the age of twenty-four, which was young even by the standards of the time. No one else has managed this in their twenties, and only four people – Grafton, Rockingham, Devonshire and North, clustered in the three decades before Pitt – have achieved it in their thirties. Even when he died at the end of his brief second term, at the age of forty-six, Pitt was still younger than all but six of his successors – Addington, Grenville, Liverpool, Goderich, Blair and Cameron – were on first entering Downing Street.

Nor was his early success some mere fluke or flash in the pan. His first term of office lasted seventeen years, and saw prodigious work reforming the nation's finances, followed by prodigious resilience in the face of revolutionary France.

He inherited from his father a name – William Pitt – which in 1759, the year of his birth, was the most illustrious in Europe. Pitt the Elder was at the height of his powers as a war leader. Great men often neglect their children: Winston Churchill was deeply hurt that his father, Lord Randolph Churchill, had so little time for him. But no such difficulty arose in the Pitt household, where father and son were on the most affectionate terms. The father had been to Eton, but said he 'scarce observed a boy who was not cowed for life' at that school, so resolved to educate his own son at home.

Pitt the Younger was immersed in politics from earliest childhood: his father served as prime minister in the 1760s, and so did his mother's brother, George Grenville. Just as Mozart (born three years earlier, in 1756) revealed a precocious genius for music, so Pitt displayed a very early talent for politics. According to his tutor, Edward Wilson, he 'seemed never to learn but merely to recollect'. His absorptive powers were astonishing. His father encouraged him to recite each day a passage from Shakespeare, Milton or some other English poet, and also to take up a book in Latin, Greek or French, and read it aloud in English. This task the boy came to be able to perform with ease. He developed his innate ability to think on his feet: the capacity to find at once and to speak the right words, which would help him time and again to lead the Commons along the path which he could show to be reasonable. Nor were his gifts limited to language: he delighted also in mathematics. His mind expanded in the company of gifted and congenial adults, without the presence of schoolfellows who would have mocked him.

At the age of eight, and with the encouragement of his father, Mozart composed his first symphony. Lady Holland met Pitt when he was seven, and realised at once that he might become a fatal rival to her brilliant son, Charles James Fox, who was ten years older: 'I have been this morning with Lady Hester Pitt, and there is little William Pitt, not eight years old and really the cleverest child I ever saw ... *Mark my words*, that little boy will be a thorn in Charles's side as long as he lives.' It was at about this time that Pitt the Elder made the blunder, on becoming prime minister, of accepting a peerage, whereupon his ability to command the Commons ceased to be a trump card. His 7-year-old son commented: 'I am glad I am not the eldest son [who would inherit the title and go to the House of Lords]. I want to speak in the House of Commons like papa.'

At the age of fourteen, Pitt went to Pembroke College, Cambridge, where he studied for several years. His health was poor, and Dr Addington, the family physician, urged him to drink port, which he did for the rest of his life in quantities even some of his contemporaries regarded as excessive. At the age of nineteen, he was with his father when the latter collapsed, mortally ill, while speaking in the House of Lords. At the age of twenty-one he defeated Edward Gibbon, the celebrated historian of the Roman Empire, in an encounter at the dinner table. A few months later, still only twenty-one, he entered the House of Commons.

That intimate chamber – smaller and narrower before the fire of 1834 than it is now – can within a few moments expose a supposedly gifted newcomer as a conceited fool. Many MPs never dared speak. Pitt delivered his maiden speech on 26 February 1781, a month after taking his seat. It was an apparently impromptu performance, delivered without a note and including a demolition of what the previous speaker had said. His listeners were astonished by the power and eloquence with which he marshalled his arguments. He dominated the House, and was at home there, as if he had already belonged to it for many years. Lord North, the prime minister, said it was the best first speech he had ever heard. Fox sang Pitt's praises, and so did Edmund Burke. A great talent was revealed.

George III loathed Fox, who in his eyes was an impudent libertine, addicted to women, gambling and the turf, and a bosom friend of the King's dissolute and detested son, the Prince of Wales. But the freedom-loving Fox was a brilliant speaker and a generous-hearted friend, who won the love and admiration of a wide circle of MPs.

Who could stop Fox becoming prime minister? Within a short period of time, it became clear to the King that only Pitt had the necessary courage and skill as a debater. But Pitt, like his father before him, guarded his independence and presented himself as the one man of principle who could rescue the nation from the bunch of self-seeking schemers who were leading it to perdition. After refusing a junior position in Lord Rockingham's government, he agreed, at the grand old age of twenty-three, to become Chancellor of the Exchequer under Lord Shelburne. But when the latter was forced to step down, Pitt declined the King's entreaties to form a government, for with Fox and North in alliance with each other, there was no prospect of controlling the Commons. George III responded by taking the first opportunity to sack the Fox–North coalition and renew his invitation to Pitt.

On 19 December 1783, Pitt became prime minister. His government was at first ridiculed as the 'mince-pie administration', for it was not expected to last beyond Christmas. All the great speakers – Fox, Burke, North and the playwright Sheridan – were ranged against him. He lost vote after vote in the Commons, yet with the King's support and to growing public approval this tall, thin young orator, with bright eyes and gawkish manner, defied them all. His fearlessness and cool judgement under fire marked him out as a leader. In January, he made an excellent impression on the country, and confounded his opponents, by declining to award himself the Clerkship of the Pells, a sinecure office worth £3,000 a year – in modern terms an enormous income. In February, he received the Freedom of the City of London, and on returning to the West End of London, had his carriage demolished by a Foxite mob: an attack which produced a further public reaction in his favour. In March, he judged that the moment had come to ask the King to dissolve Parliament, and to hold a general election, which he proceeded to win. He was still only twenty-four, but had routed his opponents and established himself with a healthy Commons majority.

Sir Nathaniel Wraxall wrote this celebrated description of the new prime minister:

> In his manners, Pitt, if not repulsive, was cold, stiff, and without suavity or amenity. He seemed never to invite approach or to encourage acquaintance, though when addressed he could be polite, communicative, and occasionally gracious ... From the instant that Pitt entered the doorway of the House of Commons, he advanced up the floor with a quick and firm step, his head erect and thrown back, looking neither to the right nor to the left, nor favouring with a nod or a glance any of the individuals seated on either side, among whom many who possessed five thousand pounds a year would have been gratified even by so slight a mark of attention. It was not thus that Lord North or Fox treated Parliament, nor from them would Parliament have so patiently endured it, but Pitt seemed made to guide and to command, even more than to persuade or to convince, the assembly that he addressed.

In his circle of intimate friends, including William Wilberforce, Pitt would unbend, and become delightful company. He never married, and on growing close, in 1797, to Eleanor Eden, drew back in fear and told her father there were 'decisive and insurmountable obstacles' to marrying her. Like Wilberforce, Pitt wanted to abolish the slave trade: an objective which was not achieved in his lifetime. But in the task of restoring prosperity, and the public finances, after the humiliation of losing the American War of Independence, he was triumphantly successful. His own personal finances were a catastrophe: he devoted no attention to them, allowed himself to be robbed in a most outrageous way by tradesmen, refused various posts which would have enabled him to pay off his enormous debts, had to be bailed out by his friends, and after his death was found to owe £40,000, which Parliament voted to pay off.

In 1788, when George III went mad, Fox hoped to come in, but was thwarted by Pitt, who severely restricted the powers the Prince of Wales could wield as Regent. Fox unwisely declared that his friend the Prince had a hereditary right to the regency. Pitt, seeing at once his opponent's blunder, remarked to his neighbour, 'I'll unwhig the gentleman for the rest of his life.' For the Whigs, led by Fox, believed in parliamentary sovereignty, not the inherited royal right to overrule Parliament. The crisis passed when the King recovered his wits.

The French Revolution, which began in 1789, brought a new and harsher atmosphere. Early hopes of peaceful constitutional development in Paris, expressed most confidently by Fox, were confounded by the Terror, and by the execution of Louis XVI and Marie Antoinette. The fear now was that the revolution would spread to London. France declared war on Britain in 1793, and was to prove invincible on land, sweeping aside the continental coalitions laboriously assembled by Pitt. As a war leader, he was less successful than his father. But he had kept the Royal Navy in good repair, which preserved the British Isles from invasion, and to pay for the war he invented income tax, which was supposed to be a temporary measure. As a parliamentarian, his gifts were undiminished, though as Sydney Smith remarked, 'At the close of every brilliant display, an expedition failed or a kingdom fell.'

In 1801, he resigned after falling out with the King over the issue of Catholic emancipation, which Pitt saw as an implied condition of the union of the British and Irish parliaments, enacted the previous year. He was replaced by Addington, the son of his father's doctor, and retired from politics for a couple of years.

But Addington was clearly not up to the job, and in 1803 Pitt reappeared in the Commons. The diarist Thomas Creevey was shocked by the change in him: 'I really think Pitt is done: his face is no longer red, but yellow; his looks are dejected; his countenance I think much changed and fallen, and every now and then he gives a hollow cough. Upon my soul, hating him as I do, I am almost moved to pity.'

Pitt was nevertheless needed at the helm. Soon after the end of his first prime ministership, when peace had been made with France, a great celebration in his honour was organised by his young disciple, George Canning, who wrote:

When our perils are past, shall our gratitude sleep?
No, – here's to the pilot that weathered the storm.

So in May 1804, Pitt the trusted pilot came back in, weaker in body and weaker politically too. The war with France broke out again in 1804, and was no nearer being won. At the start of November 1805, news arrived that Napoleon had won a great victory over the Austrians at Ulm, and the road to Vienna was now open to him.

Four days later, news reached London that Nelson had won a decisive naval victory over the combined French and Spanish fleets at Trafalgar. On receiving the news of this triumph, and of

Nelson's death in it, Pitt for once could not sleep, but had to get up, although it was three in the morning.

The victory produced wild celebrations in London. Pitt was toasted at the Lord Mayor's banquet as 'the Saviour of Europe', and in the words of a future prime minister, Wellington, 'he returned thanks in one of the best and neatest speeches I ever heard in my life', which went as follows:

I return you many thanks for the honour you have done me; but Europe is not to be saved by any single man. England has saved herself by her exertions, and will, as I trust, save Europe by her example.

Pitt himself grew weaker, and could no longer revive himself by the vast consumption of port which had seen him through so many late-night sittings in the Commons. William Hague suggests, in his biography of Pitt, that he was suffering from a stomach ulcer which today could easily be treated. In January 1806, Pitt heard the news of Napoleon's crushing victory over the Austrians and the Russians at Austerlitz, and on seeing a map of Europe is supposed to have said, 'Roll up that map; it will not be wanted these next ten years.'

By now the prime minister was dying, worn out at the age of forty-six. His last words have been variously given as 'Oh my country! How I leave my country!', 'Oh my country! How I love my country!' and (this last tradition related or perhaps invented by Benjamin Disraeli) 'I think I could eat one of Bellamy's veal pies.'

HENRY ADDINGTON

Lived 1757–1844; prime minister 1801–04

Pitt is to Addington
As London is to Paddington.

These lines, composed in 1803 by Pitt's follower George Canning, expressed a cruel truth. Addington had the chance to grow into a big figure, but instead his littleness was rendered more conspicuous by Pitt's genius. The two men were childhood friends: Addington's father was a successful doctor who treated Pitt's father, and indeed Pitt himself. Addington the younger entered the Commons in 1784, and possessed the qualities of a loyal and reliable subordinate, good at getting on with people more powerful than himself.

He was the first member of the middle class to get to the top, but was valued for his deference rather than because he represented anything new. He was a faithful friend to Pitt, who in 1789 encouraged him to become Speaker of the House of Commons. In that role Addington won the confidence of MPs, since he was a fair-minded man who took the trouble to master the details of procedure, and it did not matter that he himself was a feeble orator.

In 1801, Pitt resigned after falling out with George III about Catholic emancipation, and Addington's moment had come. Pitt had for some time regarded his friend as a possible stand-in while he himself took a break, and Addington agreed with the King that Catholic emancipation must at all costs be averted. The King in turn thought highly of Addington, dismissed his requests that someone more fitted to be prime minister be found and granted him the use for life of White Lodge in Richmond Park. People had grown weary of the war with France, which was appallingly expensive, and it was reckoned that although Addington lacked the qualities needed to lead a struggle for national survival, he was perfectly capable of making peace.

Which is what he proceeded, at the Treaty of Amiens in 1802, to do. Addington also introduced in that year a successful peace-time budget, cutting the income tax which Pitt had introduced. But peace was soon disturbed by Napoleon meddling in the affairs of Switzerland, and people started to lose confidence in Addington, who was referred to derisively as the Doctor, in reference to his father's profession.

When war with France broke out again in 1803, Addington appeared in the Commons in his militia uniform, but failed as an orator. Pitt, who had retired from public life but had gradually been losing confidence in Addington, reappeared in the Commons and spoke so brilliantly that, according to Fox, 'If Demosthenes had been present, he must have admired.' Nor had Addington managed to persuade any of the most distinguished statesmen of the day to serve with him in government. According to the diarist Creevey, they were 'the feeblest, lowest almost, of men, still more of ministers'.

In 1804, Pitt returned as prime minister, and Addington was sent to the House of Lords as Lord Sidmouth. In the last months of Pitt's life, Addington was reconciled to him, and after Pitt's death he wrote: 'May everlasting happiness await him. To me it is a comfort not to be expressed, that I have been enabled at this crisis to show, not merely attention, but the affection which has never been extinguished.'

Addington enjoyed thirty more years of political life, including a long stint as a highly reactionary Home Secretary. Once again, he demonstrated his abilities as a subordinate, but he was never a leader.

LORD GRENVILLE

Lived 1759–1834; prime minister 1806–07

Like his father, who served as prime minister in the 1760s, Lord Grenville was an intelligent, industrious, efficient, uncharming and greedy statesman. He and his many cousins attracted adverse comment for being so good at enriching themselves at public expense: in 1807, they received a total of £55,000, equivalent to many millions today. But in that year, to Grenville's lasting glory, he succeeded as prime minister in putting through Parliament the Slave Trade Abolition Act, a cause he had championed since the 1780s.

His head was abnormally large, his eyes protuberant, his gait ungainly and his bottom large, and from early in his political career he was nicknamed 'Bogy', because of his resemblance to a goblin. He took no care with his clothes, and while at Christ Church, Oxford, demonstrated exceptional abilities as a classicist and a mathematician. Literature remained his lifelong passion. He assembled a magnificent library at his house, Dropmore, in Buckinghamshire, and in retirement published a playful volume of his own translations from English, Greek and Italian into Latin verse. He seems, indeed, to have felt more at ease with books than with people, and while prime minister confessed in a letter to one of his brothers: 'I want one great and essential quality for my station and every hour increases my difficulty … I am not competent to the management of men.'

He was, however, exceptionally good at transacting ministerial business, and had a genuine interest in policy. He entered the Commons in 1782 and soon became one of the workhorses on whom his cousin, Pitt the Younger, relied. In 1791, Pitt sent him to the House of Lords, which Grenville led with success for the next ten years, while also taking a major role as Foreign Secretary in running the war with France. In 1801, he resigned with Pitt on the issue of Catholic emancipation.

While in Opposition, something very unexpected happened. Grenville fell out with Pitt, and became a close friend and ally of Charles James Fox, whom the King could not stand. In 1804, when Pitt became prime minister for the second time, he wanted to include both Grenville and Fox in the government, but the King vetoed Fox, so Grenville also refused to serve, despite Fox saying, with characteristic magnanimity, that he would have no objection.

Pitt's death in January 1806 left the King obliged, with great reluctance, to turn to Grenville, and with him to accept Fox too. Grenville, though only forty-six, had more ministerial experience than anyone else and was more respected by other parliamentarians.

But he was reluctant to accept the King's offer, for he said that becoming prime minister would reduce his income, as it would oblige him to give up a valuable sinecure.

Once Fox had arranged for the sinecure to be kept open, Grenville agreed to become prime minister, and formed what became known sarcastically as 'the Ministry of All the Talents'. Quite a few talents were missing from it, including three future prime ministers – Perceval, Liverpool and Canning – who had been followers of Pitt. Fox became Foreign Secretary and got on well with the King, but died after only seven months.

Grenville, like his father before him, had no idea how to humour George III, and soon fell out with him on the issue, yet again, of Catholic emancipation. The King considered himself obliged, by his coronation oath, to uphold the Protestant religion. Almost every statesman who understood conditions in Ireland knew that concessions to Catholic feeling must come, or unrest would almost certainly increase. The war with France was going badly, and the last thing England needed was trouble in Ireland too.

The King stood firm, so Grenville resigned. 'I am again a free man,' he exclaimed. He had been prime minister for just over a year, and the abolition of slavery was his only notable achievement. But despite the pull of his books and his garden, he remained a significant Opposition figure at Westminster for many years to come. In 1829, when Catholic emancipation at last went through, he voted for it in the Lords and remarked to one of his nephews that 'I have not lived in vain.'

SPENCER PERCEVAL

Lived 1762–1812; prime minister 1809–12

S pencer Perceval is the only prime minister to have been
assassinated. The United States, which is a more violent
country, has had four presidents – Lincoln, Garfield,
McKinley and Kennedy – murdered. Perceval was shot in the heart
at point-blank range in the lobby of the House of Commons by
John Bellingham, who had spent five years in prison in Russia in
connection with an unpaid debt and had long resented the British
government's understandable refusal to compensate him for this
ordeal. Perceval cried out, 'I am murdered, murdered', and died.

Bellingham sat down on a bench and waited to be arrested. Within a few days, he was tried, convicted and hanged. In London and the Midlands, there were popular demonstrations in his favour, but the Commons was appalled and voted an annuity of £2,000 for Perceval's widow, and the sum of £50,000 for his children.

Perceval was one of the nine children of the Earl of Egmont, and had to make his own way in the world, which he did by pursuing with tireless determination a successful career at the bar. He was thin, pale and scarcely five feet tall, and was known as 'Little P'. While still very poor, he married, against her father's wishes, Jane Spencer-Wilson, who was wearing a riding habit at the time and may have eloped, though her family were in due course reconciled to her choice. The Percevals were to have twelve children, and lived at first over a carpet shop.

At Harrow School, and Trinity College, Cambridge, Perceval acquired the evangelical convictions to which he remained faithful for the rest of his life. He opposed the fashionable pastimes of gambling and hunting, and annoyed such worldly Whigs as the Reverend Sydney Smith, who referred to him as 'an odious evangelical' and saw his hostility to Catholic emancipation as horribly intolerant. But William Wilberforce testified that Perceval had 'the sweetest of all possible tempers', and he acquired a general reputation for probity.

In 1796, when he was thirty-three, Perceval became an MP. He soon distinguished himself by an intrepid attack on Charles James Fox. Two years later, when the prime minister, Pitt the Younger, was about to fight a duel and was asked who would succeed him if he was killed, he replied, 'Perceval seems to be the most able to cope with Mr Fox.' Perceval established himself as a debater who showed no fear, and was almost as quick on his feet as Pitt himself. His opponent on the Catholic question, Henry Grattan, said of him: 'He is not a ship of the line, but he carries many guns, is tight-built, and is out in all weathers.'

Perceval introduced several bills to get curates in the Church of England paid properly, and in 1800 published a pamphlet in which he identified Napoleon as the woman in the Book of Revelation 17:3–6, who '[sits] upon a ... beast ... the mother of harlots ... drunken with the blood of the saints'. After holding various legal offices, he agreed in 1807 to become Chancellor of the Exchequer, in which role he succeeded in raising enough money to carry on the war with France.

In 1809, the prime minister, the Duke of Portland, died and Perceval came through the field as his successor. His position was at first very weak, for Portland's administration had become a complete mess, with two of its leading figures, George Canning and Lord Castlereagh, fighting a duel with each other which ruled them out of the leadership stakes.

The King delighted in Perceval's cry of 'No Popery', and praised him as 'the most straightforward man he has almost ever met'. Perceval was resilient, and even managed, after an initial falling-out, to get on with the King's heir, the Prince Regent, who took over in 1811 after George III went mad. By this time, Perceval's authority in the Commons was established. But this able, trust-worthy and narrow-minded lawyer-politician was murdered before he could make any claim to greatness. In the summer of 1812, Napoleon invaded Russia, Wellington gained the upper hand in Spain, and Perceval was laid to rest in Westminster Abbey.

LORD LIVERPOOL

Lived 1770–1828; prime minister 1812–27

Lord Liverpool was prime minister for almost fifteen years, a length of time exceeded only by Walpole and Pitt, yet his name today produces a frown of puzzlement. Disraeli dismissed him as 'the Arch-Mediocrity', which was unfair, but there is something strangely unmemorable about Liverpool. Perhaps he was so good at managing a Cabinet of formidable and quarrelsome individuals, six of whom went on to become prime minister, because he had no desire to monopolise fame.

His father was an MP and then a peer, and was ambitious for him to make his way in politics. On 14 July 1789, young Robert Jenkinson (as he was known before himself becoming a peer) witnessed, while touring the Continent, the Storming of the Bastille. Neither at the time, nor in later years, when the significance of the event became clearer, did he say anything memorable about it: an omission which confirms that he was no attention-seeker. At Oxford, he acquired a more brilliant friend, George Canning, who would certainly have had something to say.

Liverpool (as we shall call him, though he did not inherit the title until the death of his father in 1808) did soon acquire, like most members of the British Establishment, a horror of the French Revolution and a fear that the infection might cross the English Channel. He was elected to the Commons in 1790, when he was only twenty, but had to wait until he had come of age to take his seat. When it became clear that Louis XVI was about to be executed, an event that actually took place on 21 January 1793, Liverpool condemned the revolutionaries as

a band of sanguinary ruffians ... murderous regicides ... hands still reeking with the blood of a slaughtered monarch ... a set of monsters, who, while we are agitating this subject, are probably bearing through the streets of Paris – horrid spectacle – the bloody victim of their fury.

The prime minister, Pitt the Younger, was quick to spot new talent, and in 1793 brought Liverpool into government at the age of only twenty-three. For the next thirty-four years, he was continuously in office, except for thirteen months in Opposition in 1806–07. But as a Pitt protégé, he also took command of the Cinque Ports Regiment of Fencible Cavalry, a militia unit designed to help defend the country against the threat of invasion. His friend, Canning, regarded his enthusiasm for soldiering as somewhat absurd, so had some posters printed and delivered to Colonel Jenkinson (as Liverpool was known in his military incarnation) at a dinner party, together with a message that these were already on display all over London. The poster read:

> Tight lads, who would wish for a fair opportunity,
> Of defying the Frenchman, with perfect impunity,
> Tis the bold Colonel Jenkinson calls you to arm,
> And solemnly swears you shall come to no harm.

Liverpool was so mortified by this joke that he burst into tears. Not for the last time, his friendship with Canning came under severe strain.

But Liverpool's ascent continued. In 1801, when Pitt resigned the prime ministership, he was made Foreign Secretary. In 1804, when Pitt came back in, Liverpool became Home Secretary. In 1806, when Pitt died, he was offered the prime ministership, but turned it down, for he knew he would not be able to control the Commons. In 1812, when Spencer Perceval was assassinated, the offer of the prime ministership was renewed, and Liverpool accepted.

The war with France, which had already lasted, with one short gap, for almost twenty years, was at last turning in Britain's favour. Liverpool deserves some of the credit for this: as Secretary of State for War, he had given the strongest possible support to Wellington in Portugal and Spain, where British forces first achieved sustained victories over the French on land. In 1814, Napoleon was forced to make peace and was exiled to Elba. The following year, he escaped, gathered his last army and suffered his final defeat at Waterloo. Wellington's name remains imperishably associated with that victory; Liverpool's is entirely forgotten. Peace was made with France: a peace that lasted much better than the Treaty of Versailles after the First World War, for it was imposed with a degree of magnanimity towards the French, so was in their interests as well as their enemies'.

But to Liverpool now fell the heavy burden of the transition to peacetime. Bad harvests and economic stagnation led to widespread misery and discontent. Luddites broke the machines that were putting them out of work. Starving labourers fired ricks and barns. There was no police force, so magistrates ordered troops to quell disturbances, as at the Peterloo massacre in Manchester in August 1819, when at least eleven people were killed and more than 500 were injured. The Six Acts were introduced: a series of repressive measures for which Liverpool reluctantly saw the necessity. He agreed in the Lords that the summary power of arrest and detention was 'a most odious one', and saw that it was sparingly used.

He is accused by posterity of being a reactionary, and this is true. Even at the time, the best writers – Shelley, Byron, Cobbett – were opposed to the government, though they tended to attack Castlereagh, the Foreign Secretary, rather than Liverpool. In Shelley's words,

> I met murder on the way,
> He had a mask like Castlereagh.

After Castlereagh committed suicide, Byron wrote:

> Posterity will ne'er survey
> a Nobler grave than this:
> Here lie the bones of Castlereagh:
> Stop, traveller, and piss!

Liverpool did not believe in parliamentary reform in order to give representation to the huge new towns. For Liverpool, 'the landed interest is the stamina of the country': he regarded country gentlemen as far more reliable than the representatives of volatile urban voters would turn out to be.

His economic policy was successful. He got a grip on the nation's war-ravaged finances and, inspired as a young man by his reading of Adam Smith, his laissez-faire policy led after 1820 to increasing prosperity. He was, throughout his career, the reliable man of government, with an exceptional ability to weigh up political situations and work out the most sensible way forward.

In 1820, George IV became king, and greatly embarrassed his ministers, and indeed himself, by trying to divorce Queen Caroline. A spotlight was shone on his atrocious behaviour as a husband, and hers as a wife. All this Liverpool dealt with about as tactfully and astutely as it could be dealt with. He was also instrumental in the founding in 1824 of the National Gallery, but again his name is not much remembered in connection with this. In 1827, worn out from overwork, he suffered a severe stroke while opening his morning post, and had to step down. The next year he died, at the age of fifty-eight. Liverpool was instrumental in winning the war, maintaining the peace and returning the country to prosperity. But it would be surprising if one passenger in a million who passes through Liverpool Street Station, in London, ever pauses to reflect that the street in question was named after a prime minister.

GEORGE CANNING

Lived 1770–1827; prime minister 1827

Georgie Canning was prime minister for only 119 days, a shorter period than anyone else, but is one of the most fascinating figures in this book. He was quick-witted, decisive, impatient, able to see how the world was moving, brilliant at framing foreign policy, brilliant too at making his rivals look ludicrous, but also more than capable of making himself look ludicrous, by running extravagant risks, lodging unacceptable demands and taking the huff when he did not get his own way.

He was only a year old when his father died. His mother, a beautiful Irishwoman, was left destitute, and decided to try her luck on the stage. Before long, she was touring the provinces as the mistress of a rascally actor called Samuel Reddish, with whom she had several children.

From this life of seedy lodging houses, Canning was rescued at the age of eight by a rich uncle, a banker. The boy was sent to Eton, where he excelled, and to Christ Church, Oxford, where he became friends with a group of gilded youths including Robert Jenkinson, the future Lord Liverpool.

But Canning had next to no money, so could not think of entering the House of Commons, which he described to his friends as 'the only path to the only desirable thing in the world, the gratification of ambition'. He was advised that he should instead become a lawyer. This prudent course he followed for a short period of time, but he yearned for politics. So, in 1792, he took the audacious step of writing to the prime minister, William Pitt, whom he had never met, to ask for help in finding a seat.

Pitt had a keen eye for talent and was sufficiently struck by the letter to suggest a meeting. The brilliant young man and the brilliant slightly older man (the gap between them was only eleven years) got on very well. Some of Canning's Whig friends accused him of abandoning them for the Tories, but at this time some of the Whigs were so extravagantly enthusiastic about the French Revolution that others were indeed moving towards Pitt.

Although Canning was seen once to touch the prime minister on the shoulder, in a way which jealous observers regarded as overfamiliar, the relationship seems to have been that of father and son rather than lovers. Pitt found a parliamentary seat for Canning, invited him to dine with him and members of the Cabinet on his first night in the Commons, and gave him an arduous post as a junior Foreign Office minister. Here Canning confirmed his capacity for hard work and transacting business.

Pitt needed to counteract the dangerous currents of revolutionary propaganda, some of it by writers of genius such as Tom Paine. Canning helped set up a paper, *The Anti-Jacobin*, in which he poured scorn on the kind of person who supported the revolution:

A steady patriot of the world alone,
The friend of every country but his own.

George Orwell was to identify the same mentality in left-wing intellectuals in the mid twentieth century.

In 1800, Canning placed his finances on a firmer footing by marrying, for love, Joan Scott, the daughter of General Scott, who left her £100,000 from the half a million he made from gambling. Here was another stroke of good fortune, and the marriage was very happy, except for the illness and eventual death at the age of nineteen of their beloved eldest son. Until 1801, Canning's star was in the ascendant. But then his hero resigned the prime ministership, and was replaced by Henry Addington. Canning could see that Addington was nothing compared to Pitt, and had the effrontery to say so. This was embarrassing for Pitt, who wished Addington well. And while Canning refused to serve under the new prime minister, Jenkinson, his less brilliant but altogether more prudent Oxford friend and contemporary, became Foreign Secretary.

In defence of Pitt, Canning in 1802 spoke these celebrated words in the Commons:

Away with the cant of 'measures not men', the idle supposition that it is the harness and not the horses that draw the chariot along. No, Sir, if the comparison must be made, if the distinction must be taken, men are everything, measures comparatively nothing.

Canning had to wait until 1807 to enter the Cabinet, which he did as Foreign Secretary in the Duke of Portland's administration. In a daring manoeuvre, which could easily have gone wrong, he thwarted Napoleon by seizing the Danish fleet at Copenhagen, after a bombardment in which 2,000 Danes were killed. Portland could not keep order, and chaotic infighting broke out. Canning was far from blameless: he demanded that Castlereagh be sacked from the post of Secretary of State for War. When Castlereagh discovered this, he sent Canning a long letter, challenging him to a duel. Canning, who had never fired a pistol in his life, said he would rather fight than read the letter. They fought, and Canning received a light wound in the thigh. Many people thought he had been disgracefully reckless.

Yet when Portland stepped down, Canning offered to become prime minister. George III found this rather forward of him, and preferred Spencer Perceval. Three years later, when Perceval was assassinated, Canning's Oxford friend, now Lord Liverpool, became prime minister and invited Canning to become Foreign Secretary.

Canning now overplayed his hand to a quite ridiculous extent. He said he would only become Foreign Secretary if he could also be Leader of the House of Commons. Liverpool refused, Castlereagh got the job instead and Canning was consigned to the wilderness. He watched as Castlereagh made peace at the Congress of Vienna.

Only in 1822, when Castlereagh committed suicide, did Canning's fortunes revive. Now he was Foreign Secretary, and came into his own. He charmed George IV, who had previously hated him, on the probably unjustified suspicion that Canning had long ago had an affair with the King's unhappy and sexually predatory wife, Queen Charlotte. The new Foreign Secretary worked with almost unbelievable rapidity: when his writing hand was disabled by gout, he dictated two eloquent and complicated dispatches at once, on Greece and South America. He successfully promoted Greek independence from Turkey, and declared sooner than any other nation that Britain should recognise the Spanish colonies in Buenos Aires, Colombia and Mexico, which were declaring themselves republics, for here a vast British trade could ensue. In 1826, he supplied (as the prime minister, Lord Liverpool, could never have done) the phrase to explain what he was doing: 'I called the New World into existence, to redress the balance of the Old.'

He also sent a message, in a new and difficult cipher, to the British ambassador in The Hague. The ambassador stayed up all night to translate it, only to discover that the message read:

> In matters of commerce the fault of the Dutch
> Is offering too little and asking too much.
> The French are with equal advantage content,
> So we clap on Dutch bottoms just twenty per cent.

The Foreign Secretary's gift for light verse had not deserted him. But he was at the same time Leader of the House of Commons, which kept him up night after night, defending every aspect of government policy. Liverpool, his friend and chief, was the first to crack under the enormous strain: in February 1827 he suffered a disabling stroke. Canning succeeded him as prime minister, and took on also the role of Chancellor of the Exchequer. Some of the Tories, including two future prime ministers, the Duke of Wellington and Sir Robert Peel, refused to serve under Canning, whom they regarded as too liberal on the question of Catholic emancipation. Canning instead brought in some of the Whigs.

If he had been in good health, it is probable that his fertility in expedient and understanding of the times would have kept him going. He saw that 'a great struggle between property and population' was coming, which could only be averted by 'the mildest and most liberal legislation'. But time was running out for him. He was mortally ill. In January 1827, he had caught a severe cold at the funeral of the Duke of York, brother of George IV and heir presumptive. In July, he reported to the King that 'he did not know what was wrong with him but he was ill all over'. In August he died.

Canning's wit and insolence are illustrated in an anecdote about him attending a church service. The clergyman asked his opinion of the sermon, and Canning said, 'You were brief.'

'Yes,' the clergyman said, 'you know I avoid being tedious.'

'But you *were* tedious,' Canning replied.

Canning should not just be remembered as a wonderfully amusing prime minister. He was also wonderfully penetrating, and saw how the 'mighty power of Public Opinion, embodied in a Free Press', was coming by the 1820s to pervade, check and nearly govern the British constitution. He was a genius, and it is right that his statue stands today in Parliament Square, along with those of men who are today more famous than him, including Churchill, Lloyd George, Disraeli, Lincoln, Mandela and Gandhi.

LORD GODERICH

Lived 1782–1859; prime minister 1827–28

Lord Goderich could not stand the strain of being prime minister. At moments of crisis, he tended to burst into tears: George IV, who ought never to have invited him to form an administration, described him as 'a damned, snivelling, blubbering blockhead'. Goderich's amiability and willingness to take a joke against himself had deflected criticism when he was in departmental offices, but contributed to his complete inability to impose his authority once he reached the top, where he remained for only 130 days.

He was born Fred Robinson and ended his days as the Earl of Ripon, but will be known here as Goderich, the title he held while in 10 Downing Street. After entering the Commons in 1806, he served a long ministerial apprenticeship and acquired an impressive collection of nicknames. In 1814, his colleagues dubbed him 'the Grand Duke of Phussandbussle' because of the amusingly self-important way he rummaged through the papers on his desk. He saw the joke and from then on often called himself 'the Grand Duke'.

The following year, Goderich and his wife left their London house to be defended by their servants and a few soldiers, for the London mob was enraged by Goderich's support for the Corn Law, a protectionist measure which was expected to raise the price of bread. The crowd destroyed his furniture and pictures, and two innocent bystanders were fatally wounded, one by a shot fired by Goderich's butler. While relating these unhappy events in the House of Commons, Goderich burst into tears, after which he became known as 'the Blubberer'.

From 1823 to 1827, he served as Chancellor of the Exchequer, where he cut taxes and predicted prosperity, which led him to be called 'Prosperity Robinson'. He was also known in some quarters as 'Goody' Goderich, for he was a devout, well-meaning man. In 1826, he asked the prime minister, Lord Liverpool, for a less arduous post, along with a peerage, but was turned down. In 1827, Liverpool collapsed, Canning succeeded him and Goderich was duly given a peerage and made Leader of the House of Lords. Here he failed to gain the respect of such formidable figures as the Duke of Wellington, and was altogether a humiliating failure.

Yet in August 1827, when Canning died, George IV asked Goderich to become prime minister. The King supposed he could control the new prime minister, and most unwisely told him who he could and could not have in the Cabinet. Goderich even more unwisely accepted these demands, which at a stroke destroyed whatever power he might have had to resolve disputes between his colleagues, for they realised he was a weak man who would give in to pressure.

In October, the Royal Navy – whose commander, Admiral Codrington, exceeded his instructions – won a crushing victory over the Ottoman Turks at the Battle of Navarino. Back in London, ministers could not agree whether this was a good or a bad thing, for if they recognised Greek independence they would run the risk of an undesired war with Turkey.

By December, chaos reigned in the Cabinet, where a row had broken out between two strong-minded ministers about which of them had the right to appoint the chairman of the parliamentary finance committee. Threats of resignation flew to and fro. A strong prime minister would have slapped down his squabbling colleagues, but Goderich was known to be 'in a most pitiful state' of exhaustion and unable to take decisions. His wife, who had been morbidly nervous ever since the attack on their house in 1815, was now almost crazy with post-natal depression.

Goderich confessed to the King 'how deeply he feels his own inadequacy to discharge the great duties of the situation to which your Majesty's far too favourable opinion called him'. George IV interpreted this as a resignation and on 8 January 1828 informed him that his services were no longer required. Disraeli refers to him as 'a transient and embarrassed phantom', which as a description of his premiership is about right.

But six days after stepping down, Goderich was reported to be 'quite another man', who 'sleeps at nights now, and laughs and talks as usual'. His wife likewise regained her spirits and lived to a ripe old age. Goderich resumed his ministerial career, in which the mildness of his convictions enabled him to serve in governments of various hues. Their son, born in Downing Street (to their great sorrow, two other children had died), was to become, as Marquess of Ripon, a distinguished Liberal politician.

DUKE OF WELLINGTON

Lived 1769–1852; prime minister 1828–30 and 1834

Wellington is the only great soldier to become prime minister. But after crowning an almost unbroken series of victories on the battlefield by defeating Napoleon at Waterloo in 1815, he turned out to be less suited to political life. For he had an admirably honest, and also rather comic, disinclination to spend his time listening to his colleagues' worries, or as he put it, 'assuaging what gentlemen call their feelings'.

As a commander, Wellington had proved himself to be calm, brave, clear, astute, dutiful, ambitious, energetic, persistent, uningratiating, unpretentious, unconfiding, self-disciplined, incorruptible, irascible, cool in his assessment of risk, vehement in defence of his strategy, determined his orders should be obeyed and comprehensive in his grasp of the unglamorous, indispensable and innumerable details of supply. He was, in short, a paragon who, along with Cromwell and Marlborough, is one of the three greatest commanders of an army these islands have produced.

In politics, he was nowhere near being one of the three greatest prime ministers. He did, however, wield from 1815 until his death in 1852 an authority that sprang not just from his brilliant military career, but from his undeniable straightforwardness and powers of judgement. When asked once for his definition of a great general, he replied, 'To know when to retreat, and to dare to do it.' In politics too, he had the courage to retreat. He forced the Tories to accept Catholic emancipation and parliamentary reform, for he saw that the alternative was civil war.

Wellington as a boy showed no special promise. He was the fourth son of an Irish peer, Lord Mornington, who died when Wellington was twelve. The family name was Wesley, later changed to Wellesley. He was sent to Eton, but did not distinguish himself, and it is doubtful he ever said Waterloo was won on its playing fields. As a young man, he was sent to a military academy in France, after which he entered the army and also, in 1790, the Irish Parliament in Dublin, so he had some early political experience. He proposed marriage to Kitty Pakenham, but her elder brother, Lord Longford, thought Wellington's prospects too uncertain.

This blow to his pride seems to have prompted him to decide to take his military career seriously. He burned his violin (like his father, he had a talent for music) and got himself posted to India, where he greatly distinguished himself. Returning home in 1805 as a major general, he became a Westminster MP and was made

Chief Secretary for Ireland. He also agreed to marry, after a twelve-year delay during which he had not set eyes on her, Kitty Pakenham, only to find she had lost her looks and become a silly, nervous woman. Two sons were born to her, but Wellington later admitted to a friend that he had been 'a damned fool' to marry her.

He soon had an excuse to leave home. His services were needed in the field. Many years of campaigning in Portugal and Spain followed: the epic of the Peninsular War, fought from 1808 to 1814, in which with irresistible shrewdness and persistence, Wellington worked out how to defeat much larger French forces. The government made him a duke and dispatched him to Paris as British ambassador. He was a hero now, with a European reputation. Among his conquests were two of Napoleon's mistresses, one of whom reported that 'Monsieur le duc était beaucoup le plus fort.' Wellington's features were universally reproduced: the aquiline nose, piercing eyes, spare figure in a plain coat. He was five foot nine inches tall. In Lawrence's most famous portrait of him, which hangs in the National Portrait Gallery, one sees too his sensitivity. Here is an Iron Duke (his most famous nickname) with feelings.

Wellington knew that only a peace which was in everyone's interests would endure – a truth he used his reputation to enforce on Britain's allies. Napoleon alarmed all Europe by escaping from captivity on Elba and raising a new army. Wellington was placed in command of the multinational coalition ranged against him. There followed the decisive engagement at Waterloo, just outside Brussels, where Napoleon made the fatal error of underestimating Wellington. Peace had to be made afresh.

In 1819, at the age of forty-nine, the hero returned home from the Congress of Vienna. What was to be done with him? The prime minister, Lord Liverpool, prevailed on him to enter the Cabinet as Master-General of the Ordnance. Wellington, who saw himself as a public servant rather than a party politician, said he would only enter the government if he could remain above factional strife. In 1822, he had the courage to tell George IV that George Canning – to whom the King had strong objections – must be admitted to the Cabinet as Foreign Secretary. But Canning began quite soon to irritate the duke, by showing an excessive sympathy with Latin American revolutionaries who wanted to throw off Spanish and Portuguese rule and set up republics. The duke was not in politics to promote revolution.

In 1827, Liverpool suffered a disabling stroke, and the King turned to Canning rather than Wellington to become prime minister. Wellington felt snubbed by Canning and declined to serve under him. Later that year, Canning died and the King turned, not to Wellington or to the Home Secretary, Sir Robert Peel, but to the nonentity Lord Goderich. 'Our lord and master hates Peel and me,' Wellington remarked, 'and he will adopt any resource rather than send for us.'

But Goderich was simply not up to the job, and in January 1828 George IV summoned Wellington to Windsor. The King was in bed, dressed in a greasy silk jacket and a turban. 'Arthur,' he said to the duke, for that was the familiar form by which he addressed him, 'the Cabinet is defunct.'

Wellington accepted with some reluctance the royal invitation to form a government. He felt an instinctive dislike of the party management in which he was now obliged to engage: 'I hate it.' Although he was an efficient administrator, he admitted he was a poor public speaker. The idea of having anything to do with journalists – something Canning had enjoyed – was also anathema to the duke: 'What can we do with these sort of fellows? We have no power over them, and, for my part, I will have no communication with any of them.' He set a low value on public opinion, and on the whole preferred to be unpopular. As he himself put it, 'The people of England must be governed by people who are not afraid.'

Such remarks make him one of the strangest figures in this book, and in some ways one of the most admirable. To his annoyance, the entire Cabinet told him he must step down as commander in chief of the army: a step he took with great reluctance. He brought some liberal Tories, who had supported Canning, into the government, but the Tory ultras, who were implacably opposed to Catholic emancipation, suspected from the first that he was going to betray them.

And they were right. But Wellington lost the Canningites first, when he fell out with them about a minor question of parliamentary reform. Their leading member, William Huskisson, submitted a letter of resignation, which he did not expect to be taken literally. But that is exactly what Wellington proceeded to do. Four other liberal-minded ministers resigned in sympathy.

The great issue of Catholic emancipation now came to the fore. Wellington judged that to avert unrest in Ireland, emancipation must go ahead. In March 1829, the Catholic Relief Bill, which enabled Catholics to become MPs and to hold other high offices, passed through Parliament with surprisingly little difficulty, to the delight of the leader of the Irish Catholics, Daniel O'Connell, who exclaimed to his wife: 'Who would have expected such a bill from Peel and Wellington?'

But the Tory ultras were incensed, and in order to dispel 'the prevailing atmosphere of calumny', the duke challenged one of his most abusive critics, Lord Winchilsea, to a duel. They met early one morning in what is now Battersea Park. The duke tried and failed to hit his opponent in the leg, but Winchilsea realised that to kill the hero of Waterloo was simply not on, and shot wide. Winchilsea then apologised to Wellington, who touched his hat, said 'Good morning' and rode back to Westminster. There was nevertheless widespread shock that the prime minister had risked death in this way, and none of his successors ever imitated his example.

That left the great issue for the following year as parliamentary reform. In France, the July Revolution took place. In England there were great disturbances, and also the unfortunate death of Huskisson, who was notorious for his physical clumsiness and was run over by Stephenson's Rocket, an early steam locomotive, while talking to Wellington. That made the return of the Canningites to government impossible in the short term. In November 1830, Wellington denounced reform in the most uncompromising terms in the House of Lords. His unyielding attitude made his continued leadership impossible, and on 16 November he resigned.

This was not the end of the story. The Whigs now had to cope with demands for reform. Wellington was hated by the London mob as an enemy of reform. They hanged him in effigy, and twice they stoned his house and broke his windows. His response was to install iron shutters – the origin of the nickname the Iron Duke.

Yet it was not his way to go on defending a position once it had become untenable, and in June 1832 he concluded that reform had got to be allowed. He was, in the end, a concessionary conservative: a man who realised the need to yield to the spirit of the times. Right up to his death, he discouraged his fellow peers from standing in the way of the Commons.

For a few weeks in 1834, he was again prime minister, but only as a stopgap, for Sir Robert Peel was somewhere in Italy, and it took time to find him and for him to get back.

When Wellington died, he was given perhaps the grandest funeral ever seen in London, and Tennyson described him as 'The last great Englishman'. The duke's fame was so great that a capital city (Wellington, New Zealand), a tree (the Wellingtonia), a dish (beef Wellington), a regiment, a school and a boot were all named after him.

EARL GREY

Lived 1764–1845; prime minister 1830–34

E arl Grey played the leading role in one of the greatest parliamentary dramas in British history, and achieved one of the most spectacular legislative triumphs. At the age of sixty-six, when he had been out of office for twenty-four years and his career seemed over, he ascended to the prime ministership, introduced the Great Reform Bill, outwitted powerful opponents and showed that the British constitution could be adapted to meet new requirements. To find a comparable comeback from the wilderness, one has to turn to Churchill, who became prime minister in 1940 at the age of sixty-five in order to save Britain from invasion.

Grey's aim was to save Britain from revolution. The eighteenth-century House of Commons, in which about half the seats were in the gift of wealthy patrons, was no longer tolerable to the wider nation, where some of the great new industrial towns had no parliamentary representation. Reform had been delayed for forty years by the fear of change that the French Revolution induced in the British ruling class. But in 1830, when the July Revolution took place in Paris and Belgium threw off Dutch rule, a wave of unrest swept southern England, and the clamour for reform suddenly became irresistible. The Duke of Wellington nevertheless resisted, so was swept out of power. Grey's hour had come.

He was an aristocrat, not a democrat. As Byron remarked, when he first set eyes on the tall, slim, handsome, charming and rather arrogant Charles Grey: 'He has the patrician thoroughbred look ... which I dote on.' Grey was from an old Northumberland family and educated at Eton, which like many future statesmen, he did not enjoy, and Trinity College, Cambridge, which he left without taking a degree. By the time he returned from a three-year grand tour of Europe, he had been elected to the Commons as one of Northumberland's two MPs.

His family were moderate Tories and supposed he would be too, but Grey gave early evidence of his liberal inclinations, and his boldness, by joining the Whigs, who were led by the charismatic Charles James Fox. Grey's maiden speech in 1787, an intemperate attack on Pitt the Younger, made his reputation. Soon afterwards he began a passionate love affair with the glamorous Georgiana, Duchess of Devonshire, who was seven years older than himself and a great Whig hostess, at the heart of a brilliant and scandalous world. She became pregnant. On discovering this, the duke told Georgiana she would never see their three children again unless she gave up Grey and had the baby adopted. She went to Aix-en-Provence to give birth, and the child, a daughter called Eliza, was brought up in Northumberland by Grey's parents, who pretended she was theirs.

In the 1790s, Grey campaigned for parliamentary reform: an unfashionable cause, heavily defeated on the two occasions he introduced it in the Commons. His lofty disinterestedness could not be doubted: he was not the kind of careerist who would take office on any terms. Power, if it came, would be on his terms. After marrying in 1794 the 18-year-old Mary Ponsonby, with whom he was very happy and had fifteen children, he retired for long periods to Howick, his estate in Northumberland, where he delighted in being. He was furious with his father, a distinguished general, for accepting a peerage, since this meant he himself would have to go to the Lords in due course.

When Fox died in 1806, Grey succeeded him for a brief period as Foreign Secretary. The following year, Grey found himself in the Lords, from where he complained in a letter to his wife that it was 'like speaking in a vault by a sepulchral light to the dead. It is impossible I should ever do anything there worth thinking of.'

For many years, he led the Whigs in Opposition. In 1820, he incurred the undying enmity of George IV by siding with Queen Caroline during the King's unbelievably embarrassing attempt to divorce her. In 1827, Grey declined an invitation to serve under George Canning, whom he privately dismissed as 'the son of an actress', so 'disqualified from being prime minister'.

But in 1830, everything changed. George IV died, the country was in turmoil, reform was suddenly in the air and the new king, William IV, held no prejudice against Grey. In November of that year, the King invited him to form a government after Wellington had declared in the Lords that the system of parliamentary representation could not be improved.

The new prime minster set out to show that it could be. He formed a Cabinet of landowners: every member of it held a hereditary title and, according to Grey, between them they owned more acres in England than any previous government. But it included four future prime ministers – Lord Melbourne, Lord John Russell, Lord Derby and Lord Palmerston – and Grey at once set up a subcommittee to draw up proposals for reform. 'Radical Jack' Durham, his own son-in-law, was keen on sweeping change and abused him in Cabinet for not going further. Lord Melbourne later remarked: 'If I'd been Lord Grey, I'd have knocked him down.'

But although Grey was tolerant, he was not weak. He espoused a set of compromise proposals which were sufficient to satisfy the more respectable, middle-class reformers, but fell so far short of pure democracy that they did not entirely alienate the parliamentarians who would have to enact them. At the same time, he imposed harsh penalties on rural unrest.

In March 1831, the First Reform Bill passed by a single vote in the Commons, only to be voted down by eight votes on a wrecking amendment the following month. Grey called a general election, which he won by a landslide. The Second Reform Bill now passed through the Commons and was thrown out in the Lords, despite a brilliant speech by Grey himself. The country was swept by riots. Grey introduced the Third Reform Bill, got it through the Commons and tried to persuade the King to create more peers to get it through the Lords. Throughout this desperate struggle, Grey preserved his sangfroid: he was what would now be called a big-match player, who could relax under extreme pressure. His handling of the King was recognised to be masterly. In May 1832, he resigned, when William IV refused his request to create fifty to sixty new peers to get the Bill through the Lords. The King asked Wellington to form a Tory government. Wellington tried and failed to do so, and the King now promised to create the peers needed to enable the Bill to pass despite diehard Tory opposition. But Wellington could tell when he was beaten, and persuaded a hundred peers to abstain. In June 1832, the Third Reform Bill passed the Lords by 106 votes to 22; three days later it received the Royal Assent and became law. Almost all the rotten boroughs, which contained very few voters, were abolished, and over 40 towns gained either one or two MPs. The size of the electorate in England increased from about 400,000 to 650,000.

It is hard, while relating these events, not to become swept away by a mood of Whig triumphalism. As a corrective to this, let it be stated that Grey saw the Great Reform Bill as a final settlement which would preserve the power of landowners, not as the first instalment on the road to 'one man, one vote', let alone 'one woman, one vote'.

His government's reforming zeal was not yet spent. In 1833, slavery was abolished throughout the British Empire, and the Factory Act began to regulate the use of child labour. In 1834, the Poor Law was reformed, in what turned out to be a harsh, utilitarian manner which would soon draw condemnation from Dickens. At the same time, the government started to disintegrate, riven by differences about how to reform the Irish Church. Grey had no desire to hang on to the bitter end. He too resigned, and was granted eleven years of retirement in his beloved Northumberland. Here his friend Thomas Creevey described his manner in his final years:

A most natural, unaffected, upright man, hospitable and domestic; far surpassing any man one knows in his noble appearance and beautiful simplicity of manner and equally surpassing all his contemporaries as a splendid public speaker. Take him all in all I never saw his fellow; nor can I see any imitation of him on the stocks.

Earl Grey brought in one of the great reforms, and his name survives as a type of tea.

LORD MELBOURNE

Lived 1779–1848; prime minister 1834 and 1835–41

On being asked to become prime minister, Lord Melbourne said he thought it 'a damned bore', and was 'in many minds as to what to do'.

His private secretary, Tom Young, retorted: 'Why, damn it all, such a position was never held by any Greek or Roman; and if it only last three months, it will be worth while to have been prime minister of England.'

'By God that's true,' Melbourne said. 'I'll go!'

We have this story from the diarist Charles Greville, who saw a great deal of Melbourne but, like most people, could not quite make him out: 'Everybody wonders what Melbourne will do. He is certainly a queer fellow to be prime minister.' To the world in general, Melbourne concealed his thoughts and emotions behind an affable, witty, tolerant, teasing exterior. As a young man, he had suffered the most notorious marital difficulties of any future prime minister. Yet he still loved and needed the company of spirited women, and became in the first years of her reign the adored prime minister and mentor of Queen Victoria. She saw at once that he was 'straightforward, clever, honest and good'.

He was born William Lamb. His mother established herself as a great Whig hostess: beautiful, intelligent, vivacious, ambitious and promiscuous, she had children by several men while remaining married to the rich but unremarkable Lord Melbourne. William, her second son, was generally supposed to have been fathered by Lord Egremont and was educated at Eton, Trinity College, Cambridge, and Glasgow University. He grew into a tall, dark, handsome, amusing and unpushy young man, who was liked by everyone he met. The death of his elder brother enabled him to renounce the legal career on which, with no enthusiasm, he had embarked and to enter in 1806, at the age of twenty-six, the House of Commons.

It also enabled him to propose marriage to the 19-year-old Lady Caroline Ponsonby, daughter of the Earl and Countess of Bessborough and niece of the Duchess of Devonshire, with whom he was in love. She was an upper-class wild child – slim, high-spirited and used on all occasions to getting her own way or else throwing a tantrum. For a few years they were happy, then they were unhappy. In 1812, she began a conspicuous affair with Lord Byron, a month after the poet awoke one morning and found himself famous, thanks to the publication of *Childe Harold*. It was Lady Caroline who described Byron as 'mad, bad and dangerous to know'. He called her 'the cleverest, most agreeable, absurd, amiable, perplexing, fascinating little being'. But he soon tired of her impetuous rages, realised her parading of their affair was doing him social harm and decided to break it off. She was infatuated with him, and refused to let him go. Her rages grew ever more extreme and culminated at Lady Heathcote's ball in July 1813, where Byron refused to dance with her, so she broke a glass and began gashing her naked arms.

The scandal was the talk of London and was followed by Lady Caroline's excruciatingly embarrassing autobiographical novel, *Glenarvon*. Melbourne's family urged him to separate from a woman who had heaped humiliation on them all, and most particularly on him. He agreed, but could not bring himself to leave her until 1825, and even after that, with tender good humour took what care he could of her until her death in 1828. They had one son, who was mentally handicapped, to whom Melbourne was devoted and who died in 1836 at the age of twenty-nine.

For many years, his political career seemed no happier than his marriage. In 1812, he left the Commons, unable to stand the heavy cost of getting himself re-elected. He told his mother that leaving Parliament felt like 'actually cutting my throat', for it deprived him of 'the greatest object of my life'. He cared about politics more deeply than he would generally admit. In 1816, he returned to Parliament, but these were the long years of Tory domination under Lord Liverpool, when there was no place for even a moderate, middle-of-the-road Whig like Melbourne.

In 1827, Canning became prime minister and needed some moderate Whigs to serve in place of the stern unbending Tories who refused to join. In came Melbourne as Chief Secretary for Ireland. It was his first real job, and he demonstrated his ability to conciliate Catholics as well as Protestants, and also his well-hidden capacity for hard work. In Dublin, he relaxed in the company of the young, beautiful and animated Lady Elizabeth Brandon. Her husband, the Reverend Lord Brandon, attempted to get a bishopric for himself out of this, and having failed to do so, sued Melbourne, but was unable to prove that anything improper had occurred.

The following year, Melbourne was one of the Whigs who resigned in sympathy with William Huskisson from the Duke of Wellington's government. But at the end of 1830, when Lord Grey replaced Wellington, he appointed Melbourne to the vital post of Home Secretary. For while the Reform Bill made its tempestuous passage through Parliament, the country had to be saved from sliding into civil war. This Melbourne did with energy and firmness. He avoided sending in troops, but urged magistrates to use their powers to the full. Once again, he had given proof of his executive abilities.

By 1834, the government was disintegrating and Lord Grey retired to Northumberland. William IV had to decide which of the Whigs to invite to take over as prime minister. His choice fell on the dependable Melbourne, for he seemed best placed to preserve the still-precarious order. His Cabinet colleague, Lord Durham, offered another reason for choosing Melbourne: 'He is the only man to be prime minister because he is the only one of whom none of us would be jealous.'

So in came the amiable Melbourne. He was fifty-five and lasted for 121 days before the King decided to replace him with the Tory leader, Sir Robert Peel. The most memorable event at this time was the burning down, in October 1834, of the Houses of Parliament, an event greeted with cheers by the London mob. Peel had no majority in the Commons, so called an election, but made insufficient progress to gain control, so in April 1835 resigned.

Melbourne, with some reluctance, was back. Few people expected him to last long, and he had renewed difficulties in his private life. He had for several years cheered himself by calling on his way home in the evenings on Mrs Caroline Norton, a beautiful and high-spirited young novelist who had established herself in rooms at Storey's Gate, not far from Parliament. She was the granddaughter of the playwright Sheridan, a famous Whig whom Melbourne had known in his youth.

George Norton, her villainous husband, decided to sue Mrs Norton for divorce, with Melbourne cited as co-respondent. But there was no evidence whatever that she had slept with him. When she was ill, Mr Norton had actually accompanied Melbourne to his wife's bedroom. On another occasion, Mr and Mrs Norton had visited Melbourne together in his house in South Street, Mayfair, where he continued to live even after becoming prime minister.

Melbourne asked William IV if he should resign. The King said definitely not. He and the Duke of Wellington suspected a shady plot to discredit Melbourne, and neither of them wanted anything to do with it. So Melbourne fought the case, though he did not appear in court himself, but sent the attorney general to make the case on his behalf. The court proceeedings caused huge excitement but only lasted a day, for the main witness Mr Norton had managed to recruit was a drunken groom called Fluke, whose ludicrous evidence fell to pieces under cross-examination. The jury acquitted Melbourne without even leaving their box to confer.

This was a success of a kind, and one which showed the prime minister's resilience under pressure. But it also left a gap in his emotional life, for while he remained anxious for Mrs Norton's welfare, he could no longer risk visiting her. This void was to be filled in a most unexpected way.

In June 1837, William IV died, and was succeeded by his niece, the 18-year-old Princess Victoria. She was on bad terms with her mother, the Duchess of Kent, whose husband, the duke, had died when their daughter was only one year old. During Victoria's childhood, the duchess, prompted by the unscrupulous Sir John Conroy, cut her off from other sources of advice and tried to lay the foundations for permanent control over her.

Victoria was determined to resist them. But to whom could she turn for help and comfort in this endeavour? As soon as she met Melbourne, she knew she could count on him. And on whom could it be more proper to rely than on her prime minister? He became her private secretary, spent six hours a day with her and soon had his own bedroom at Windsor. Ministers were allowed to do pretty much as they pleased. Lord Palmerston, the Foreign Secretary, nearly started a war with France. Melbourne was engaged in the vital work of tutoring the young Queen, for which he was entirely suited. As she herself wrote, 'he alone inspires me with that feeling of great confidence and I may say security, for I feel so safe when he speaks to me and is with me'.

His conversation was fascinating. He dropped the swear words, but was as witty as ever. He had known everyone worth knowing for the last forty years, including her own family. Her uncle George IV had been as, Prince Regent, a regular visitor, and something more than a visitor, to Melbourne's mother, and had become very fond of Melbourne himself.

For although Victoria was Queen, the Victorian age had not yet set in. Melbourne remained, in his manners and sense of humour, a man of the eighteenth century, who detested earnestness and refused to admire the middle classes. His attitude is caught in his remark after hearing an evangelical sermon: 'Things have come to a pretty pass when religion is allowed to invade the sphere of private life.' He was deeply interested in religion, and had read widely on the subject. But he was not pious.

Nor was he abstemious. He ate and drank huge amounts. In 1838, Lady Lyttelton observed that he was quite safe in office 'unless he contrives to displace himself by dint of consommés, truffles, pears, ices and anchovies, which he does his best to revolutionise his stomach with every day'.

In 1839, he made a dreadful error of judgement. One of the Duchess of Kent's maids of honour, Lady Flora Hastings, had been unkind about Baroness Lehzen, who ran the queen's household. Now Lady Flora grew unexpectedly large, and Melbourne encouraged the Queen in the idea that Lady Flora might be pregnant. When Lady Flora died, she was found, at the postmortem, to have an enormous liver tumour. The Hastings family were furious, and Victoria became for a time very unpopular.

In the same year, Sir Robert Peel seemed about to become prime minister, but indicated that he would expect the Queen to replace some of her ladies-in-waiting. Victoria said she could not bear this, and Melbourne encouraged her in her resistance. Somewhat irregularly, he remained prime minister for another two years.

In his offhand way, he helped to clarify the doctrine of Cabinet responsibility. For when he and his colleagues were discussing the Corn Laws, he told them: 'Now, is it to lower the price of corn, or isn't it? It is not much matter which we say, but mind, we must all say *the same*.'

But in 1840, he became superfluous to the Queen. She married her cousin, Albert of Saxe-Coburg and Gotha, who transported her to a state of married bliss, and quickly became her chief adviser too. She wanted to make Albert a King Consort, an idea against which Melbourne quite rightly warned: 'For God's sake, let's have no more of it, Ma'am. If you once get the English people into the way of making Kings, you'll get them into the way of unmaking them.'

The following year, he called a general election, lost it and resigned. A year later, he suffered a stroke from which he never fully recovered. He died in 1848. Anyone who likes the sound of him is urged to read Lord David Cecil's wonderful two-volume biography of him, which captures better than any other the Whig attitude to politics.

SIR ROBERT PEEL

Lived 1788–1850; prime minister 1834–35 and 1841–46

Sir Robert Peel was a statesman of transcendent ability, who fell from power because his own backbenchers came to regard him as a traitor. In the 1830s, he laid the foundations of the modern Conservative Party, but in 1846 he wrecked his own work by forcing through the repeal of the Corn Laws. He was a great reformer, but his uneasy manner meant he was seldom greatly loved.

Peel's family had new money, and lots of it. His father made a fortune as a cotton spinner in Lancashire, bought an estate near Tamworth in Staffordshire, became a Tory MP and told his son:

'Bob, you dog, if you are not prime minister some day, I'll disinherit you.' To this end the boy was sent to Harrow School, where he demonstrated such gifts that his tutor embarrassed him by telling the class, 'You boys will one day see Peel prime minister.' At school he became a close friend of Lord Byron, who recalled, 'I was always in scrapes, Peel never.'

At Oxford, the industrious Peel was the first person ever to take a double First: the curriculum having recently been divided into classics and mathematics, with students usually opting to be examined in one or the other. What an admirable young man he was – tall, strong, blue-eyed and conscientious. His father arranged for him to go straight into the Commons, where his maiden speech, delivered in 1810, was hailed as the best since Pitt the Younger's. In 1812, at the age of twenty-four, he was made Chief Secretary for Ireland, in which onerous role he served for six years, taking only one proper holiday. Daniel O'Connell, the Irish nationalist leader, dubbed him Orange Peel, for the Chief Secretary was a determined upholder of Protestant rule in Ireland. O'Connell even challenged Peel to a duel, which was to be fought in Ostend, but which never came off because O'Connell was temporarily detained in London.

In 1817, Peel made a wider name for himself by delivering a powerful speech in the Commons against Catholic emancipation. In the 1820s, he became the greatest of all Home Secretaries, his reforms culminating in the foundation of the Metropolitan Police, whose officers were known after him as Peelers or Bobbies. But in 1829, O'Connell got himself elected to the Commons despite being forbidden, as a Roman Catholic, from sitting there. The mood in Ireland was explosive, and Peel agreed with the prime minister, the Duke of Wellington, that Catholic emancipation had become necessary in order to avert civil war. At the duke's request, Peel reluctantly agreed to see the necessary legislation through the Commons: an act that saw him condemned by many Tories as a traitor. The Duchess of Richmond decorated her drawing room with stuffed rats called Wellington and Peel. By the end of 1830, Wellington was out of power, and to Peel fell the task of leading the Opposition in the Commons to the Reform Bill. After a titanic struggle, the Tories were defeated, and at the subsequent general election they gained only 179 out of 658 MPs. They had tried and failed to defy the national mood, and it seemed they must be out of office for many years.

Yet the period was just beginning in which Peel would adapt the Conservative Party (as it became known in the early 1830s: the name was of French derivation) to new conditions and lead it back to power. For in 1834, William IV dismissed the new Whig prime minister, Lord Melbourne, and looked to the Tories to form a government. Peel, somewhat uncharacteristically, was on holiday in Italy with his beloved wife, Julia, and their eldest daughter. Wellington said Peel was nevertheless the only possible choice to lead the Tories. The duke stood in while Peel was discovered in Rome and made his way home, a journey which in the pre-railway age took fourteen days.

A general election now took place, in which Peel stood for Tamworth, the local Staffordshire seat he had taken on from his father. It was clearly necessary to clarify the Tory attitude to the Reform Bill, which they had so bitterly opposed only two years before. So at the end of 1834, Peel issued the Tamworth Manifesto, an address to his constituents which was printed in The Times and other leading newspapers. In this he appealed 'to that great and intelligent class of society ... which is far less interested in the contentions of party, than in the maintenance of order and the cause of good government', and affirmed that he regarded the Reform Bill as 'a final and irrevocable settlement of a great constitutional question'. He promised too 'the correction of proved abuses and the redress of real grievances'.

This was the first manifesto ever issued by the leader of a British political party. It confirmed that Peel, as his record in the 1820s showed, was more than ready to make reforms where these were warranted. In the ensuing election, held in 1835, the Conservatives gained a hundred seats. But that was not enough to give Peel control of the Commons, and in April that year he made way for the return of the Whigs under Lord Melbourne.

In 1839, Melbourne resigned and Queen Victoria sent for Peel. But he struck her as a chilly figure, and when he tried to insist that as a demonstration of her confidence in him, she get rid of some of her Whig ladies of the bedchamber, she dug in her heels and refused. The Queen was only twenty years old, and she wanted to keep her beloved Melbourne. Peel had no idea how to deal with her, and gave way.

So it was only in 1841 that Peel came in as prime minister. Victoria was by now married to Prince Albert, an earnest German who saw in Peel a kindred spirit. An election was held, in which Peel obtained a convincing majority. He recruited able men to his government, including Edward Stanley and William Gladstone.

But the new prime minister faced a troubling situation. There was widespread economic distress in the country. The Chartist agitation for annual parliaments and universal male suffrage was at its height. Peel faced these problems with his usual boldness. Among many other subjects, he had a good grasp of economics: in 1819 he had helped to get the country back on the gold standard. He now cut indirect taxes and made up the lost revenue by reintroducing income tax, hitherto regarded as the sort of emergency measure only acceptable in wartime. Within a short time, he was vindicated: the economy improved, and with growing prosperity the Chartist demands evaporated.

But in 1845, the potato harvest failed, and Ireland was faced by imminent disaster. Peel saw at once that relief must be sent, or people would starve to death. He was convinced that the Corn Laws, which kept the price of grain artificially high, must be repealed.

Most of his Cabinet colleagues disagreed with him. The Conservatives represented the landed interest and were committed to upholding the Corn Laws. A great battle ensued, in which Peel decided to defy his own party. In truth, he did not take much trouble to win over his backbenchers, for whom he felt a considerable degree of scorn. On the contrary, he exulted in defying these dullards and set out to bounce them into backing his policy. He was by now very tired, for he had maintained, by an almost superhuman effort, a supervision of every government department. Nor was he well: a shooting accident in the 1820s had given him a perpetual sound like boiling water in his left ear.

The opposition to Peel was led by Lord George Bentinck, a man hitherto more interested in the turf than in politics. He said: 'I keep horses in three counties, and they tell me I shall save fifteen hundred a year by free trade. I don't care for that: what I cannot bear is being sold.'

And an exotic young MP called Benjamin Disraeli stepped forward to debate against Peel. In 1841, Disraeli had applied to Peel for a job and been turned down. Now he had the effrontery to deny having made any such application and to dismiss Peel as 'a man who never originates an idea – a watcher of the atmosphere, a man who, as he says, takes his observations, and when he finds the wind in a certain quarter trims to it'.

Never had a prime minister been treated with such scorn by his own followers. Nor did he feel any greater respect for them, dismissing them in a letter to a friend as 'men who have not access to your knowledge, and could not profit from it if they had, who spend their time in eating and drinking, and hunting, shooting, gambling, horse-racing and so forth'.

There spoke the puritan in Peel. He knew that abolishing the Corn Laws was the right thing to do, and with Opposition votes he went ahead and did it. But two-thirds of his own party voted against him, and out he went. In his resignation speech he declared, in words that were long remembered:

I shall leave a name execrated by every monopolist who … clamours for protection because it accrues to his individual benefit; but it may be that I shall leave a name sometimes remembered with expressions of goodwill in the abodes of those whose lot it is to labour, and to earn their daily bread by the sweat of their brow, when they shall recruit their exhausted strength with abundant and untaxed food, the sweeter because it is no longer leavened by a sense of injustice.

Here was a Conservative who rose above class interest and at a moment of tragedy, of horror, of bitter suffering in Ireland, strove to do the right thing and cut the price of food.

Wellington once said of Peel: 'How are we to get on? I have no small talk and Peel has no manners.' And it is true that Peel's manner to his colleagues tended to be cold and gauche. With Wellington himself, this did not matter: like Peel, the duke had a lofty yet pragmatic conception of the national interest, so supported the repeal of the Corn Laws, despite having hitherto approved of them. And so did other Peelites, including Gladstone.

But most Tories were neither so intelligent nor so adaptable. To them, Peel was a scoundrel. And in the folk memory of the party, he has gone down as the man who made the unforgiveable error of splitting it and therefore casting it into the political wilderness for a generation. Peel deserves to be remembered as a great and high-minded moderniser, who epitomised the turn in early Victorian times towards a more moral conception of politics. But from 1846 to the present day he has also served as a dreadful reminder to Conservative leaders that whatever else they do, they must at all costs avoid splitting the party.

He died in 1850, a few days after being thrown from his horse. The Peelites remained for some years a considerable factor in politics, before being absorbed in 1859 into the Liberal Party. Peel's most gifted follower, and his political heir, turned out to be Gladstone.

LORD JOHN RUSSELL

Lived 1792–1878; prime minister 1846–52 and 1865–66

Lord John Russell thought he was right about everything, and was certainly right about some things. He was a clever, fearless, irascible reformer, whose most remarkable work was done before he became prime minister. He has been described as the last of the Whigs and the first of the Liberals. Both descriptions are true. He was a great Whig aristocrat, a younger son of the Duke of Bedford, proud of his family's leading role in the Glorious Revolution of 1688, which had defended the people's ancient liberties against the crown. Throughout his life, he worked with a statue of Charles James Fox, the Whig hero of the late eighteenth century, on his desk. But he also recognised the need for further constitutional change, to get rid of rotten boroughs and widen the franchise, and over a period of forty years, from the 1820s to the 1860s, he drove that process forward and helped to found the Liberal Party.

Throughout his life, he also demonstrated a capacity for giving needless offence. A characteristic story has him at a party, leaving the Duchess of Inverness to go and talk to the Duchess of Sutherland, because the latter was further away from the fire and he felt too hot. 'I hope you told the Duchess of Inverness why you left her,' a friend of Russell said. 'No,' Russell replied, 'but I did tell the Duchess of Sutherland.' His own father, the Duke of Bedford, warned him that he gave 'great offence' to his followers in the Commons 'by treating them superciliously, and de haut en bas'.

But on first meeting Russell, people were most struck by the oddities of his appearance. He had an unusually large head, and was only five foot four and three-quarter inches tall, which makes him the second smallest British prime minister after Perceval. Although he suffered from lifelong ill health, he lived to the age of eighty-five.

On Christmas Eve 1814, the 22-year-old Russell had a private audience with Napoleon on the island of Elba. According to family tradition, he told the deposed emperor at length about the Russells. Napoleon remained silent, but went to the corner of the room and relieved himself. But in old age, Russell supplied a highly circumstantial account in which, on the contrary, Napoleon sought, during a conversation lasting an hour and a half, to extract as much information as possible from him about the state of European politics.

Russell had already been elected to the Commons for the family seat of Tavistock. He was ambitious to distinguish himself as a writer and, among other works, composed a novel, a five-act play in blank verse, a constitutional history and a life of his kinsman, William Lord Russell, a Whig martyr who had died on the scaffold under Charles II. But it was as an outspoken advocate of parliamentary reform, and of toleration for nonconformists, that he made his name.

In 1830, the Whigs came into office under Lord Grey, who deputed Russell and three others to draw up proposals for getting rid of the rotten boroughs. This they did under conditions of great secrecy, and in March 1831 Russell introduced the Reform Bill in the Commons, with results that were described by his colleague John Cam Hobhouse:

> Lord John Russell began his speech at six o'clock. Never shall I forget the astonishment of my neighbours as he developed his plan. Indeed, all the House seemed perfectly astounded; and when he read the long list of the boroughs to be either wholly or partially disfranchised there was a sort of wild ironical laughter. Baring Wall turned to me, said, 'They are mad they are mad!' and others made use of similar expressions – all but Sir Robert Peel; he looked serious and angry.

The country was wildly enthusiastic about Russell's proposals, which after great parliamentary battles at last became law, substantially unchanged, in June 1832.

From 1834, Russell led the Whigs in the Commons. Soon afterwards, already in his forties and having had many proposals of marriage turned down, he got happily married to a charming young widow, which led him to be called the Widow's Mite. But she died after only three years. Russell soon after married again, to a woman of a somewhat pious disposition twenty-three years younger than himself. He enjoyed family life and had six children of his own, as well as several stepchildren.

From 1835 he served as Home Secretary under Lord Melbourne. Gladstone, who was at this stage still a Tory, later said of him: 'No man ever led the House of Commons with a more many-sided activity or more indomitable pluck.' An American visitor, Charles Sumner, observed that Russell looked 'diminutive and rickety', and his voice was 'small and thin', but 'a House of five hundred members was hushed to catch his smallest accents'. Russell was always thinking up imaginative new schemes of reform, and his indifference to whether or not he was liked was one reason why many people trusted him.

The Whigs went out in 1841, but in 1846, Peel was only able to repeal the Corn Laws with their help. The Tory Party was wrecked, and in came Russell as prime minister. There could not have been a more difficult moment to take over. The Irish famine was taking hold: in the next two years, about a million people died and another million emigrated. Russell told the government machine to provide relief, but it was not equal to the task. He acquired a reputation for being personally disorganised, often losing papers, forgetting to finish letters and sending them to the wrong recipient. Colleagues would arrive for appointments in Downing Street only to find the prime minister had gone out. Russell was a curious combination of upper-class eccentric and absent-minded professor.

On the plus side, he managed in 1848 to defuse the Chartist demands without a revolution. While many parts of the Continent saw revolutions, London experienced nothing worse than an enormous demonstration at Kennington, from which the protesters dispersed peacefully. Russell also managed to put through educational reforms.

But he affronted the Roman Catholic Church, which the Whigs had traditionally seen as an enemy of freedom, by criticising its creation of bishops in England. He was bad at managing his colleagues, especially the Foreign Secretary, Lord Palmerston, who was, essentially, unmanageable. In December

1851, Palmerston went too far, by recognising, without consulting the prime minister or the Cabinet, the *coup d'état* carried out in Paris by Napoleon's grandson, Louis Napoleon. Russell sacked Palmerston, who took revenge by ensuring that in February 1852, Russell lost a vote in the Commons and had to resign as prime minister. A man of less vitality than Russell might have decided to retire from the scene, but that was not his way. He remained leader in the Commons, was annoyed by his successor, Lord Aberdeen, who did not take his advice, and in 1855 precipitated that prime minister's downfall by refusing to defend the conduct of the Crimean War. At a meeting of 274 MPs held at Willis's Rooms in 1859, Russell helped to unite the Whigs, led by himself, the Peelites and the Radicals into the new Liberal Party.

Queen Victoria now found herself faced with a choice between 'two terrible old men' as prime minister: Russell and Palmerston. She plumped for Palmerston, who carried on until 1865, when he died. In came Russell – who had served harmoniously as Foreign Secretary and in 1861 had entered the Lords as Earl Russell – for a second go at being prime minister. He had for years been saying that a new reform bill to widen the franchise was required, and now he tried and failed to get one through. In June 1866, he resigned. It was the end of his ministerial career, but he remained active in the Lords until his death in 1878.

Dickens dedicated *A Tale of Two Cities* to Lord Russell, 'In remembrance of many public services and private kindnesses.' He was at home with writers and intellectuals, and his grandson, who became the third earl and remembered him as 'a kindly old man in a wheelchair', was the philosopher Bertrand Russell, who would become at least as well known.

EARL OF DERBY

Lived 1799–1869; prime minister 1852, 1858–59 and
1866–68

L ord Derby was a brilliant orator who never quite fulfilled
his promise, and is today almost completely forgotten. He
was the first person to become prime minister on three
separate occasions, but served a total of only three years and 280
days in that office. For although he led the Conservative Party for
twenty-two years, longer than anyone else, he could never
persuade its gifted former members, the Peelites, to return to the
fold after the disastrous split of 1846. And this in turn meant that

for the entire period of Derby's leadership, the Conservatives were unable to gain a Commons majority.

He was a man of high birth – his family, the Stanleys, had established their fortune by helping Henry Tudor to defeat Richard III at the Battle of Bosworth Field in 1485 – and also of high ability. The Times said after his death that he was the only 'brilliant eldest son produced by the British peerage for a hundred years'. He was an excellent classicist, whose translation of Homer's Iliad ran through six editions. He was also a passionate devotee of the turf, his grandfather, the 12th earl, having founded the Derby. His father, the 13th earl, spent vast sums building up a collection of animals at Knowsley, the family seat outside Liverpool, and was the patron of Edward Lear, whose most famous poem, The Owl and the Pussycat, was dedicated to the Stanley children.

In 1822, the Derby with whom we are here concerned, who would become the 14th earl, entered the Commons as MP for the rotten borough of Stockbridge, bought for him by his grandfather. At this point he was called Edward Stanley, for he did not inherit the earldom until 1851, but in keeping with this volume's policy on names, we shall call him Derby from the first. He was soon identified as a coming man. Lord Melbourne told the young Benjamin Disraeli to forget about being prime minister, for that palm would go by 'the mere force of superior will and eloquence' to Derby, 'a young eagle above them all'.

Here was a man who could sway the Commons, as he showed in 1830–32 when he served in Lord Grey's government and was one of the leading Whig speakers who got the Reform Bill through Parliament. Yet Disraeli noted from the first that things did not always turn out well for Derby: 'The noble Lord is the Prince Rupert of Parliamentary discussion; his charge is resistless; but when he returns from pursuit he always finds his camp in the possession of the enemy.' That image was taken up in the description of Derby by Disraeli's friend, Edward Bulwer-Lytton:

The brilliant chief, irregularly great,
Frank, haughty, rash, the Rupert of Debate.

Haughty he certainly was: a grand seigneur, and not much disposed to accommodate other points of view. He was an intransigent defender of the privileges of the Anglican Church in Ireland, and in 1834 resigned rather than go along with Lord John Russell's plan to devote some of its surplus revenues to secular purposes. 'Johnny has upset the coach,' Derby said.

After a vain attempt to create his own group, the so-called Derby Dilly, he joined the Conservatives and served from 1841 as Secretary of State for War and the Colonies in Sir Robert Peel's government. In the great smash over the repeal of the Corn Laws, Derby parted from his Cabinet colleagues with the grim words, 'We cannot do this as gentlemen.' He became the leader of the mass of Tory backwoodsmen who saw Peel as a turncoat.

But by now, Derby was in the Lords: he had gone there in 1844, at his own request, because his health was poor. So the Conservatives needed a leader in the Commons, and only Disraeli had the ability to play that role. For the next twenty-two years, he was Derby's manager in the Commons. Relations between the two of them were, as John Vincent has written, 'frigid'. Derby's authority was unassailable, but he was appallingly rude to Disraeli's wife, making fun of her in front of other guests at Knowsley. Nor did he ever do his second-in-command the honour of visiting him at Hughenden, the country house Disraeli had set up near High Wycombe. Derby was cruel even to his own son, who was a disciple of Disraeli, but once arrived unexpectedly at Knowsley, only to receive the crushing retort: 'What the devil brings you here, Edward? Are you going to get married, or has Disraeli cut his throat?' And when another Tory grandee wrote to Derby, denouncing Disraeli as 'that nasty, oily, slimy Jew', Derby read those words out with relish, for the amusement of his friends at White's Club.

The agonising gout from which he suffered from his late thirties can have done nothing to improve his temper. But his arrogant manner did nothing to encourage Peel's followers, a gifted group which in William Gladstone and Lord Aberdeen included two future prime ministers, to return to the Conservative Party. As the Duke of Wellington remarked to Queen Victoria, 'There are two sections of the Conservative Party: on one side officers without men, on the other men without officers.'

So in February 1852, when Lord John Russell's Whig government fell and Queen Victoria invited Derby to form an administration, there was an embarrassing shortage of talent with which to do so. It became known as the 'Who? Who?' Cabinet, for that was how Wellington, who was by now very deaf, greeted in a loud voice the list of ministerial names as it was read out in the House of Lords. Disraeli was made Chancellor of the Exchequer, Derby brushing aside his objection that he knew nothing about finance.

That patrician attitude was not sufficient to see the government through. At the general election held in the summer of 1852, the Conservatives made gains, but not enough to get a Commons majority. In November, Derby said he would no longer seek to reimpose the Corn Laws: 'I bow to the decision of the country.' But the Peelites were unimpressed: they were already doing a deal with the Whigs, under which Aberdeen would become prime minister. In December, Disraeli's Budget was eviscerated by Gladstone and defeated in the Commons. The Conservatives were out.

Their next chance came in 1855, with the fall of Aberdeen. But Derby, to his followers' distress, missed it. They thought he was too devoted to the politics of 'masterly inactivity', and too inclined to go racing or shooting. In 1858, the Conservatives did come back in. Lord Derby launched the new administration with an exposition of his political philosophy:

My Lords, there can be no greater mistake than to suppose that a Conservative ministry necessarily means a stationary ministry. We live in an age of constant progress, moral, social and political ... our constitution itself is the result of a series of perpetual changes. Like the venerable old country houses of England, it has been framed from time to time by successive occupants, with no great regard for architectural uniformity or regularity of outline, but adding a window here, throwing out a gable there, and making some fresh accommodation in another place, as might appear to suit, not the beauty of the external structure, but the convenience and comfort of the inhabitants.

All this was true, no doubt, but there was no overwhelming demand in the country for the Conservatives to be the ones who carried out the alterations. They had time to place the government of India on a new footing and to allow Jews to sit in Parliament, but they could not get through their wider proposals for constitutional reform. Nor could they gain a majority at the 1859 general election: the newly formed Liberal Party narrowly beat them.

Derby spent another eight years in Opposition. He contemplated giving up, but did not wish to make way for Disraeli. From 1862, he performed great acts of public benevolence in his home county of Lancashire, in order to relieve the distress caused by the collapse of cotton imports during the American Civil War. His own donation of £10,000 was said to be the largest ever given by a private individual for a single purpose.

In 1866, the failure of Lord John Russell to widen the franchise gave Derby his last and greatest chance. In he came, and he and Disraeli cooked up the Second Reform Bill: a far more audacious measure than they themselves had just voted against, for it more than doubled the proportion of the adult male population who could vote, from 7 per cent to 16 per cent. Derby himself admitted this was 'taking a leap in the dark'. But the political temptation to do so was overwhelming. As he put it to one of his own discontented followers: 'Don't you see how it has dished the Whigs?' Here was a last great gamble worthy of a lover of the turf, and it came off.

But Derby's health was exhausted, and in February 1868 he made way for Disraeli. The following year he died at Knowsley. Disraeli said of him, when unveiling a statue of him some years later in Parliament Square: 'He abolished slavery, he educated Ireland, he reformed Parliament.' It is true that Derby promoted measures to achieve those things. But although he was an Olympian figure to his contemporaries, posterity regards him as a mere footnote to Disraeli.

EARL OF ABERDEEN

Lived 1784–1860; prime minister 1852–55

Lord Aberdeen's prime ministership was cut short by the disaster of the Crimean War. In the exceptionally severe winter of 1854–55, the British army, which had been assumed since the Battle of Waterloo in 1815 to be invincible, suffered appalling losses, amounting to over half the original force, as it strove while ravaged by disease to take Sebastopol from the Russians. The incompetence of the British commanders, and grotesque inadequacy of the supply and medical services, were conveyed to an indignant public by William Howard Russell of *The Times*, whose reports reached London with unprecedented speed thanks to the newly invented telegraph system. 'Someone had blundered,' as Alfred Tennyson put it in *The Charge of the Light Brigade*, his tribute to the courage of British soldiers whose lives were thrown away in a futile attack.

The public decided that, from a political point of view, Aberdeen was the blunderer. It is certainly true that this able, conscientious and peace-loving man was not cut out to be a war leader. He was an elderly expert on foreign affairs who allowed himself to be pushed by his more forceful colleagues into a conflict he was desperate to avoid.

Aberdeen's parents died while he was still a child. William Pitt, who was prime minister, became one of his guardians and encouraged him to pursue a political career. He travelled as a young man to Greece, where he excavated classical sites and, like Lord Elgin, acquired a collection of antiquities which ended up in the British Museum. Lord Byron – a cousin of Aberdeen – ridiculed their activities:

> Let Aberdeen and Elgin still pursue
> The shade of fame through regions of Virtu;
> Waste useless thousands on the Phidean freaks;
> Misshapen monuments and maim'd antiques;
> And make their grand saloons a general mart
> For all the mutilated blocks of art.

Aberdeen was actually a serious scholar. He also became an exemplary landlord of his estate in Aberdeenshire, where in the course of his life he planted 14 million trees, and was proud never to have turned out a tenant for failing to pay the rent. He married, very happily, Catherine Hamilton, and after her early death went into lifelong mourning for her, which included a diary in Latin of her appearances to him: '*Tota nocta vidi, ut in vita*' – 'The whole night I saw her, as in life.' His second marriage, which he was induced to make despite having once described his bride as 'one of the most stupid persons I have ever met with', was unhappy, and after she too died, he remained for the last thirty-seven years of his life a widower.

He never sat in the Commons: a grave drawback for a future prime minister, which in the nineteenth century he shared only with Rosebery. Nor was Aberdeen any good as a speaker in the Lords, which he joined in 1806 as a Scottish Representative Peer. In 1813, he undertook an important diplomatic mission to Austria, during which, as he hastened through the night, his coach overturned and he suffered concussion, to which he attributed the headaches from which he suffered for the rest of his life.

During this expedition, he also shared a hayloft with Metternich, Austrian Foreign Minister from 1809 to 1848, and witnessed the aftermath of the huge Battle of the Nations in which Napoleon was defeated at Leipzig:

> For three or four miles the ground is covered with bodies of men and horses, many not dead. Wretches wounded unable to crawl, crying for water amidst heaps of putrefying bodies. Their screams are heard at an immense distance, and still ring in my ears.

Aberdeen acquired a deep horror of war, and during his two terms of office as Foreign Secretary, from 1828 to 1830 and 1841 to 1846, became known as a safe pair of hands, who managed to heal the wounds opened by the bellicose Lord Palmerston in the late 1830s and to form the first *entente cordiale* with France. Aberdeen was the Conservatives' most trusted authority on foreign affairs, and in the great split of 1846 he sided, like other men of weight and judgement, with the outgoing prime minister, Sir Robert Peel.

The Peelites, as they were called, went into Opposition with their chief, and after Peel himself died in 1850, Aberdeen became their leader. At the start of 1852, Lord John Russell's Whig government went out, brought down by the truculent Palmerston, and Lord Derby came in as prime minister at the head of a minority Conservative government. He tried in vain to get the Peelites to join him. In the course of that year, a more tempting offer came their way. Although there were only thirty of them, they found they could take just over half the Cabinet posts, including the prime ministership, by forming a coalition with the 200 Whigs.

In December 1852, Aberdeen entered office at the head of a formidable group of ministers, including Russell and Palmerston from the Whigs, and William Gladstone and Sir James Graham from the Peelites. The latter wrote in his diary:

It is a powerful team, but it will require good driving. There are some odd tempers and queer ways among them, but on the whole they are gentlemen, and they will have a perfect gentleman at their head, who is honest and direct, and who will not brook insincerity in others.

It was his innate decency that made Aberdeen so acceptable to his colleagues. This was not, however, accompanied by the force of character needed to control them. He was a conciliator rather than a leader. Disraeli, chief spokesman for the Conservatives in the Commons, perceived this weakness and in the summer of 1853 wrote a savage description of the new prime minister:

Now that he is placed in a prominent position, and forced to lead English gentlemen, instead of glozing and intriguing with foreign diplomatists, not a night passes that his language or his demeanour does not shock and jar upon the frank and genial spirit of our British Parliament. His manner, arrogant and yet timid – his words, insolent and yet obscure – offend even his political supporters. His hesitating speech, his contracted sympathies, his sneer, icy as Siberia, his sarcasms, drear and barren as the Steppes, are all characteristic of the bureau and the chancery, and not of popular and aristocratic assemblies animated by the spirit of honour and the pride of gentlemen. If war breaks out – and the present prospect is that war will break out – this dread calamity must be placed to the account of this man, and of this man alone.

How very unpleasant Disraeli could be, when trying to destroy a rival. But he was right that Aberdeen often failed to make clear what the government was trying to do, that war was on the way and that the blame would be pinned on the prime minister. The Russian tsar, Nicholas I, believed he could get away with grabbing some Turkish territory, for Aberdeen wanted to appease him. The Turks believed they could defy the tsar, because Palmerston (who had been put in charge of the Home Office, where it was thought he could do less harm) was implacably determined to make the Russians back down, as were the French.

In March 1854, Britain and France declared war on Russia, after the Russians had sunk a Turkish naval squadron. Palmerston, who had frenziedly anti-Russian public opinion on his side, had got his way. Aberdeen wanted to step aside, but Queen Victoria begged him to carry on, as otherwise she would be left in the hands of Palmerston and the war party. Against his better judgement, Aberdeen carried on. He proposed that the Royal Navy bombard Sebastopol, which was the Russian naval base, but the decision was instead taken to capture it from the land. In the mid-nineteenth-century suburbs of most English towns can be found Alma, Balaclava and Inkerman Roads, commemorating the costly victories on the way to Sebastopol. Then came the horrors of the siege itself. Public fury mounted, Aberdeen proved pitifully incapable of defending himself against Lord Derby's attacks and Lord John Russell, who had all along thought that he rather than Aberdeen should be prime minister, resigned from the Cabinet rather than support the government. In January 1855, a Commons motion calling for a committee of inquiry into the conduct of the war was passed by 157 votes, and Aberdeen was forced to resign. He had been in office for only two years and 42 days. He died in 1860 at the age of seventy-six and although he still had many friends and many estimable qualities, his reputation has never recovered.

LORD PALMERSTON

Lived 1784–1865; prime minister 1855–58 and 1859–65

Lord Palmerston was a bold, jaunty, high-handed minister, who expressed the almost overpowering vitality of mid-Victorian England and always backed his own quick judgement against the slow, dreary, methodical timidity of his colleagues. He was rude, unpunctual, industrious, adventurous, licentious and refused to treat anyone, no matter how grand and especially if foreign, with exaggerated respect. That was Palmerston's idea of freedom, and the British public loved him for it.

He possessed astonishing stamina. Entering the Commons at the age of twenty-two, for as an Irish peer he had no seat in the Lords, he served almost continuously in various arduous roles before becoming prime minister at the age of seventy, the oldest at which anyone has ever done so for the first time. He then remained in power for most of the next ten years.

His speciality was foreign affairs. As a child, he learned excellent French and good Italian while travelling with his family on the Continent. In his maiden speech, delivered in 1808, he supported the bombardment of Copenhagen. The following year, he was offered the post of Chancellor of the Exchequer, but declined it, pleading inexperience. Throughout his life, he possessed a well-hidden streak of prudence: he was daring, but not reckless. For seventeen years he served as Secretary at War, followed by a total of seventeen years as Foreign Secretary.

In the early 1830s, Palmerston overcame huge difficulties to negotiate the creation of Belgium. He was a professional diplomatist with a detailed knowledge of every court and Cabinet in Europe, and worked so hard that his staff complained about him. Yet he also found the time and energy to conduct love affairs with, among others, three of the seven 'lady patronesses' who controlled access to Almack's, where fashionable society gathered in the West End of London.

The love of his life was Lady Cowper, whose brother, Lord Melbourne, became prime minister, and said of her that she was 'a remarkable woman, a devoted mother, an excellent wife – but not chaste, not chaste'. After Lady Cowper's first husband died, Palmerston married her. He was fifty-five and she fifty-two, but they still made a handsome couple. She was for half a century one of the most notable hostesses in London, whose morals were out of keeping with the new Victorian age, but whose invitations were highly prized.

Queen Victoria and her husband, Prince Albert, were appalled by Palmerston. He did not value Albert's expert knowledge of foreign affairs and enraged Victoria by sending off dispatches which she had not even been shown. In 1850, the prince informed the prime minister, Lord John Russell, that while a guest under the Queen's roof at Windsor Castle, the Foreign Secretary, Palmerston, had

> committed a brutal attack upon one of her ladies-in-waiting, had at night by stealth, introduced himself into her apartment, barricaded afterwards the door and would have consummated his fiendish scheme by violence had not the miraculous efforts of his victim and assistance attracted by her screams saved her.

Albert omitted to mention that this incident had occurred many years earlier, before Palmerston got married. Cecil Woodham-Smith explains, in her life of Victoria, how the mistake occurred: 'There had been a change in accommodation at Windsor and the room entered by Lord Palmerston was normally occupied by a lady not averse from his attentions, whom he was accustomed to visit there.'

Palmerston started out in politics as a Tory, became a Whig and ended up as leader of the Liberal Party, but these party labels reveal very little about him. In domestic politics, his views tended towards the conservative: he could not see much need for reform, as Britain already possessed an admirable constitution. In foreign policy, he tended to be much more liberal and to sympathise, for example, with those Italians who wanted to liberate and unify their nation and set up their own parliamentary system. When the Austrians, who under Metternich's guidance had long resisted change, protested that he was interfering in Italy, a considerable part of which was in their hands, he replied: 'Prince Metternich thinks he is a conservative in clinging obstinately to the status quo ... We think ourselves conservatives in preaching and advising everywhere concessions, reforms and improvements, where public opinion demands them.'

But above all, Palmerston was identified with the robust assertion of the British national interest, to be pursued in accordance with the circumstances of the moment, for as he told the Commons in 1848: 'We have no eternal allies and no perpetual enemies. Our interests are eternal and perpetual and those interests it is our duty to follow.'

In 1850, Palmerston seemed to overreach himself. Don Pacifico was a Portuguese Jew living in Athens, who happened to have been born in Gibraltar, so was a British subject. When an anti-Semitic mob burned down his house, he demanded the preposterous sum of £81,000 in compensation from the Greek government, and appealed to London for help. After fruitless negotiations, Palmerston dispatched the British Mediterranean fleet to Piraeus and forced the Greeks to pay up: a step generally seen as a gross overreaction which left Britain on the brink of war. A torrent of condemnation poured over the Foreign Secretary, but he turned the tables on his critics by delivering, with scarcely a note, a brilliant four-and-a-half-hour speech in the Commons which ended with one of the most famous appeals to national pride ever uttered by a British statesman:

as the Roman, in days of old, held himself free from indignity, when he could say Civis Romanus sum; so also a British subject, in whatever land he may be, shall feel confident that the watchful eye and the strong arm of England, will protect him against injustice and wrong.

Palmerston was a popular hero, yet his colleagues continued to distrust him, and at the end of 1851, Lord John Russell dismissed him as Foreign Secretary. Palmerston was entirely unabashed by this setback, and soon afterward got in his 'tit for tat', as he called it, by engineering Russell's downfall. Lord Derby formed a short-lived Conservative government, after which Lord Aberdeen came in at the head of a coalition, in which Palmerston was confined to the role of Home Secretary.

But he could not be confined there for long. The slide into the Crimean War had begun, and after Aberdeen had been forced, in January 1855, to step down and to take the blame for the British army's appalling unpreparedness, the Queen was obliged, most reluctantly, to ask Palmerston to take over. He was seen by the public as the one man with the drive and determination to retrieve the situation and defeat Russia. Disraeli attempted, for the Conservatives, to dismiss Palmerston as 'an old painted pantaloon – very deaf, very blind and with false teeth'. The charge did not stick. Palmerston greatly improved the army's supplies, backed Florence Nightingale as she transformed its medical services and soon brought the war to a relatively successful conclusion, assisted by the French storming of Sebastopol. He adopted a forward policy in China, where he protested that 'an insolent barbarian wielding authority in Canton has violated the British flag', and in 1857, when the Commons voted against this policy, he called a general election, which he won. He proceeded to handle the Indian Mutiny with steadfast moderation, resisting calls, after it had been suppressed, for vengeance to be wreaked on the Muslims and Hindus.

In 1858, he agreed that would-be assassins in London who had plotted an attempt on the life of Napoleon III should be more effectually suppressed. His Conservative opponents seized the chance to condemn him for yielding to French pressure and defeated him in the Commons. Palmerston was out, but his replacement, Lord Derby, did not command a majority, and was very soon out too. In the summer of 1859, Palmerston came back in at the age of seventy-five, at the head of the newly formed Liberal Party, and governed for another six years. He refused to contemplate any parliamentary reforms and held in check all attempts by William Gladstone, the brilliant and imperious Chancellor of the Exchequer, to range beyond that brief. Palmerston said of his colleague: 'Gladstone will soon have it all his own way, and whenever he gets my place we shall have strange doings.'

At the start of the American Civil War in 1861, Palmerston supported the southern states without actually recognising the sovereignty of the Confederacy. In 1863, during a visit to Scotland to be installed as Rector of Glasgow University, the 78-year-old prime minister demonstrated his continued health and energy by climbing Arthur's Seat in Edinburgh. He also rode an hour from Westminster to his old school, Harrow, to take part in speech day. Best of all, he found himself accused, by the wife of an Irish journalist, of having committed adultery with her. This story delighted the public and raised his popularity to new heights.

Palmerston grappled in vain with the Schleswig-Holstein problem, which he claimed only three people had ever understood: Prince Albert, who was dead, a Danish professor, who had gone mad, and he himself, who had forgotten all about it. In 1864, Bismarck, at the head of Prussia and in alliance with Austria, proceeded in a short war to deprive Denmark of Schleswig-Holstein. This was a severe humiliation for Palmerston, who had assured the Danes that if it came to war, they would not fight alone. The problem was that the Royal Navy, which had so often underwritten his assertive foreign policy, was of no value in stopping the Prussian army.

His popularity with the British public remained to the end intact. In the summer of 1865, he called a general election and was returned with an increased majority. But in October, before Parliament met, he caught a chill while out driving in an open carriage and died, two days before his eighty-first birthday, of pneumonia. His last words are supposed to have been the characteristic retort: 'Die, my dear doctor, that's the last thing I'll do!'

Florence Nightingale said of him: 'He will be a great loss to us. Tho' he made a joke when asked to do the right thing, he always did it.' There too, Palmerston was a very English figure: a man who refused to adopt a serious tone of voice, even when he was doing serious and well-calculated things.

In old age, Gladstone told a story of a Frenchman, 'thinking to be highly complimentary', who told Palmerston: 'If I were not a Frenchman, I should wish to be an Englishman.' To this Palmerston coolly replied: 'If I were not an Englishman, I should wish to be an Englishman.' He is in some ways the most English of all prime ministers, and his popularity survives to this day as the name of a pub.

BENJAMIN DISRAELI

Lived 1804–81; prime minister 1868 and 1874–80

Benjamin Disraeli's career was a triumph of highly coloured imagination over earnest respectability. Conservatives were intoxicated by him, and long after his death still thrilled to his name, because he gave them the romance of politics, not just the practicalities. He was as vivid as one of the preposterously overdone aristocrats in his novels and became, after humiliations which would have destroyed a less courageous and shameless man, the most improbable prime minister in this book.

He grew up as an outsider. Every other prime minister in the nineteenth century attended a famous school, usually Eton or Harrow, while Disraeli went to Higham Hall School, Walthamstow. Nor did Disraeli attend either Oxford or Cambridge, an omission which in that century he shares only with Wellington. But Wellington was born into the ruling class, while Disraeli was born a Jew, at a time when Jews could not even become MPs, a restriction which remained in force until 1858.

In 1817, at the age of twelve, Disraeli was baptised into the Church of England. But he always regarded himself as Jewish and, far from downplaying his race, was immensely proud of it, and insisted it made him at least as aristocratic as any Englishman: 'I am not disposed for a moment to admit that my pedigree is not as good as that of the Cavendishes [the Duke of Devonshire's family]', as he put it when standing for election against one of them. His father, Isaac D'Israeli, was a man of letters, well known as the author of *Curiosities of Literature*, published in six volumes from 1791 to 1834, and himself the son of a merchant who had emigrated from Italy to London in 1748, and had prospered as an importer of straw hats.

Isaac arranged for Benjamin to train from the age of seventeen as a solicitor. This did not accord with the youth's craving to cut a dash in the world. He spent two years as a trainee lawyer, after which he began a series of speculations in South American mining shares and launched a newspaper to compete with *The Times*. The shares collapsed, as did the newspaper, and for the rest of his life Disraeli was mired in debt. In great haste, he wrote a novel in which he enraged his fellow investors by making fun of them, after which he had a nervous breakdown, from which he recuperated during a course of foreign travel.

Back in London, he was mocked for his absurdly dandified dress. From 1832 onwards, he stood and lost three times in Wycombe for Parliament as an 'independent Radical'. It became evident to him that he must have the support of a party. In 1835, he joined the Conservatives, for whom he had one more electoral failure, but in 1837, at the age of thirty-two, he at last entered the Commons, as one of the two members for Maidstone. His colleague there soon died, and Disraeli married the man's voluble, warm-hearted, ill-educated widow, Mary Anne, who was forty-five years old and had a life income of £5,000 a year. They became deeply fond of each other, and he dedicated one of his novels to 'a perfect Wife!'

His maiden speech was delivered in December 1837. Greville, the diarist, described its reception, using the apostrophe which Disraeli had dropped from his name in 1822, but which many who wished to emphasise his Jewishness continued to use:

> D'Israeli made his first exhibition this night, beginning with florid assurance, speedily degenerating into ludicrous absurdity, and being at last put down with inextinguishable shouts of laughter.

The new member was reduced to shouting above the din, which came mainly from some Irish MPs he had annoyed: 'I will sit down now, but the time will come when you will hear me.'

In 1841, the Conservative leader, Sir Robert Peel, became prime minister, and Disraeli applied to him for a ministerial post, but received a polite refusal. Disraeli instead wrote more novels, including *Coningsby* (1844) and *Sybil* (1845), which can still be read with enjoyment today, for they are by turns spirited and ludicrous, comic and romantic, and the author's gusto carries the reader through the passages which are trumpery stuff. Disraeli has a keen eye for the humour of ambition, and of political hack-work, and of young idealism, and of love, and confounds them all together. He is full of penetrating insights about power, but to try to divine a political philosophy from these novels is a fool's errand. They are remarkable for their style, and for a kind of hopeless longing for a patrician, paternalistic England that existed mainly in Disraeli's superheated imagination, though he cultivated the friendship of those few young noblemen who could glimpse what he meant.

Within a few years, Sir Robert had decided on the repeal of the Corn Laws, a form of protection to which he had previously been committed, for it kept grain prices up and was very dear to the landed gentlemen who formed the great majority of Conservative MPs. Disraeli now became, in a series of unbelievably impertinent speeches delivered in an impassive drawl, their champion against the traitor Peel, who had no idea how to reply.

In his first great onslaught, delivered on 22 January 1846, after a long and dreary explanation by Peel had been received in dead silence, Disraeli compared the prime minister to a nurse, who had been entrusted with the baby of protection:

> Who can forgot how its nurse dandled it, fondled it? What a charming babe! Delicious little thing! so thriving! Did you ever see such a beauty for its years? This was the tone, the innocent prattle. And then the nurse, in a fit of patriotic frenzy, dashes its brains out, and comes down to give master and mistress an account of this terrible murder. The nurse, too, a person of a very orderly demeanour; not given to drink; and never showing any emotion except of late, when kicking against protection.

Peel was goaded into pointing out that Disraeli, despite now condemning his entire career, had once been willing to enter office with him. Disraeli responded with a flat lie, which Peel for some reason declined to expose, despite possessing the letter in which Disraeli had solicited a job.

In June 1846, Peel got the repeal of the Corn Laws through, with the votes of the Whig Opposition. But as leader of the

Conservative Party, he was finished. Disraeli had, however, done his work so well that the party was very nearly finished too. It would not win a majority for another twenty-eight years.

Disraeli set out to acquire some of the appurtenances of a traditional political leader. He borrowed the substantial sum needed to buy Hughenden, a country house in Buckinghamshire, and there he planted trees and entered into county life. He also toned down his wardrobe a bit. As the Conservatives' most gifted debater, Disraeli had established the right, despite the distaste some people felt for him as a reckless parvenu, to lead them in the Commons. But Lord Derby was the undisputed leader of the party as a whole. In February 1852, Derby formed the first of his three short-lived minority administrations and invited Disraeli to serve as Chancellor of the Exchequer. Disraeli objected that he did not know much about the Treasury, to which Derby replied: 'You know as much as Mr Canning did. They give you the figures.'

Canning had served simultaneously as prime minister and Chancellor in 1827. Disraeli's first chancellorship ended in December 1852, when his Budget was ripped to pieces by William Gladstone: the start of the parliamentary duel between the two men which would last for almost thirty years. It was in response to Gladstone that Disraeli – about to be voted out of office by an alliance of opposition parties – made his famous assertion: 'England does not love coalitions.' On stepping down, Disraeli refused to hand over the Chancellor's robe to Gladstone, who succeeded him at the Treasury.

Disraeli's next chance, in the same office, came in 1858, but only lasted until 1859. These were years of frustration: Lord Palmerston, who was prime minister, pursued such conservative policies that the Conservatives found themselves redundant. Only in June 1866, by which time Palmerston was dead, did Disraeli come in for a third turn at the Treasury. With Derby, he saw through the Second Reform Bill, which more than doubled the size of the electorate, and then in February 1868 Derby retired through ill health. Disraeli became prime minister at the age of sixty-four, remarking to friends that he had reached the top of the greasy pole.

Greasy was the right word, for he soon slid back down again, having lost the general election of November 1868 to Gladstone. Disraeli settled down to write *Lothair*, which enjoyed a huge success: the first novel ever written by an ex-prime minister, and a performance none of his successors has tried to emulate.

By 1874, Gladstone's reforming zeal had blown itself out and the Conservatives managed to win a general election, their first since Peel had led them to victory in 1841. No longer did they seem condemned to eternal minority status. Disraeli had led them back into the promised land.

But he was sixty-nine, and in declining health. His beloved wife was dead. He wrote indefatigably to Lady Bradford, with whom he was now in love. The new Conservative government passed a number of pieces of social legislation, but without Disraeli showing any conspicuous enthusiasm. He was much more excited by questions of national prestige. His patriotism owed much to the example set by Lord Palmerston. He bought a controlling share in the Suez Canal from under the noses of the French: a coup that delighted the nation, and Queen Victoria in particular. With her, he exercised all his flattering arts, persuading her to resume public duties, which she had long neglected, and obtaining for her the title of Empress of India. Gorgeous oriental spectacles had always delighted him. He became the only prime minister regularly to receive flowers from the sovereign. In 1876, for the sake of his health, he moved to the House of Lords, allowing the Queen to make him Earl of Beaconsfield. On being welcomed by a peer who expressed the fear that he might miss the excitement of the Commons, Disraeli replied, 'I am dead: dead, but in the Elysian fields.'

Atrocities occurred in the Balkans, where the Turks were reported to be massacring Christians. Gladstone had a fit of moral indignation, but Disraeli remained calm. Because he was not a moralist, he was able to behave as a realist. In 1878, he went to the Congress of Berlin to settle the trouble, and was the celebrity of the conference, and got on well with Bismarck, who had unified Germany, was of a similarly unsentimental disposition, and said of Disraeli, 'Der alte Jude, das ist der Mann.' The old Jew was indeed the man, and returned amid scenes of wild enthusiasm to London, where he informed a grateful nation that he had obtained 'peace with honour', and also the island of Cyprus.

In 1880, he called a general election, and the Conservatives were overwhelmed by the Liberals under Gladstone. Disraeli completed the last of his novels, Endymion, which contains the remark: 'The British People being subject to fogs and possessing a powerful Middle Class require grave statesmen.' He could be grave when it suited him, but even when he was grave, he preserved a light tone of voice and was alert to the ironies of a situation. He was prime minister for a total of just under seven years, yet impressed his personality on the nation in a way few others have. After his death in 1881, the Primrose League, an enormous voluntary organisation founded by Lord Randolph Churchill, the father of Winston, perpetuated Disraeli's fame for many years, and laid primroses at his statue each year on 19 April, the anniversary of his death. Lord Randolph provided this summary of Disraeli's career: 'Failure, failure, failure, partial success, renewed failure, ultimate and complete triumph.'

WILLIAM GLADSTONE

*Lived 1809–98; prime minister 1868–74, 1880–85, 1886
and 1892–94*

William Gladstone turned politics into a morality play
starring himself as God's right-hand man, and
brought it to mass audiences. No other prime minister
has striven with such titanic energy, sincerity and eloquence to
apply Christian principles to political life. Lord Kilbracken, who
worked for him as his principal private secretary, said if a figure
of 100 represented the energy of an ordinary man, and 200 that

of an exceptional man, Gladstone's energy was represented by a figure of at least 1,000.

To his admirers, he had the strength and conviction of an Old Testament prophet. To his opponents, he was Judas Iscariot: a traitor who betrayed the causes he had once held dear and inflicted deep wounds on his own party by trying to push through Irish Home Rule. And to many people of a less earnest temperament than himself, he seemed absurd. The MP and journalist Henry Labouchere said that while he had no objection to Gladstone's habit of concealing the ace of trumps up his sleeve, he did object to his repeated claim that it had been put there by Almighty God. Like the conflict in the English Civil War between Roundheads and Cavaliers, the rivalry between Gladstone and Disraeli expressed an unbridgeable temperamental divide.

Born in 1809, Gladstone became an MP at the age of twenty-two and formed his fourth and last administration in 1892, at the age of eighty-two. His father, John Gladstone, was from Leith, near Edinburgh, and made a fortune as a merchant in Liverpool. When William was only three, he was brought into a dinner his father was giving for Canning, then a Liverpool MP, was placed on a chair, and gave what in later life it amused him to call his first speech: 'Ladies and gentlemen.' He was sent to Eton and to Christ Church, Oxford, where he took a double First in classics and mathematics. He was also President of the Union, where he made a tremendous speech denouncing the Great Reform Bill.

This speech led directly to Gladstone becoming, at the invitation of the Duke of Newcastle, the Tory candidate in Newark, where despite the passing of the Reform Bill, the duke still had a preponderant influence. In later life, when mocked by Disraeli and others for having been at this point not just a Tory but an arch-reactionary, Gladstone admitted that 'there was to my eyes an element of the anti-Christ in the Reform Act'.

There is no doubt that at this early stage in his career, Gladstone favoured every reactionary cause. Not for nothing did Macaulay refer to him as 'the rising hope' of the 'stern and unbending Tories'. He defended his father's record as an owner of slaves in the West Indies and said that, while he would not defend the institution of slavery, for it was a system which 'unquestionably began in crime, in atrocious crime', 'I do not admit that holding slaves necessarily involves sin, though it does necessarily involve the deepest and heaviest responsibility.' He advocated ruthless coercion in Ireland and the maintenance of all the privileges of the Anglican Church Establishment in that country.

But more important than Gladstone's political opinions were his religious convictions. In 1838, when he was twenty-nine years old, he published his first book, *The State in its Relations with the Church*. He argued that the State possessed a conscience and had a duty to distinguish between truth and error in religion. Doctrinal differences were, therefore, matters of supreme importance. The Established Church was the conscience of the English State, and that State was bound to give an active, informed, consistent and exclusive financial and general support to the Anglican religion, which was of the purest and most direct Apostolic descent.

The book was torn to pieces by Macaulay, who remarked that 'he deludes first himself and then his readers'. Gladstone himself soon realised that no one agreed with his medieval ideal of a Christian society possessing a monopoly of truth: as he later admitted, 'I found myself the last man on a sinking ship.' In 1839, he began a long and happy marriage to Catherine Glynne, who was closely related to four former prime ministers, the Pitts and the Grenvilles. Thanks to her, he acquired the Hawarden estate in North Wales, which with characteristic resourcefulness he rescued from bankruptcy after unwise speculations by her brother.

Gladstone began to adapt his political ideas to the way the world was going, which was towards greater freedom and wider opportunities for Catholics, Jews, the lower classes, the Irish and other groups hitherto excluded from the Anglican Establishment. He became a strong supporter of Sir Robert Peel, who in 1843 invited him to join the Cabinet as President of the Board of Trade, in which role Gladstone acquired his astounding mastery of fiscal policy and especially of the measures needed to promote free trade. He was a follower of Peel, and like Peel he ended by dividing his own party. In 1846, when the great bust-up over the Corn Laws occurred, Gladstone was one of the gifted group of Conservative ministers who stayed loyal to Peel.

In a great speech delivered late at night in December 1852, and lit by flashes of lightning from a storm outside, Gladstone destroyed the Budget just introduced by Disraeli: the start of a rivalry which ended only with the latter's death. Lord Aberdeen, who at this point became prime minister, invited Gladstone to become Chancellor of the Exchequer. In his first Budget, delivered in April 1853, Gladstone declared that income tax is, in its essence, immoral, for it tempts statesmen to extravagance and taxpayers to fraudulent evasions. He laid out a plan to abolish it over a period of years and, although he did not succeed in this ambition, he did reduce it from tenpence to fourpence in the pound: in modern terms, the unbelievably low rate of 1.7 per cent. Opinion will always be divided about Gladstone's record as prime minister, but no one will seek to deny that he is the greatest ever Chancellor of the Exchequer. Money, he declared, should 'fructify in the pockets of the people' rather than being taken by the State. He gave the Treasury a dominance over all other departments which it has never lost.

In 1868, he became prime minister for the first time. Disraeli, his great Tory rival, had just trumped him by widening the franchise: a parliamentary humiliation for Gladstone, who found himself comprehensively outwitted by his subtle and unscrupulous opponent. But it was the Liberal Party, formed as recently as

1859, which now triumphed under Gladstone's leadership at the polls. He led from the front, introducing all the main measures of this great reforming administration himself. These included universal education up to the age of thirteen; competitive exams for entry to the civil service; the abolition of the purchase of commissions in the army; and voting by secret ballot. But he found his great new mission in Ireland, a country to which he only ever paid one proper visit, but which he intended to pacify by overthrowing the Protestant ascendancy, in the first place by disestablishing the Anglican Church in Ireland and pushing through land reform. This alienated some of his most prominent supporters, including a number of great Whig landowners, but Gladstone pushed on regardless. His style of politics was incredibly forceful, because everyone could see it was not just a style. He had what would now be called authenticity.

His refusal to be put off by practical considerations which would have deterred almost anyone else can be seen in his nocturnal work to rescue and rehabilitate prostitutes. This began in 1840, the year after he had got married, and clearly rendered him vulnerable to blackmailers. But he spent about £83,000 of his own money on this work, and no one who knew him well, not even his enemies, accused him of getting the prostitutes to indulge his sexual appetites. He was instead trying to persuade them to join his great battle for self-control and, like him, to repress or channel their passions. As he admitted in his diary, he 'courted evil'. Rather than break his marriage vows, he flagellated himself.

Disraeli said of him, 'He has not a single redeeming defect.' To Disraeli, Gladstone was a prig and a hypocrite, and vindictive too. In a famous passage, he called him 'a sophistical rhetorician, inebriated with the exuberance of his own verbosity, and gifted with an egotistical imagination that can at all times command an interminable and inconsistent series of arguments to malign an opponent and to glorify himself'.

During his first term, Gladstone antagonised the drinks trade by trying to bring in a Licensing Bill. It took its revenge at the election of 1874 by backing the Tories, and Gladstone claimed 'we have been borne down in a torrent of gin and beer'. He envisaged retiring from politics. But for the next two decades, he discovered reasons to defer this withdrawal. The first was the 'Bulgarian atrocities' committed in the European part of their empire by the Ottoman Turks, which in 1876 he denounced in a bestselling pamphlet. Foreign policy was for Gladstone a moral question. Disraeli provoked him to paroxysms of indignation by refusing, as prime minister, to share this approach. But Gladstone took his case to the masses, which thrilled to his speeches in the Midlothian campaign of 1879.

During his second administration, which began in 1880, Queen Victoria came to loathe Gladstone, for he had no idea how to handle her: she complained that he addressed her as if she were a public meeting. She implored him to send an expedition to save General Gordon, who had got into trouble in the Sudan by disobeying orders to withdraw. Gladstone resisted sending help until it was too late, and in early 1885 Gordon was slain by the Mahdi in Khartoum. The Queen was not alone in regarding Gladstone as a murderer, and soon afterwards his second government came to an end.

His prescriptions for Ireland became more and more radical: in 1886, he returned to office intent on bringing Home Rule to Ireland, a measure which he sprang on his followers without any preparation. Joe Chamberlain, the greatest politician ever to come out of Birmingham, led the dismayed Liberal Unionists into the arms of the Conservatives, and Gladstone's third prime ministership lasted only 169 days. Lord Randolph Churchill said the Liberal Party had been 'shivered into fragments to gratify the ambitions of an old man in a hurry'.

But Gladstone did not give up. In 1892, he began his fourth prime ministership and, in a final parliamentary tour de force, got

Home Rule through the Commons. The measure fell in the Lords, and his colleagues were by now desperate for him to retire, which in 1894 he did, having fallen out with them about naval expenditure, which he was determined to restrict. He left the Commons the following year, died in 1898 of cancer and was buried in Westminster Abbey. To Queen Victoria's distress, the Prince of Wales, soon to become Edward VII, was among the pall-bearers when the greatest of Victorian Liberals was laid to rest.

One of the many paradoxes in this extraordinary figure's life was that although he said he would always 'back the masses against the classes', he was by no means an egalitarian. When John Ruskin was staying with Gladstone at Hawarden, he accused him of being the kind of person who thinks 'one man as good as another'. 'Oh dear, no!' Gladstone replied. 'I am nothing of the sort. I am a firm believer in the aristocratic principle – the rule of the best. I am an out-and-out *inequalitarian*.'

His other activities, pursued so strenuously that the word 'recreations' would convey the wrong impression, included translating Homer, on whom he developed idiosyncratic theories published at ample length. It can be estimated, from his diaries, that he read the *Iliad* at least thirty-six times. He was fluent in Latin, Greek, Italian, French and German, which last language he used in debate with German theologians. Until an advanced age, he enjoyed going on very long walks, and he also loved cutting down trees: as Lord Randolph put it, 'The forest laments in order that Mr Gladstone may perspire.' Lord Randolph's wife, Jennie Jerome, summed up the difference between the two greatest parliamentarians of the Victorian period: 'When I left the dining room after sitting next to Gladstone, I thought he was the cleverest man in England. But when I sat next to Disraeli I left feeling that I was the cleverest woman.'

MARQUESS OF SALISBURY

Lived 1830–1903; prime minister 1885–86, 1886–92
and 1895–1902

L ord Salisbury was one of the ablest men in this book but
lacked the flamboyance required to achieve lasting fame.
He was shy, badly dressed, suffered from fits of depression,
had no small talk and locked himself away behind double doors
when working on an important despatch. His daughter, Lady
Gwendolen Cecil, said in her wonderful Life of him that the
unfailing courtesy with which he greeted his guests at Hatfield,
his great house north of London, was 'rendered a trifle impersonal

by his constant incapacity to identify them'. For faces, and for visual beauty, this short-sighted man had no eye at all.

Yet into power and the motives of other politicians, domestic and foreign, he had the keenest insight. He succeeded Disraeli as the leader of the Conservative Party and became the most formidable statesman of the day, outwitting Gladstone and serving for almost fourteen years as prime minister, a record exceeded in earlier times only by Walpole, Pitt the Younger and Lord Liverpool, and by no one since. He was deeply perturbed, as were most members of the ruling class, by the growth of democracy, which he feared would lead to a complete divorce between power and responsibility, whereupon 'the rich would pay all the taxes and the poor make all the laws'. Yet to his own surprise, he turned out to be a successful practitioner of democratic politics, who led his party to victory at three general elections by identifying and tapping the great new reservoir of suburban Tory support.

Lord Robert Cecil, as he was known for the first thirty-five years of his life, was a younger son of the 2nd Marquess of Salisbury, who was a great landowner and a minor politician. They were descended from the two illustrious Cecils, William and Robert, who had served as chief minister to Elizabeth I and James I, but the family had done nothing noteworthy since. Lord Robert was sent to Eton, where he was so badly bullied that he had to be taken away. From an early age, he was fascinated by theology and other intellectual pursuits, and uninterested in field sports. After a period spent at home at Hatfield with a tutor, he went up to Christ Church, Oxford, which he liked much better, but had to leave after two years because of ill health. He was about six foot four inches tall, very thin and stooped, and pessimistic both about the way the world was going and about his own prospects. In 1853, at the age of twenty-three, he became an MP for the family seat of Stamford and was elected a fellow of All Souls College, Oxford.

His life became much happier a few years later when he met and married Georgina Alderson, the daughter of a judge. She was an ideal companion for him, as convinced an Anglican as he was but considerably lighter-hearted, and together they had eight children. His father, who had tried to avert the match and still strongly disapproved of it, refused to increase his allowance. MPs did not begin to be paid until the early twentieth century, so Lord Robert supplemented his income, and provided for his growing family, by writing a large quantity of political journalism, which can still be read with pleasure today, at least by those who like to see reactionary ideas argued with bracing intelligence, candour and ferocity. He could not see a liberal piety without wishing to explode it.

In 1865, Lord Robert's elder brother died. This meant he could in due course expect to inherit his father's title and estates, and would have to leave the Commons for the Lords. Meanwhile he acquired the courtesy title of Lord Cranborne. The following year, Lord Derby came in at the head of a minority Conservative government, and asked Lord Cranborne to serve as Secretary of State for India.

The great issue of the day was widening the franchise. Gladstone had just tried and failed to get a Reform Bill through the Commons. Now Disraeli, for the Conservatives, proceeded to wangle a Reform Bill through the House which gave the vote to about twice as many people as Gladstone had been denounced for trying to give it to. This brilliant but unscrupulous parliamentary exploit aroused Cranborne's deep disgust. He saw it as a complete betrayal, made a swift but detailed study of the statistics, which confirmed this view and along with two colleagues, tendered his resignation.

Some days later, his wife met Lord Derby, the prime minister, on the crowded staircase of an evening party. Lady Gwendolen relates the exchange which took place:

'Is Robert still doing his sums?' enquired the great man grimly as he passed her. Lady Cranborne declined to be put out of countenance and defiantly threw back her retort across the heads of intervening guests, 'Yes, – and he has reached rather a curious result; – take three from fifteen and nothing remains.'

Actually, however insignificant the other members of the Cabinet might be, Disraeli remained. But Salisbury (as he became on the death of his father in 1868) was determined never again to serve under that 'adventurer', who was 'without principles or honesty'.

Seven years later, when Disraeli was forming a government after winning the election of 1874, he persuaded Salisbury to return as Secretary of State for India. Salisbury described the prospect of working with him as a 'nightmare', but he was wrong. He started to get on well with Disraeli, who in turn knew how to charm his independent-minded colleague and make use of his very considerable abilities. In 1876, he sent Salisbury to represent Britain at the conference held in Constantinople, to try to settle the hostilities which had broken out between Russia and the Ottoman Empire. It is amazing to see, from his dispatches, the rapidity with which Salisbury got to grips with the intractable problems of foreign policy. On his way out, he visited many of the main players in European affairs and quickly saw how they might be induced to behave in a more reasonable manner.

Although the conference settled nothing, Salisbury was surprised to find himself greeted, on his return to London, as a hero. In April 1878, he became Foreign Secretary and at once issued the Salisbury Circular, which Lord Rosebery later described as one of the 'historic state papers of the English language' and which made Salisbury one of the architects of the Congress of Berlin. Here a settlement of the Eastern Question, as the Russian–Turkish conflict was known, was reached and was guaranteed by the other European powers. Disraeli was the social lion of the conference: a side of things Salisbury did not relish. He said the most enjoyable thing about being in Berlin was discussing electromagnetism with Hermann von Helmholtz, the great German physicist. Salisbury was deeply interested in scientific research and built his own laboratory at Hatfield, which was the first private house in England to have electric light. Like other great conservatives, Salisbury was also a great innovator.

In 1881, Disraeli died and Salisbury succeeded him, first as joint leader of the Conservatives, and from 1885 to 1902 as sole leader. For while Sir Stafford Northcote, who at first led the Conservatives in the Commons, was not up to coping with Gladstone, Salisbury certainly was. As early as 1882, Salisbury noted that 'there is a great deal in Villa Toryism which requires organisation'. The owner of Hatfield was not some out-of-touch grandee, who took no interest in the new suburbs which in the age of the railways were spreading round every prosperous town. He saw that the upwardly mobile occupants of these villas were often attracted to the Conservatives, as the party of property and respectability, and were alarmed by the growing radicalism of the Liberals under Gladstone.

So in 1884, when Gladstone as prime minister proposed the Third Reform Bill, Salisbury ensured in negotiation that it included the replacement of many two-member constituencies with single-member seats in the suburbs, which in the years to come would most often vote Tory. In June 1885, Gladstone fell. Salisbury was in his laboratory at Hatfield when the summons came from Queen Victoria to form a government. He complied with reluctance, and decided to serve as Foreign Secretary too: a combination he maintained for most of his prime ministership. Rather than move into Downing Street, he ran the government from the Foreign Office, from his own London house in Arlington Street, or from Hatfield.

But this first Salisbury government was of short duration. In the general election of December 1885, the Conservatives failed to obtain a majority; in January they lost a vote to the combined Liberals and Irish Nationalists, and Salisbury resigned. Gladstone now made a precipitate and reckless attempt to drive through Home Rule for Ireland. Affronted by his attempt to bounce them into supporting a policy of which they heartily disapproved, some of his most distinguished followers now deserted him. So soon afterwards did Joe Chamberlain, leader of the Radicals, who found himself undervalued by Gladstone, and indeed treated with grotesque though unintentional rudeness.

These angry Liberal Unionists came over to Salisbury, who treated them with the utmost consideration. He made only one mistake, which was to say in a strong speech in May against Home Rule that some people, Hottentots for example, were incapable of self-government. The Liberals naturally accused him of regarding the Irish as Hottentots.

In the early hours of 8 June 1886, Gladstone made a last great appeal to the Commons: 'Ireland stands at your bar, expectant, hopeful, almost suppliant ... She asks a blessed oblivion of the past, and in that oblivion our interest is deeper even than hers.' He lost the vote, called a general election and lost that too.

Salisbury came back in as prime minister, but had to make Lord Randolph Churchill, who was only thirty-six, leader of the Commons and Chancellor of the Exchequer. There was a clear danger that the restive Lord Randolph would quite soon overthrow Salisbury, who was twenty years older and not nearly so given to being atrociously rude about people, though in younger days Disraeli had described him as 'a great master of flouts and jeers and taunts'. Salisbury remarked at this time, 'I have four departments – the prime minister's, the foreign office, the Queen and Randolph Churchill; the burden of them increases in that order.' But the young troublemaker overplayed his hand, as young troublemakers so often do. In December 1886, Lord Randolph demanded defence cuts, which Salisbury, who was dealing with trouble in the Balkans and in Egypt, was certainly not prepared to allow. Lord Randolph threatened to resign – and found to his dismay that Salisbury accepted his resignation, and nobody missed him. Lord Randolph remarked, ruefully, that he 'forgot Goschen'.

Not long afterwards, Salisbury made his nephew, Arthur Balfour, Chief Secretary for Ireland. This act of nepotism is said – plausibly enough, but without actual evidence – to be the origin of the expression 'Bob's your uncle', Robert being the prime minister's Christian name.

Salisbury took the view that 'there is always a pass through the mountains'. He often discovered that pass: a large part of his genius was to defuse difficulties which in clumsier hands could have led to serious trouble. War between the colonial powers who competed to carve up Africa was averted partly by Salisbury. His main interest remained foreign policy, with the Royal Navy kept as strong as any two of the next largest navies, and the army as far as possible not risked in action. At home, he made modest reforms, such as the introduction of county councils and the clearance of slums, in order to ward off more radical measures.

He narrowly lost the general election of 1892, and stood aside to allow Gladstone one last attempt at Home Rule for Ireland. Gladstone failed and departed, so did his successor Lord Rosebery, and in 1895 Salisbury was back. His powers were not quite what they were, and he was notoriously lax in the management of his colleagues. 'I must take up bridge so that I can meet the Duke of Devonshire,' he remarked of one of them. In order to give Joe Chamberlain something to do, Salisbury made him Colonial Secretary. Unfortunately, Chamberlain started the Boer War, which from 1899 exposed the incompetence of British commanders and the feebleness of British recruits. In order to get enough men, the army had to lower its minimum height requirement from five foot three inches to five foot.

Salisbury gained his final victory at the polls by calling the Khaki election of 1900, at which the Conservatives presented themselves as the patriotic party: a vote for the Liberals was a vote for the Boers. He saw the war through to its end. Queen Victoria died in 1901. She had trusted Salisbury, and had communicated with him behind Gladstone's back, in a manner that was frankly improper. He saw Edward VII into office, and in the summer of 1902 he resigned, handing over to his nephew, Balfour. A year later, Salisbury died. Towards the end, he was so heavy that he had to sleep in a special chair, in order to be able to breathe. He was the last prime minister to govern while in the House of Lords.

Tories of an intellectual disposition, who admire the candid, caustic writings of his youth and the authoritative pragmatism he displayed in high office, sometimes try to establish him as the greatest of all Conservative prime ministers. But they never quite succeed, for one of the many admirable characteristics of this Christian pessimist is that he was not a populist.

EARL OF ROSEBERY

Lived 1847–1929; prime minster 1894–95

Lord Rosebery is the most glittering failure in this book. He had a profusion of gifts, including wealth, eloquence, intellect and charm. He also had many eminent admirers: Gladstone at the end of his third prime ministership in 1886 told the Liberal Party that Rosebery, who had just completed a short but successful stint as Foreign Secretary, was 'the man of the future'. And Rosebery was certainly ambitious to distinguish himself. As a young man he told his boon companions during a visit to the United States that he wanted to marry an heiress, win the Derby and become prime minister. This unlikely triple he achieved, yet having glided without difficulty to the top, he found himself quite unable to cope with the pressures of being there.

His rise had been too effortless to acclimatise him to the petty drudgeries and vexatious compromises which are an inescapable part of politics. From these, he had always been inclined to opt out. His father, who doted on him, died when he was three, and he was not close to his mother, who remarried. His own daughter later wrote, 'Hardly anyone ever suspected his almost pathetic hunger for affection, only known to his family circle.' He loved Eton, but his tutor, William Johnson, a brilliant teacher who recognised his abilities and was passionately fond of him, lamented that 'he is one of those who like the palm without the dust'. Throughout his life, Rosebery was thin-skinned, easily disheartened by criticism and inclined to sulk.

In 1868, his grandfather, the 4th Earl of Rosebery, died. The new earl was twenty and reading history at Christ Church, Oxford. He inherited about 15,000 acres in Midlothian, including Dalmeny on the Firth of Forth, and decided to buy his first racehorse, Ladas, which he believed would win the Derby. The authorities at Christ Church, already vexed by his disinclination to attend lectures, told him he must either give up the horse or leave. He surprised them by leaving, after which Ladas surprised him by coming last out of twenty-two runners in the Derby.

Rosebery was now a member of the House of Lords, where he took his seat just after his twenty-first birthday. He was the first prime minister since Lord Aberdeen never to have sat in the Commons: an ominous precedent, for Aberdeen had failed. Rosebery's political education was stunted. He did, however, display early talent as a showman, successfully transplanting to Scotland the melodrama of the mass political meetings he had observed in the United States, which he reproduced with Gladstone as the star in the great Midlothian campaign of 1879.

The year before that triumph he had married Hannah de Rothschild, an heiress who brought him the treasure house of Mentmore, in Buckinghamshire, and retained her Jewish faith. She was devoted to Rosebery, and together they had four children, but in 1890 she died of typhoid, after which the insomnia from which he was already suffering grew worse. Until his own death in 1929 he was a widower, and as his young friend Winston Churchill wrote, 'When he was out of humour, he could cast a chill over all, and did not hesitate to freeze and snub.' Addressing huge audiences, Rosebery was brilliant. He mastered them, and they loved being mastered. With individuals, he was impenetrable, guarding his privacy and hiding his feelings. In 1910, fifteen years after he had been prime minister, he published a book on Pitt the Elder, entitled *Chatham: His Early Life and Connections*. Rosebery was descended on his Stanhope mother's side from the Pitts, and could have been describing himself when he says at the start of the book:

> The life of Chatham is extremely difficult to write, and, strictly speaking, never can be written at all. It is difficult because of the artificial atmosphere in which he thought it well to envelop himself, and because the rare glimpses which are obtainable of the real man reveal a nature so complex, so violent, and so repressed.

Yet when Rosebery wished to be, he was a princely host and a wonderful conversationalist too, who touched with wit and knowledge on every subject from racing, where he was for forty years a major figure, to literature and history, which he wrote himself as well as collecting great libraries.

Gladstone persuaded him, with some difficulty, into government. Rosebery was not much inclined to take subordinate posts in which he could learn the ropes. In 1884, he gave a celebrated speech in Adelaide, in Australia, in which he expounded the doctrine of Liberal Imperialism: 'There is no need for any nation, however great, to leave the Empire, for the Empire is a Commonwealth of Nations.' Rosebery's gifts were such that he was soon rewarded with the office of Foreign Secretary, which he held briefly in 1886 and again in 1892–94. Between those two stints, while the Liberals were out of office, he helped, somewhat incongruously but with complete success, to set up the London County Council. The name Rosebery is perpetuated in the streets and buildings of late Victorian London.

By the time Gladstone retired in 1894, he had ridden the Liberal Party into the ground. Joe Chamberlain, who might have succeeded him, had instead gone into alliance with the Conservatives. Sir Charles Dilke, another possible successor, had been ruined by a spectacular scandal in which he was accused in the divorce court not only of seducing a fellow MP's wife, but of possessing such an unbounded sexual appetite that he also slept with her mother, and with the housemaid too. Sir William Harcourt, the biggest Liberal figure in the Commons apart from Gladstone himself, had managed to alienate all his Cabinet colleagues.

Without consulting Gladstone, whom she could not abide, Queen Victoria decided to invite Rosebery to form a government. He was not obliged to accept: with the benefit of hindsight, it is clear he would have done better to suggest she sent instead for Harcourt, under whom he could have carried on as Foreign Secretary. But Rosebery took the prize, and it was Harcourt who had to carry on as Chancellor of the Exchequer under him. From the first, the government was irreparably divided, with Harcourt deeply miffed that he had not been given the top job and demanding to be consulted on everything including patronage and foreign policy. He thirsted for revenge, as did his son, Loulou Harcourt, who went around stirring up trouble and making bitchy remarks about the new prime minister. At Mentmore, he reported, truffles were treated like potatoes in other households.

Within a few days, Rosebery made a blunder he would have been unlikely to commit if he had spent some time in the rough and tumble of the Commons. Replying to a point made by Lord Salisbury, he remarked that Home Rule could not be conceded to Ireland until England, 'the predominant partner in the Union', agreed to it: a remark which deeply insulted Scottish, Welsh and Irish MPs, and this at a time when the government depended in the Commons on the votes of the Irish Nationalists.

Nor did Rosebery manage to mend fences with Harcourt. Instead he had a pointless row with him about the Budget, submitting a memorandum to him in which he opposed the proposal to increase the level of death duties on land. Harcourt responded with a memorandum of his own, in which he contemptuously rejected Rosebery's objections and challenged him to fight the matter out in Cabinet. Rosebery ducked the challenge and the Budget was then very well received. But Harcourt would not lift a finger in the Commons to defend Rosebery, and in private referred to himself as not belonging to the government.

A lighter moment was provided when Rosebery's horse, Ladas II, won the Derby. That was recognised as an extraordinary triumph, though the chapel-going wing of the Liberals claimed to be scandalised by their leader's connection with gambling. The following year, 1895, he won it again, with Sir Visto. But in February, he had already threatened his Cabinet colleagues with resignation. They talked him out of it, but his insomnia was terrible. In April, he got influenza, returned to work too soon and suffered a relapse. In June, he threw in the towel after the government suffered an unexpected defeat in the Commons. The Queen sent for the Conservative leader, Lord Salisbury, who called a general election and won a resounding victory.

So Lord Rosebery was a very unsuccessful prime minister. He had a weak hand and played it badly. 'Great leaders thrive in adversity,' his biographer Leo McKinstry remarks; 'Rosebery slid into wounded narcissism.' Margot Asquith, who married his colleague Henry Asquith, wrote: 'I think Lord Rosebery would have had a better nervous system and been a happier man if he had not been so rich.' Rosebery himself said he had expected politics to be 'a chivalrous adventure', and having discovered it was an 'evil-smelling bog', was always trying to extricate himself: 'That is what people used to call my lost opportunities and so forth.'

At the end of his prime ministership, he was only forty-seven, and for a long time his admirers hoped he would come back. He still displayed, at unpredictable intervals, star quality, and shafts of insight which showed an admirable independence of mind. In 1904, when everyone else was cheering the *entente cordiale* with France, Rosebery greeted Lloyd George with the words: 'You are all wrong. It means war with Germany in the end.'

Towards the end of the First World War, his beloved younger son, Neil Primrose, was killed, and he himself had a stroke. Yet he lived on for another ten years. On his deathbed, his instruction that the 'Eton Boating Song' be played to him on the gramophone was obeyed. The words had been composed by his tutor, William Johnson, who was afterwards driven out of Eton for becoming excessively fond of the boys. At school, Rosebery had been happy. In later life, he was often miserable, for he never quite fulfilled his early promise, and never quite grew up.

ARTHUR BALFOUR

Lived 1848–1930; prime minister 1902–05

Arthur James Balfour was seen as the inevitable successor to his uncle, Lord Salisbury, as prime minister in 1902, yet led the Conservatives to a crushing defeat at the general election of 1906. His MPs accepted him as leader because he was an exceptionally able and charming member of the traditional ruling class. They preferred him to Joe Chamberlain, the middle-class manufacturer from Birmingham who had led the Liberal Unionists into alliance with the Conservatives in 1886 and was the most dynamic member of the Cabinet. Chamberlain was, in Winston Churchill's phrase, 'the one who made the weather', and in 1903 he created a storm so violent that even Balfour, with his fearless detachment and sinuous mastery of the Commons, could not restore calm.

Balfour had two weaknesses which made him a failure as prime minister. One was that, unlike Chamberlain, he could not connect with the masses. Indeed, Balfour did not want to connect with the masses. While some politicians take what the papers say about them too seriously, Balfour went to the opposite extreme. For a long time, he did not read the papers at all and did not trouble to conceal his scorn for public opinion, or indeed for the opinions of his own rank and file: 'I would as soon be guided by the views of my valet as by the Conservative Party conference.'

Balfour's other weakness was a fatal disinclination to commit himself. In the great crisis which arose a year after he became prime minister, 'He nailed his colours to the fence', as his friend Harry Cust remarked.

His father, who died young, was an MP, businessman and landowner at Whittingehame, east of Edinburgh. His mother, Lady Blanche Balfour, was Lord Salisbury's sister, and at the age of twenty-six wrote a prayer: 'From the dangers of metaphysical subtleties and from profitless speculation on the origin of evil – Good Lord deliver me.' Thanks in part to her, several of her eight children, including Arthur, the eldest, attained intellectual distinction, and delighted in metaphysical subtleties. His first book was called A Defence of Philosophic Doubt. His interests were not, however, exclusively intellectual. For many years, he devoted the month of September to playing golf.

He never married, but was said to have been going to marry May Lyttelton, who died young. When someone asked if he was going to marry Margot Tennant – there being a rumour that he had become engaged to that brilliant but headstrong figure – he replied: 'No, that is not so. I rather think of having a career of my own.' He was one of the most distinguished members of the Souls, a young aristocratic coterie of high-minded, high-spirited friends which attracted the derision of duller figures. All his life, he was in demand as a conversationalist. When Frank Harris declared to him over lunch, 'The fact is, Mr Balfour, all the faults of the age come from Christianity and journalism,' Balfour replied with a childlike air: 'Christianity, of course ... but why journalism?'

In 1874, he entered the Commons as MP for Hertford, a seat within the sphere of influence of his uncle, Lord Salisbury. The two men got on extremely well, and in 1878 he attended the Congress of Berlin as Salisbury's private secretary.

Almost a decade later, Salisbury made him Chief Secretary for Ireland: an appointment greeted with hilarity, for Balfour, who at Trinity College, Cambridge, had been known as Pretty Fanny, was not supposed to be tough enough for that assignment. Only a few years before, one of his predecessors, Lord Frederick Cavendish, had been murdered in Phoenix Park in Dublin. Balfour silenced his critics and earned the nickname Bloody Balfour by taking resolute measures to suppress crime, while introducing constructive reforms such as the Land Purchase Act and facing down the Irish Nationalists in the Commons. In Ireland, his deafness to public opinion was an advantage, for he intended to pacify that island by doing the right thing, not by appeasing his opponents. He was promoted to Leader of the Commons and First Lord of the Treasury, and well before 1902 had come to be seen as his uncle's natural successor.

But it is not easy to take over from a long-serving and widely admired prime minister. The end of Salisbury's tenure had, more-over, been clouded by the Boer War, a minor colonial conflict which Britain had only been able to win after enormous efforts, with help from volunteers from Australia and Canada who knew how to handle a horse and a gun. The internment of Boer civilians in ill-run concentration camps where many of them died from disease turned this into a moral defeat, and left Britain isolated. How was the British Empire going to be able to compete in future against the rising industrial powers of Germany and the United States?

Balfour realised that better education was needed, to enable British industry to rise to the challenge, and in the face of enormous opposition he saw through the 1902 Education Act. This measure aroused the wrath of nonconformists who complained that it handed an unfair advantage to the Church of England, which could fund its schools 'on the rates'. Balfour realised with equal lucidity that far-reaching reforms were needed to render the British Empire defensible, and he set up the Committee of Imperial Defence to drive these through.

But it was Chamberlain who developed much the most exciting proposal. In May 1903, in a speech in Birmingham, he came out in favour of tariff reform. The British Empire would be bound together by a system of imperial preference, with goods from other countries subjected to duties which would protect industry and provide revenue for social reform. Free trade was the policy on which British prosperity in the second half of the nineteenth century had been founded, but Chamberlain wanted to overthrow it.

His speech was recognised, in the words of Leo Amery, one of his many Tory admirers, as 'a challenge to free trade as direct and provocative as the theses Luther nailed to the church door in Wittenberg'. It split the Conservative party, and the Cabinet, from top to bottom. What was Balfour to do? The great danger of Chamberlain's proposal was that it would mean 'taxes on food': a policy which could easily alienate the working class and lead to electoral disaster. But tariff reform exercised an irresistible appeal to imperial-minded politicians who thought it was the only way to ensure British greatness.

Balfour strove at all costs to avoid what he called 'the unforgiveable sin' of splitting the Conservative Party, as Peel had split it in 1846. But by trying to please everyone, he ended up pleasing no one. He devised a middle way which no one could understand and which entailed the admission that he himself had no 'settled convictions'. Chamberlain resigned from the Cabinet in order to be free to campaign for tariff reform, but four other ministers resigned because the prime minister no longer defended free trade. Everyone felt let down by Balfour, who committed the final tactical error of resigning without calling a general election.

He hoped the Liberals would make a mess of things, but they didn't. They were united round the policy of free trade and gained new adherents, including the young Winston Churchill, who 'ratted' from the Conservatives. In the election held in 1906, the Conservatives were reduced to only 156 MPs. Balfour himself lost his seat in Manchester.

It is a tribute to his resilience, and a sign of the respect in which he was held, that he carried on as leader and was soon found another seat. He at once enunciated the provocative doctrine that the Unionist Party – as the Conservatives were often known at this time, because of their determination to preserve the Union with Ireland – 'should still control, whether in power or in opposition, the destinies of this great Empire'. The House of Lords, which had an enormous Conservative majority, would decide which Liberal measures to allow through. This contentious view proved unsustainable, and in 1911, Balfour stepped down as leader.

And yet he was soon back in office as a senior Cabinet minister, and remained one almost until his death in 1930. During the First World War, he was resolute and sagacious in pursuit of victory, and helped bring about the change of prime minister from Asquith to Lloyd George. Winston Churchill compared the way Balfour conducted this manoeuvre to 'a powerful graceful cat walking delicately and unsoiled across a rather muddy street'.

His prime ministership is today forgotten, but while serving as Foreign Secretary he acquired lasting fame as the author of the Balfour Declaration of 2 November 1917, which favoured the setting up of what became the state of Israel. This was a subject Balfour had already discussed with Chaim Weizmann, the founder of Zionism, in Manchester in 1906. But as usual, he attempted to please both sides, an aim which a century later is still a long way from being achieved:

> His Majesty's Government view with favour the establish-
> ment in Palestine of a national home for the Jewish people,
> and will use their best endeavours to facilitate the achieve-
> ment of this object, it being clearly understood that nothing
> shall be done which may prejudice the civil and religious
> rights of existing non-Jewish communities in Palestine.

SIR HENRY CAMPBELL-BANNERMAN

Lived 1836–1908; prime minister 1905–08

S ir Henry Campbell-Bannerman was the first prime minister from the Glasgow commercial classes. He was born plain Henry Campbell, a tenacious, trustworthy, unpretentious, imperturbable man, who wore his deepest convictions lightly and was reputed to be rather idle. In the manner of an affable tortoise, he was impervious to vituperation and at length reached Downing Street ahead of more flamboyant figures. For he possessed the good humour needed to unite the fractious Liberals, and in 1906 led them to the greatest victory in their party's history.

His family ran a successful firm of warehousemen and wholesale drapers, and he was educated at Glasgow High School, after which he went to Glasgow University and Trinity College, Cambridge. In

1858, he joined the family firm and in 1860 became a partner, but he soon diverged from business into politics, being elected for the Liberals as MP for Stirling Burghs in 1868. He and his wife, Charlotte Bruce, who was a semi-invalid, had no children but shared a passion for French literature, food and furniture, and spent two months a year on the Continent. He spoke French, Italian and German, was averse to all forms of physical exercise and regarded chess not as a game but as a disease: 'When I see people with their eyes straining for long minutes together, staring at a board with every symptom of acute mental distress, I can only pity them.'

In 1871, he received a substantial bequest from an uncle on condition that he add Bannerman to his surname, after which he encouraged people to call him 'CB' rather than the more cumbersome Campbell-Bannerman. Gladstone made him Chief Secretary for Ireland and then Secretary of State for War. He was an able minister but a poor orator, and his highest ambition was to become Speaker of the House of Commons. His colleagues told him they could not manage without him in the Liberal team, and in 1899 he ascended to the leadership of the party, first in the Commons and then overall, for he had fewer enemies than Lord Rosebery or any of the other possible candidates.

In 1901, after hearing an eye-witness report on the appalling levels of death from disease, as high as 430 per 1,000, in the concentration camps for civilians set up by the British during the Boer War, CB denounced the 'methods of barbarism' employed in that conflict. For this, he himself was denounced as 'a cad, a coward and a murderer', and a traitor to the British army. But he stuck to his views, and once the passions of the war, which ended the following year, had cooled, many people came to think he was right.

His own party was divided between imperialists and anti-war campaigners, but he held them together, and took the additional precaution of making a pact with the fledgling Labour Party, under which it was granted a free run in 31 seats, in return for not opposing the Liberals in many other places. Balfour, meanwhile, could not hold the Conservative government together, and at the end of 1905 stood down.

Edward VII proceeded to ask CB to form a government, with the words 'prime minister' used for the first time in an official document: until that point, the usual term had been 'First Lord of the Treasury'. Three of CB's colleagues, including Henry Asquith, who would succeed him as prime minister, tried to force him to go to the House of Lords for the sake of his health. He held out against this conspiracy, and at once called a general election, in which the Liberals won a landslide victory.

CB now dominated the scene. Balfour had previously held the upper hand in Commons debates: now CB routed one of his somewhat mannered attacks by retorting 'enough of this foolishness'. And CB appointed a Cabinet which encompassed the full range of Liberal opinion, from Asquith to Lloyd George. He achieved reconciliation with the Boers, who were granted self-government in the Transvaal and Orange River colonies, and who as a result supported Britain during the two world wars. He also maintained friendly relations with the Labour Party, and with the suffragette movement.

But his wife was by now very ill, and would only be nursed by him. He stayed up night after night doing so, which exhausted him, and in August 1906 she died in Marienbad. From the summer of 1907, he suffered a series of increasingly severe heart attacks, and on 5 April 1908, by which time he was confined to bed in Downing Street, composed a letter of resignation to Edward VII. He had been prime minister for just over two years, but after signing the letter, CB turned to his private secretary and said: 'There's the last kick. My dear fellow, I don't mind. I've been prime minister for longer than I deserve.' He died seventeen days later, still in Downing Street, the only prime minister to have perished there. He was outlived by his grey African parrot, which he had bought on first becoming an MP in 1868.

HERBERT HENRY ASQUITH

Lived 1852–1928; prime minister 1908–16

Herbert Henry Asquith had a brilliant intellect, transacted official business with almost unbelievable rapidity and rose without apparent difficulty to the prime ministership, which he retained for eight turbulent years. Yet there was also something limited or even frivolous about him. Leo Amery, for the Conservatives, accused this Liberal prime minister of taking 'a season ticket on the line of least resistance'. Critics said he was 'incapable of doing anything except drift', because of his attachment to 'drink, bridge and holding girls' hands', in all of which pastimes he sought daily relief from the pressures of high office. His love letters to Venetia Stanley are the strangest case known to history of a prime ministerial infatuation, yet even in these he seems to be playing a role which hides as much as it reveals.

But his ascent was undeniably impressive. His father, a weaver and devout Congregationalist, who was involved in a modest way in the wool trade in Yorkshire, died when Asquith was only eight. His uncle paid for him to go to City of London School, from which he won a classical scholarship to Balliol College, Oxford. Here he took a First, became president of the Oxford Union and was awarded a prize fellowship.

He went to the Bar, after a slow start made substantial sums, entered Parliament as a Liberal in 1886 and caught the eye of Gladstone, who made him Home Secretary only six years later. This was Asquith's first ministerial post, yet he carried it off brilliantly. Long before the Liberal landslide of 1906, when they returned to power after a decade in Opposition, he was seen as their future leader. For two years he served as Chancellor of the Exchequer, and took on more and more of the work of the ailing Sir Henry Campbell-Bannerman, who resigned in April 1908. There was no doubt who would now become prime minister: King Edward VII, who was taking a six-week holiday in Biarritz and incurred some criticism for not coming home, sent for Asquith.

Soon after becoming prime minister, Asquith referred in a light-hearted but nevertheless revealing speech at Balliol to 'the tranquil consciousness of effortless superiority which is the mark of the Balliol man'. Effortless superiority was certainly the mark of H. H. Asquith, as he was always known, somewhat cryptically, to the wider world. His first wife, Helen Melland, the shy, retiring daughter of a doctor, whom he had married when he was only twenty-four and with whom he had five children, called him Herbert. In 1891, she died of typhoid.

Asquith's second wife, Margot Tennant, was neither shy nor retiring, and called him Henry. She was the daughter of a rich Scottish industrialist, Sir Charles Tennant, and had been launched 'more like a rocket than a ship' into London society. Her friends implored her not to marry Asquith, with whom they thought she had nothing in common, for she adored fox-hunting and was compulsively indiscreet, while he abhorred all forms of outdoor exercise and wore a mask of philosophic detachment. But in 1894 they married, with the register signed by four prime ministers: Gladstone, Rosebery, Balfour and Asquith himself. He moved now in much grander circles, of which not all his fellow Liberals approved.

But as prime minister, his seeming imperturbability made him an admirable chairman of a Cabinet which included, in David Lloyd George and Winston Churchill, two future prime ministers who had an impressive capacity for causing trouble, not all of it intentional. This Liberal government laid the foundations of the welfare state by bringing in old-age pensions and other measures; strengthened Britain's defences in preparation for a possible war with Germany by building dreadnoughts; curbed the powers of the House of Lords under the Parliament Act of 1911; and pushed with renewed energy for Home Rule in Ireland, a cause first espoused by Gladstone in 1886. This last measure had by the summer of 1914 led the United Kingdom to the brink of civil war, for the Protestants of Ulster refused to be coerced into a united Ireland.

Asquith came under intense strain, and Margot was not much help in relieving that strain, for instead of calming things down and telling him not to worry, she took it upon herself to attack anyone who had attacked him and to draw his attention to unfavourable newspaper coverage which, left to his own devices, he would have ignored. He tended to drink rather more than he could take – the term 'squiffy' is supposed to be a corruption of his name, and he was noticed sometimes to be the worse for wear at the Dispatch Box. He had already, as he admitted, 'a slight weakness for the companionship of clever and attractive women', who could enter 10 Downing Street quite naturally as the friends of his brilliant eldest daughter, Violet, who was herself a rival to Margot for his attention.

Margot tried to make light of these young women, referring to them as his 'harem'. But in 1912, he became besotted by one of them, Venetia Stanley, to whom over the next three years he wrote almost 600 letters, some composed during Cabinet meetings, amounting to 300,000 words. The letters are a baffling mixture of emotional craving and boasting by an elderly man of power who wants to impress a young woman by sharing Britain's most sensitive secrets with her.

In July 1914, he reassured her that Britain would not be drawn into the European crisis. The following month, the country went to war with Germany. Asquith at first found himself popular, the beneficiary of a wave of patriotism. But as casualties mounted to almost unimaginable levels, his detachment began to grate on public opinion. People wanted a warrior at their head, and instead found their destinies being guided by a man who preferred to remain above the battle.

In 1915, Venetia stunned him by revealing she was engaged to be married to a member of his Cabinet, Edwin Montagu. In the same year, he tried to defuse criticism by entering into a coalition with the Conservatives. The following year, his beloved eldest son, Raymond, a man as gifted as himself, was killed at the Battle of the Somme.

The pressure on Asquith grew greater and greater, and with it his need for relaxation. One Monday morning in the summer of 1916, the Conservative leader, Bonar Law, needing urgently to consult with the prime minister before making a visit to France, was told to visit him at the Wharf, his house on the Thames near Abingdon. This Bonar Law did, at considerable personal inconvenience. On arriving, he found the prime minister of a country which was fighting for survival playing bridge with three young women.

By such methods did Asquith wear out his colleagues' patience. He supposed himself to be indispensable, but the country wanted a more energetic leader. In December 1916, he found himself supplanted by Lloyd George. Asquith went into Opposition, expected soon to be recalled and never was. He would not serve under Lloyd George, came off worse having accused him of refusing to send sufficient reinforcements to France during the last great German offensive of the war, and lost his seat in the general election of 1918, when his supporters gained only 36 seats. Although Asquith returned to the Commons at a by-election in 1920, his career was over. In 1924, he accepted a peerage and became the Earl of Oxford and Asquith. In 1928, he died.

DAVID LLOYD GEORGE

Lived 1863–1945; prime minister 1916–22

David Lloyd George was the greatest Welshman since the Tudors, and one of the most dynamic figures ever to force his way into 10 Downing Street. After laying the foundations of the welfare state, he helped win the First World War. The Welsh wizard, as he was known, was throughout his career an instinctive radical. He enchanted great crowds with his oratory and cast his spell over some of the most forceful individuals in politics, including Winston Churchill, one of whose friends wrote: 'His was the only personal leadership I have ever known Winston to accept unquestioningly.' Yet the more successful he became, the deeper the mistrust he inspired, and by the time of his downfall he was regarded as a disreputable opportunist. In the words of Lord Beaverbrook, a press baron who was himself by no means devoid of opportunistic impulses, 'He did not seem to care which way he travelled providing he was in the driving seat.'

David George was born in 1863 in Manchester, where his father, William George, was unhappily employed as a school-master. The family returned to Pembrokeshire, where George intended to farm, but instead died of pneumonia. His widow, Elizabeth, took David, who was only seventeen months old, and his even younger brother to live at Llanystumdwy, near Criccieth in North Wales, with her own brother, Richard Lloyd, a master-cobbler who was an unpaid minister in a Baptist sect, the Disciples of Christ. Uncle Lloyd idolised the young David and gave the spoiled child a lifelong taste for unconditional praise, some of which was deserved, for the boy did very well at the excellent local school. In the cottage hung a portrait of Abraham Lincoln, offering the example of a country lawyer who rose from humble origins to become the greatest man of his time.

This example David set out to follow. He qualified as a lawyer, set up his own firm and married a local woman, Margaret Owen, whom he told in a letter: 'My supreme idea is to get on. To this idea I shall sacrifice everything – except, I trust, honesty. I am prepared to thrust even love itself under the wheels of my Juggernaut.' So she had her warning, not that her husband was to prove honest about the innumerable affairs he was to have in the years to come.

He was bilingual in Welsh and English, and heir to a rich Welsh nonconformist culture, so his way in politics was clear: it was as a defender of the Welsh people against the landowners and the Church of England. At the age of twenty-seven, the handsome and eloquent young lawyer, already well known for a case in which he had upheld the right of a Nonconformist to be buried in an Anglican graveyard, became Liberal candidate for Caernarvon Boroughs. His candidacy was nearly derailed when the local Liberal leadership discovered he had 'fathered a child on a very charming widow in Caernarvon'. But somehow this lapse was covered up, and by a narrow margin he was elected to the seat he would represent for the next fifty-five years.

His wife remained in Criccieth, despite his urgings that she come with their five children to live with him in London, and in 1897 he complained in a letter to her: 'I have scores of times come home in the dead of night to a cold, dark and comfortless flat without a soul to greet me, when you were surrounded by your pets [i.e. their children].'

In 1899, he leaped to national attention as a passionate opponent of the Boer War. The rights of small nations always appealed to him, and the pious, pastoral, unfashionable Boers had obvious similarities to the Welsh. He accused Joe Chamberlain, the great promoter of the war, of profiting personally from the conflict. At a rally in Birmingham, Chamberlain's citadel, a mob yelling 'Pro Boer! Traitor! Kill him!' invaded the hall where Lloyd George was about to speak, and he was lucky to escape with his life, smuggled out disguised as a police officer.

His gift for picking fights propelled him upwards. At the end of 1905, when the Liberals came back into government, he entered the Cabinet, and soon he was attacking the House of Lords, which considered itself entitled to veto various measures, as the 'poodle' of the Conservative leader, Arthur Balfour: 'It fetches and carries for him. It barks for him. It bites anybody that he sets it on to.'

From 1908, he served as Chancellor of the Exchequer, and in 1909 he presented the People's Budget, launching a tremendous series of attacks on the House of Lords: 'Five hundred men chosen at random from among the ranks of the unemployed'. In order to pay for the introduction of old-age pensions, and the building of dreadnoughts to meet the German naval threat, Lloyd George brought in heavier taxes on the rich, including a tax on land used for development. By later standards, the increases seem moderate, but he personalised the fight by pouring scorn on the dukes: 'A fully equipped duke costs just as much to keep up as two dreadnoughts; and dukes are just as great a terror, and last longer.'

The Lords vetoed the Budget. The prime minister, H. H. Asquith, gave staunch support to Lloyd George and in 1910 called not one but two general elections on the issue. In 1911, George V promised to create as many new peers as might be needed to make the Lords back down, which it did. Its powers had been curbed, but the atmosphere of political crisis continued, for the Lords now wished to stop Home Rule for Ireland.

Lloyd George became embroiled in the Marconi scandal, in which he and other ministers were accused of profiting from their inside knowledge of a government contract which was to be awarded to that firm. He was fortunate to escape from this embarrassing episode as lightly as he did. At about the same time, he made his secretary, Frances Stevenson, his mistress, a post she was to occupy for thirty years before becoming his second wife.

At the outbreak of war in 1914, he attracted praise in the City for being quick-witted and astute enough to help ward off a collapse of the financial system, which was centred on London. Some observers supposed, because of his opposition to the Boer War, that he would come out against this new conflict. He was instead persuaded by the German violation of Belgian neutrality – another attack on a small country – that Britain must fight. To this end, he delivered in September 1914 a celebrated rallying cry in which he said: 'The stern hand of fate has scourged us to an elevation where we can see the great everlasting things that matter for a nation; the great peaks of honour we had forgotten – duty and patriotism clad in glittering white; the great pinnacle of sacrifice pointing like a rugged finger to Heaven.'

His love of battle was now directed against the Germans. Asquith, as prime minister, was less good at evincing the required dynamism. It emerged that British forces on the Western Front were suffering from a severe shortage of shells. In May 1915, Lloyd George was made Minister of Munitions and transformed the situation by bringing about an enormous increase in production. Asquith, who had been forced to form a wartime coalition with the Conservatives, claimed Lloyd George could not supplant him as prime minister, for 'he does not inspire trust'. But nor, increasingly, did people trust Asquith to get the war won. In December 1916, the Conservatives decided they would rather serve under Lloyd George, the very man they had regarded before the war as a mortal threat to the established order.

When Lloyd George put his mind to getting on with someone, he could do it, and he formed a strong partnership with the Conservative leader, Bonar Law. The new prime minister's relations with the generals were much less happy: he regarded them as incompetent butchers, while they considered him an amateur strategist whose suggestions it was their duty to ignore. There was an element of gangsterism in his conduct that gave pause for thought. As he said one day to Bonar Law, when instructing him to sack a middle-ranking minister: 'I don't mind if he is drowned in Malmsey wine, but he must be dead chicken by midnight.' Nevertheless, the war was won and so was the election that followed, in which the coalition between the Lloyd George Liberals and much larger numbers of Conservatives won a thumping victory, with the Asquithian Liberals reduced to a rump.

Lloyd George's personal prestige was such that he survived in office with Conservative support until 1922. John Maynard Keynes, who saw much of him during the negotiations in Paris that led to the Treaty of Versailles, has left a memorable sketch: 'How can

I convey to the reader, who does not know him, any impression of this extraordinary figure of our time, this siren, this goat-footed bard, this half-human visitor to our age from the hag-ridden magic and enchanted woods of Celtic antiquity?'

For although people felt inspired by Lloyd George, they did not feel they knew him, or even that he was stable enough to be knowable. At Versailles, he could not avert the making of a vengeful peace, imposing huge reparations on the Germans, which Keynes and others pointed out they could not pay. At home, Lloyd George said he wanted to make 'a land fit for heroes', but here too, the reality was less comforting. A post-war boom was followed by a slump. In Ireland, he made the best peace he could, though it precipitated a savage civil war, and a less skilful nego-tiator might well have done worse.

Lloyd George needed to fill the coffers of his part of the Liberal Party and did so by selling peerages and other honours in a more and more flagrant fashion, with the proceeds under his personal control. Stanley Baldwin, who was an obscure but emerging Tory MP, said Lloyd George had a 'morally disintegrating effect' on all who dealt with him. Men who were less inspiring but more reli-able than the prime minister were preparing to replace him. In 1922, he gave them a very good reason to do so, by leading the country to the brink of war with Turkey. Out he went.

He was only fifty-nine years old, and thought he would soon be back. But his ill-gotten election fund, which he refused to share with the rest of the Liberals, was now a mortal handicap to him, for it advertised his unscrupulousness. He could not heal the rift in his own party. In vain he promoted Keynes's economic ideas: the nation would no longer listen to him. In 1936, Lloyd George visited Hitler and hailed him in public as 'a born leader of men', with a 'dynamic personality'. A. J. Sylvester, who worked for Lloyd George from 1922 until the end, wrote of him: 'If LlG gave his mind to thinking how best he could help his country, instead of thinking cunt and women, he would be a better man.' In another diary entry, Sylvester speculated on the cause of his employer's obsession with women: 'There he stood as naked as when he was born with the biggest organ I have ever seen. It resembled a donkey's more than anything else ... No wonder they are always after him and he after them.'

In January 1941, Lloyd George's long-suffering wife, Margaret, died in Criccieth. He was prevented by a blizzard from reaching her. In 1943, he at last married Frances Stevenson, with whom he had a 12-year-old daughter. In January 1945, he accepted a hereditary peerage, becoming Earl Lloyd George of Dwyfor, and two months later he died. He was buried under a boulder he had chosen beside the River Dwyfor, which flowed past his childhood home.

ANDREW BONAR LAW

Lived 1858–1923; prime minister 1922–23

Andrew Bonar Law was disparaged by Asquith, his predecessor but one, as 'the gilded tradesman'. He had no charisma and served for only 209 days, a shorter stint than anyone but Goderich and Canning. Yet for the dozen years from his unexpected elevation to the Conservative leadership in 1911 he exercised a pervasive influence, and when the time came to end the careers first of Asquith and then of Lloyd George, the altogether less stylish figure of Bonar Law was not found wanting. For here was an able but unimaginative businessman who did not mind being called an able but unimaginative businessman, and who often saw the next moves more clearly than his flashier rivals.

He is the only prime minister to have been born outside the British Isles. The first twelve years of his life were spent in a remote district of New Brunswick, in Canada, where his father, an Ulster Scot, served as Presbyterian minister. His mother died when he was two, and when his father remarried, Bonar was entrusted to some well-off cousins outside Glasgow. He attended Glasgow High School, the only day school to have educated two prime ministers (the other being Campbell-Bannerman), and at the age of sixteen he started work in the family bank, Kidston's. When that was absorbed into the Clydesdale Bank, he joined a firm which traded on the Glasgow iron market. He brought to it an astounding memory for figures and a reputation for straight dealing, and achieved success in a highly speculative business with frequent violent fluctuations in prices: experience which he afterwards said had prepared him better than most of his competitors for the violent fluctuations in politics.

By the age of forty he had made, and inherited, enough money to go into politics. In 1900, he was elected to the Commons for one of the Glasgow seats. His maiden speech was overshadowed by Winston Churchill's, but Law was soon in demand and was given junior ministerial office, because he was one of the few Conservatives who understood figures. The great issue of the day, rousing passions at least as deep as the European Union a century later, was tariff reform, and on this he could speak with authority and without notes. Law's hero was Joe Chamberlain, the larger-than-life promoter of that cause, who held that it would unite the British Empire and secure Britain's future as a great power. Its immediate effect, however, was to split the Conservatives and enable the Liberals to smash them at the polls.

Law was one of the many Tory MPs who lost their seats in the 1906 election, but he soon returned to the Commons at a by-election.

A much worse disaster for him, from which he never really recovered his spirits, was the death in 1909, aged only forty-three, of his beloved wife, Annie, with whom he had six children. His range of recreations was limited: he was a teetotaller who was completely uninterested in food, detested dinner parties, disliked music and took no interest in scenery. He was, however, a heavy smoker and an excellent chess player, and also played golf and bridge. In 1910, he formed an improbable friendship with an ebullient young Canadian tycoon, Max Aitken, who pushed his career.

The following year, the Conservatives needed a new leader, but were bitterly divided between two candidates, Austen Chamberlain (son of Joe) and Walter Long. They were persuaded to stand down in favour of Law, after which Aitken told him: 'You are a great man now. You must talk like a great man, behave like a great man.'

To this, Law replied: 'If I am a great man, then a good many great men must have been frauds.' He decided the best way to reunite the party – which he knew was his first and most important duty – was to launch a series of ferocious attacks on the government, and therefore remarked to the prime minister as they walked back to the Commons after hearing the King's Speech: 'I am afraid I shall have to show myself very vicious, Mr Asquith, this session. I hope you will understand.' Roy Jenkins claims, in an essay published in *The Chancellors* in 1998, that Law 'was the first leader to exhibit some aspect of the "poor white" mentality which has been a growing and marked feature of the Conservative party in much more recent times'.

Law possessed a hereditary streak of Ulster intransigence and was ready to take Britain to the brink of civil war in order to save the province from being made to accept Irish Home Rule. In 1913, he assured Protestant Ulstermen who were busy importing weapons to defend themselves that 'whatever steps they might feel compelled to take, whether they were constitutional, or whether in the long run they were unconstitutional', they would have the whole of the Conservative and Unionist party behind them. He had a particular dislike and distrust of Winston Churchill, and referred to 'the coat which he has turned so often', for Churchill had started out as a Conservative, but had crossed the floor and was now a rising Liberal star.

In August 1914, the outbreak of the First World War led Law to become a loyal supporter of the government. In 1915, he led the Conservatives into coalition with the Liberals. By the end of 1916, he knew the general feeling in his party was that Asquith should be replaced by Lloyd George, and this he helped to arrange. Law could have attempted to become prime minister himself during this crisis, but was instead content to serve as Chancellor of the Exchequer, and in effect as deputy prime minister, under Lloyd George. In 1917, Law's two eldest sons were killed on the Western Front: a grievous blow to him. But he continued the wartime coalition into peace and himself carried on as Chancellor until 1921, when his doctors told him that unless he took several months of complete rest, he would kill himself.

While Law was away, the coalition started to unravel. Conservative MPs grew restive at supporting Lloyd George as prime minister, for he inspired in a growing number of them a sense of moral revulsion. 'That is the difference between Bonar Law and me,' Lloyd George once remarked to Stanley Baldwin. 'Poor Bonar can't bear being called a liar. Now I don't mind.' Baldwin was not cynical enough to find that sort of thing funny.

Law, who as he himself once remarked was not quite so simple as he looked, sensed this change of opinion in his own party. Austen Chamberlain, who had taken over from Law as party leader, did not understand the trouble that was brewing and in October 1922 called a meeting of all Conservative MPs at the Carlton Club. He thought he could bounce them into fighting another general election in alliance with Lloyd George. Instead he found himself facing a revolt. Law warned that the needs of the party, not the coalition, must come first. Otherwise it would face a split as disastrous as had occurred under Peel in 1846. 'The party elects a leader,' Law warned, 'and that leader chooses the policy, and if the party does not like it, they have to get another leader.'

Chamberlain pushed the question of whether the Conservatives should resume their independence to a vote, and lost by 187 to 88, whereupon he resigned. Lloyd George resigned too, and the King sent for Law and asked him to form a government. But Law insisted that before he could do so, he must be re-elected as Conservative leader. This he duly was, by unanimity, at a further meeting of Conservative MPs. His odd mixture of loyalty, tenacity and humility made him one of the best servants his party has ever had.

The grandees who had wanted to remain in government with Lloyd George were very angry indeed with Law. Churchill accused him of forming 'a government of the second eleven', while Lord Birkenhead lamented that 'first-class problems' were going to be tackled by 'second-class brains'. Lord Robert Cecil replied, on Law's behalf, that second-class brains were better than 'second-class character'.

The country seemed to agree. Law called an election in November 1922 in which the Conservatives won 344 seats, Labour 142, Lloyd George's Liberals 62 and Asquith's Liberals 54. It was clear from this what happened to divided parties: the Liberals, who had dominated politics since their great victory of 1906, were in desperate trouble.

Law had fought the election on the promise of 'tranquillity': something the country yearned for after the horrors of war. But a prime minister's life is seldom tranquil. He made Baldwin Chancellor, and sent him off to negotiate with the Americans about Britain's war debts. Baldwin returned in January 1923 with such an unfavourable settlement that Law almost resigned and was only dissuaded from doing so when the rest of the Cabinet backed the Chancellor.

The prime minister was having trouble with his throat. He was extremely good at managing the Commons, but in April his voice became so weak he could not make himself heard. His doctor advised a Mediterranean cruise, which had to be broken off at Genoa, for Law was suffering an acute pain in the side of his face. His friend Aitken, who by now was Lord Beaverbrook, summoned the doctor to meet them in Paris, and here incurable throat cancer was diagnosed, though the word 'cancer' was not mentioned in the patient's presence.

In May 1923, Law resigned as prime minister. He was by now very ill, and declined to recommend who his successor should be. He died in October, and although he had asked to be buried next to his wife at Helensburgh, his family consented to have him buried in Westminster Abbey. 'It is fitting,' Asquith is supposed to have said, 'that we should have buried the Unknown Prime Minister by the side of the Unknown Soldier.'

STANLEY BALDWIN

Lived 1867–1947; prime minister 1923–24, 1924–29 and
1935–37

Stanley Baldwin dominated politics between the two world
wars by overthrowing the Lloyd George coalition and
supplying instead the unadventurous and emollient
leadership most people wanted. He won great victories for the
Conservatives and made Labour welcome as it formed its first two
minority governments. There was a kind of sincerity about him:
he was genuinely disgusted by Lloyd George, genuinely wanted
peace and in the 1930s genuinely out of his depth as he watched
the rise of Hitler. On stepping down in 1937, he was still popular,
and in a letter written a year later was able to say: 'I knew that I
had been chosen as God's instrument for the healing of the nation.'

But when people saw in 1940 how unprepared he had left
Britain for the fight for national survival against Nazi Germany,

he became one of the guilty men who took the blame for failing to rearm with the necessary speed and determination. George Orwell wrote in an essay published at the end of that year: 'As for Baldwin, one could not even dignify him with the name of stuffed shirt. He was simply a hole in the air.'

Baldwin was the only child of a Worcestershire ironmaster who established a thriving business, and sent him to Harrow and Trinity College, Cambridge. For many years after leaving university, Baldwin helped run the family firm, which grew to employ 4,000 people and was conducted on paternalistic lines. Only on the death of his father in 1908 did he enter the Commons, succeeding him as Conservative MP for the local Worcestershire seat of Bewdley. At first, Baldwin made little impression at Westminster, and until becoming a minister in 1917 he continued to run Baldwin's, but in December 1916 he was taken on as parliamentary private secretary by Bonar Law, the leader of the Conservative Party, who had just become Chancellor of the Exchequer. There was an affinity between these two businessmen, and rapid promotion followed. In 1919, he wrote a letter to The Times, signed with the cryptic initials FST (they stood for Financial Secretary to the Treasury, the office he then held), in which he urged the rich to impose a voluntary tax on themselves in order to relieve the heavy burden of debt accumulated during the First World War. He himself donated, anonymously, £120,000, or a fifth of his wealth, for this purpose.

Almost no one followed his example, and Baldwin grew increasingly disgusted by the state of public life. He described the Conservative MPs elected in 1918 as 'a lot of hard-faced men who look as if they had done very well out of the war', and was appalled by the behaviour of the prime minister, Lloyd George, who was selling honours with impudent openness. In October 1922, Baldwin demonstrated his usually dormant capacity for independent action by rebelling against the coalition between the

Conservatives and Lloyd George. He seized on the defence of Lloyd George as 'a dynamic force', and warned his fellow Conservative MPs when they met at the Carlton Club:

> A dynamic force is a very terrible thing; it may crush you but it is not necessarily right. It is owing to that dynamic force, and that remarkable personality, that the Liberal Party, to which he formerly belonged, had been smashed to pieces; and it is my firm conviction that, in time, the same thing will happen to our party.

The Conservatives voted to withdraw their support from Lloyd George, who was finished. The grandees who had stuck by him were sidelined too: they had backed the wrong horse. In came the unassuming Bonar Law as prime minister, persuaded by Baldwin to return from a period of illness.

Baldwin's reward was to become Chancellor of the Exchequer. After the Conservatives had won the general election of November 1922, he set off for the United States, in order to negotiate a repayment schedule for Britain's enormous war debts. The deal he reached was in Law's opinion unacceptable, but Baldwin revealed details of it to the press, got the rest of the Cabinet to agree to it and talked Law out of resigning.

There was at this time, in the immediate aftermath of the Russian Revolution, great fear of Communism. In February 1923, Baldwin sought to reassure people that it could not happen here:

> I am myself of that somewhat flabby nature that always prefers agreement to disagreement ... When the Labour Party sit on these benches, we shall all wish them well in their effort to govern the country. But I am quite certain that whether they succeed or fail there will never in this country be a Communist Government, and for this reason, that no

gospel founded on hate will ever seize the hearts of our
people – the people of Great Britain.

This was the kind of preaching millions of people wanted to hear.
British decency would bring salvation.

In May 1923, Law was obliged by ill health to step down. Would
George V send for the Foreign Secretary, Lord Curzon, a statesman
of high ability and vast experience, or for the relatively obscure
and untested Baldwin? Law offered no advice, so the King turned
for guidance to Arthur Balfour, the only other former Conservative
prime minister still alive. Balfour distrusted Curzon, who had
antagonised people by his grand manner and was in the Lords,
which was felt in a democratic age to be less and less acceptable.
Curzon nevertheless expected to become prime minister and was
shocked to find himself beaten by 'a man of the utmost insignif-
icance', as he described Baldwin.

The new prime minister was actually a man of considerable
ability, who would hold high office for most of the next fourteen
years. He began, however, by making a mistake. He was worried
Lloyd George would stage a comeback by espousing tariff reform,
a policy still dear to the hearts of many Conservatives. So Baldwin
decided he must espouse it too. But Law had promised that before
implementing tariff reform, he would hold a general election. So
this is what Baldwin proceeded in December 1923 to do. The
Conservatives lost the comfortable majority which they had
attained only a year before: a dreadful shock to Baldwin, and one
which discouraged him from running unnecessary risks in future.

But he had shown himself to be an asset on the campaign trail,
and his recovery was masterly. He allowed Ramsay MacDonald to
form a minority Labour government, and the Liberals to take the
blame for bringing about its downfall nine months later. In the third
general election in two years, held in October 1924, the Conservatives
won 412 seats, Labour 151 and the Liberals a mere 40.

Baldwin had reunited the party and brought in some of the big figures, including Winston Churchill, who had wanted to continue with Lloyd George as prime minister. Churchill was pinned down by being made Chancellor of the Exchequer, the office his father, Lord Randolph, had held, but not one for which he himself possessed any very obvious suitability. He put the country back on the gold standard, which was not what the economy needed, but which conformed to pre-war orthodoxy. Baldwin now had his own mandate, and could develop his own political persona. Few leaders have ever been so skilful at playing the game of being an unpolitical politician, who aspired, as he put it, to be 'the leader of the people who do not belong to any party'.

The prime minister rehearsed in front of a mirror the best angle at which to hold his pipe, and let it be known that his favourite tobacco – a masterpiece of unfashionability – was Dr Gale's Glasgow Presbyterian Mixture. He had a genius for the fireside chat delivered straight into people's homes by way of the radio, which was the newest form of political communication. Although a businessman, his favoured recreation was known to be going for country walks, and he gave frankly preposterous speeches about 'the sight of a plough team coming over the brow of a hill', which he claimed was 'the one eternal sight of England'.

When did anyone last see a plough team coming over the brow of a hill? But in this age of bogus Tudor architecture, plenty of people wanted to believe England had not really changed. The prime minister was studiously unglamorous, uncondescending and inclusive, determined to avert class conflict, and attained, at times, a sort of willed complacency. Perhaps his bromides helped the country to get through the General Strike, which occurred in 1926, and into which two other future prime ministers, Neville Chamberlain and Churchill, flung themselves with greater partisanship. Baldwin was the first Tory to proclaim the need for 'One Nation' conservatism, a term he adapted from Disraeli's novels.

Much to his surprise, he lost the general election of 1929, and Labour formed a minority government which was almost at once knocked off course by the Wall Street Crash and ensuing Great Depression. In that year, Baldwin's eldest son, Oliver, gained election as a Labour MP: the only time a party leader has faced his own son across the Commons. Baldwin carried this off with his usual amiability. Meanwhile the press lords, Rothermere and Beaverbrook (the latter the former Max Aitken, who had been such an ally of Bonar Law), mounted a determined campaign to get rid of Baldwin as Conservative party leader, at a point when he was out of power and plainly vulnerable. His wife Lucy spurred him to resistance by exhorting him to be a tiger, her nickname for him. And resist he did, routing his persecutors with a famous rebuke composed for him by his cousin, Rudyard Kipling: 'What the proprietorship of these newspapers is aiming at is power, and power without responsibility – the prerogative of the harlot throughout the ages.' His Tory colleague the Duke of Devonshire commented: 'That's done it. He's lost us the tarts' vote.'

In 1931, a national government was formed to try to cope with the economic emergency that was unfolding. Baldwin as Tory leader commanded the overwhelming majority of its MPs, though MacDonald remained prime minister. Lord Dunglass, a newly elected Tory MP who thirty years later would become, as Sir Alec Douglas-Home, prime minister, admired Baldwin's skill, but reported that in the Commons he behaved in a very odd way:

His sympathetic treatment of Mr Lansbury, who, in 1931, was left to lead a weak rump of Socialists with a vocal Left wing, forced the Opposition to be constitutional. Baldwin did it all by kindness. He had an extraordinary habit while sitting on the Bench of making an excruciating grimace, and then planting a smacking kiss on the Order paper. The psychologists must have been hard put to it to find an explanation.

In January 1933, Hitler became German Chancellor. Baldwin recognised the danger posed by German air power and warned that 'the bomber will always get through', but did not promote rearmament with any great dynamism. That was, after all, a quality of which he had disapproved when it was shown by Lloyd George. In his own defence, Baldwin asserted as early as 1936 that he could not have gone faster, because if he had, he would have lost the 1935 general election. Churchill in this period was kept very firmly out of power, and in his book about the Second World War, the index carries the damning words 'Baldwin, Stanley . . . confesses putting party before country'. Baldwin said leading the Conservative Party was about as difficult as driving pigs to market, but he was remarkably good at it, and achieved overwhelming election victories in 1931 and 1935.

Baldwin wished to move no faster than public opinion would allow him to move. He preferred to wait on events, and was known for taking long holidays at Aix-les-Bains, in Savoy, where he went walking in the hills. In 1935, when MacDonald's feebleness became impossible to conceal, Baldwin resumed the prime ministership, but hoped soon to retire. That plan was delayed by the abdication crisis in 1936, during which with masterly skill he united the British and Imperial Establishment behind the policy of replacing the feckless Edward VIII with the dutiful George VI. The following year, he did step down, and became a Knight of the Garter and Earl Baldwin of Bewdley.

Three years later, he was so unpopular he did not care to appear in public, and was denied a seat when travelling on a train, despite by now being old and infirm. Lord Beaverbrook, in an act of spite, had the gates removed from Baldwin's house, a gift from Worcester Conservative Association when their leader retired, under the pretence that the metal was needed to make aeroplanes. At his final appearance in public, for the unveiling in 1947 of a statue of George V, a feeble cheer was raised in his honour, and he asked whether he was being booed.

PRINCIPLE
INTEGRITY
SOCIALISM

RAMSAY MACDONALD

Lived 1866–1937; prime minister 1924 and 1929–35

Ramsay MacDonald rose from humble origins to become the first Labour prime minister, yet went down in sorrow to the grave, denounced as a traitor to his own cause. Having done more than anyone else to build the party up, he became detached from it, and in the crisis of 1931 allowed himself to be persuaded that it was his duty to form a National Government in which the Conservatives had the predominant share. The hatred he inspired on his own side for accommodating himself to the ideas of its opponents far exceeded what Tony Blair was to experience a few generations later.

MacDonald was born in a two-room cottage at Lossiemouth, a port looking north across the Moray Firth. He was the illegitimate son of Annie Ramsay, who worked for a time as a servant at the same farm as his father, John Macdonald, a ploughman who vanishes from the pages of history. Why Annie and John did not marry is unclear, but it is possible that Annie's mother, Bella, thought the ploughman not good enough for her daughter, and drove him away.

Young Ramsay MacDonald was brought up as an only child by his mother and grandmother, two women of spirit and independence, both of whom earned their living as seamstresses. He went to school four miles away, at Drainie, where he received a good, thorough education and worked for the last four years as the pupil teacher. On travelling first to Bristol and then to London, where he managed to find clerical work, he became a socialist, a keen member of various socialist organisations and a prolific freelance journalist. His eloquence started to bring him to the fore as a man who could express socialist views with an attractive mixture of romance and patriotism. He was assisted by his striking good looks, his nervous energy and his Scots background, which by putting him outside the English class system gave him a kind of classlessness.

Unlike some socialists, he was not a revolutionary: for him the path to power lay through Parliament. He contested the general election of 1895 as a candidate for the Independent Labour Party, came bottom of the poll, but received a campaign donation from an ardent young socialist called Margaret Gladstone. In 1896, they married. She was the daughter of a distinguished scientist and had a private income of several hundred pounds a year, enabling them to rent a flat in Lincoln's Inn Fields, which became a busy centre of socialist activity as well as home to their six children.

In 1900, MacDonald helped found the Labour Representation Committee, run by him, with the aim of getting MPs into Parliament. The election of that year saw only two Labour candidates victorious: Keir Hardie and one other. When Labour candidates stood, there was a danger they would take votes off the Liberals and allow the Conservatives to get in. MacDonald accordingly negotiated a secret pact, under which the Liberals and Labour agreed not to oppose each other in seats where this was likely to happen. Thanks to this pact, 29 Labour MPs were elected in 1906, including MacDonald himself in Leicester.

Within a few years, MacDonald became the foremost figure among the Labour MPs. But in 1911, he suffered an irreparable loss with the death of his wife, Margaret, leaving him the father of five young children: their son David had already died the previous year. This loss left him grief-stricken and inflicted on him a loneliness which was never fully lifted. In later life, he was mocked for having amorous friendships with various grand Tory ladies, of whom the most fatuous was Lady Londonderry. Had Margaret survived, it is unlikely this would have occurred, or that he would ever have found himself in coalition with the Conservatives.

In 1914 he had the moral courage to oppose British participation in the First World War. He and his wife had travelled widely in order to inform themselves about world affairs, and MacDonald had warned that constructing the alliances needed to maintain a balance of power in Europe would lead to war. He could not carry most of his Labour colleagues with him, and his relations with some of them never recovered. He came under sustained and vitriolic attack in the press, and the Moray Golf Club passed a critical resolution. He never again played on its links at Lossiemouth, and in the general election of 1918 lost his seat.

It took him until 1922 to get back into the Commons, but Labour now had 142 MPs, and MacDonald as their outstanding figure became leader of the Opposition. The following year, the new Conservative prime minister, Stanley Baldwin, threw away his parliamentary majority by holding an unnecessary election. No party now controlled the Commons, but in January 1924 MacDonald became, with the help of the Liberals, prime minister at the head of a minority Labour government.

Because it had no majority, it could not be expected to do very much or last very long, and Labour in any case had not worked out plans for transforming the British State. MacDonald and his ministerial team instead set about proving how respectable they were. For their meetings with George V, they took great care to wear the correct court dress, and their wives were even keener to go to Buckingham Palace than they were. David Marquand, himself a former Labour MP, remarks on the 'incredulous delight' of these representatives of the working class 'at having been incorporated into the political class'. Philip Snowden proved as orthodox a Chancellor of the Exchequer as any Treasury official could wish. MacDonald served as Foreign Secretary as well as prime minister, and conducted a successful allied conference in London on German reparations. In October 1924, the Liberals voted the government out of power, and in the ensuing general election, the Zinoviev Letter, later exposed as a forgery, was used to suggest that Labour was subject to sinister Soviet influence.

Labour lost 40 seats, but was still the largest opposition party, with MacDonald at its head. In 1926, he disapproved of the General Strike, for any kind of extra-parliamentary action was anathema to him. He also disapproved of quite a few of his colleagues in the Labour Party, and was not inclined to take them into his confidence. They in turn observed with a hostile eye his fondness for moving in aristocratic circles. Lady Londonderry, the greatest political hostess of the day, was said to be trying to cater her husband into the Cabinet, and was certainly very keen on MacDonald, and he on her.

In the general election of 1929, Labour became for the first time the party with the largest number of seats, though once again it did not have a majority. In MacDonald came for his second term. Sixteen weeks later, the Wall Street Crash – the plunge in the stock market which heralded the start of the Great Depression – took place, and six months after that, unemployment in Britain began to climb from the already worrying level of one million to over three and a half million by the middle of 1932, with areas dependent on traditional heavy industries suffering devastating levels of worklessness. Snowden, as Chancellor, responded with orthodox attempts to balance the books and thereby keep Britain on the gold standard. For him, austerity was a moral virtue. He wore his hair shirt with pride, and set out to cut unemployment benefit. A few voices were raised in protest: Sir Oswald Mosley, who was at this time a Labour MP, thought that great programmes of public works, as recommended by Maynard Keynes, were the way to cope with unemployment. Lloyd George, for the Liberals, took up that cry too. But Lloyd George was now in the wilderness, a discredited figure, and MacDonald backed Snowden.

MacDonald was sixty-three when he embarked on his second prime ministership, and in physical and mental decline. His eyes gave him trouble, he felt exhausted and sometimes he forgot people's names. In October 1930, Harold Nicolson and his wife, Vita Sackville-West, visited him at Chequers:

> The PM pours out to Vita the miseries of his soul: he cannot sleep: two hours a night is all he gets: he can do no work: 'the moment I disentangle my foot from one strand of barbed wire it becomes entangled in another. If God were to come to me and say "Ramsay, would you rather be a country gentleman than Prime Minister?", I should reply, "Please God, a country gentleman."'

Paralysis set in: the government had no answers to the Crash. In August 1931, there was a run on the pound, and the Cabinet could not unite round the benefit cuts which were needed to restore confidence. Ministers instead decided, with MacDonald at their head, to submit their resignations to the King. The prime minister's personal expectation was that they would go into Opposition, and would support from there whatever emergency measures proved necessary to rescue the pound. But the King instead asked him to lead a National Government, and MacDonald allowed himself to be persuaded. He thought it was his patriotic duty to agree to this.

Most of his MPs were appalled. In September 1931, they expelled MacDonald and Snowden from the party. A general election was called, in which Snowden deepened the rift by condemning the Labour manifesto: 'This is not Socialism. It is Bolshevism run mad.' The general expectation was that MacDonald, who now sat for the mining seat of Seaham, in County Durham, would himself be defeated. But thanks to a brilliant Tory organiser, Dorothy Brant, who rallied the women's vote, he hung on, as one of only thirteen National Labour MPs.

MacDonald was now the prisoner of the 473 Conservatives who had been returned. On the Opposition benches sat fifty-two Labour MPs who regarded him as a traitor. The country was forced off the gold standard, with Sidney Webb, a member of the outgoing Labour Cabinet, complaining: 'Nobody told us we could do this.' The British economy started to recover, with new industries such as cars and electronics doing well. But unemployment in traditional trades such as mining, shipbuilding and textiles was still appallingly high, and MacDonald would never be forgiven. Nor in his special field of foreign policy could he achieve any countervailing successes: Hitler and Mussolini posed problems to which he did not have the answer. His parliamentary performances had become pitiful and in June 1935, on grounds of health, he at last asked to be relieved of the prime ministership. But still he lingered in the Cabinet in the meaningless role of Lord President of the Council.

In the general election of November 1935, he lost Seaham to the Labour candidate Manny Shinwell. But another seat, the Combined Scottish Universities, was found for MacDonald, and he remained a minister until Baldwin stepped down in May 1937. In November of that year, MacDonald died suddenly while on a holiday voyage to South America, where he was hoping to recover his health.

To this day, his immense contribution to the creation of the Labour Party is undervalued or unknown, and he is thought of, quite unfairly, as a scoundrel.

NEVILLE CHAMBERLAIN

Lived 1869–1940; prime minister 1937–40

Neville Chamberlain has the worst reputation of any prime minister since Lord North. He took personal charge of the attempt in the late 1930s to appease Hitler, and was foolish enough on his return to London from negotiating with the dictator in Munich, in September 1938, to declare 'peace for our time'. When this announcement, greeted with unbounded enthusiasm, turned out to be sorely mistaken, Chamberlain took the blame, and as soon as a warlike prime minister was required, was forced to stand down. His supporters urge that as a peacetime politician, he has great achievements to his name, but even they cannot pretend his meticulous and rigid mind was well adapted to comprehending, let alone surmounting, the danger posed by Nazi Germany.

Neville's father was the illustrious Joe Chamberlain, an irrepressible figure in national politics from 1886 to 1906, but never prime minister. Neville's elder brother, Austen Chamberlain, was given the education in Cambridge, Paris and Berlin befitting a statesman, but although he served as Foreign Secretary, he could never quite grasp his chances to go even higher. Neville was sent as a young man to manage the sisal plantation which Joe had decided to set up on the island of Andros in the Bahamas, in the confident expectation that it would make money. After seven years of lonely toil, Neville was forced to admit the investment had been a total failure. This ordeal intensified his secretive, solitary, self-willed approach to problems. Even his friends said he was 'by no means easy to get to know'.

On returning to the Chamberlain family mansion of Highbury, in Birmingham, Neville pursued a successful career as a businessman and entered municipal politics. In 1915, he became the eleventh member of the family to serve as Lord Mayor, and the following year he accepted in London the new post of director general of national service. Here he fell victim to bureaucratic infighting and blamed the prime minister, David Lloyd George, whom he described as 'a degraded little skunk', for failing to back him. In 1918, at the age of forty-nine, he at last entered the House of Commons.

Chamberlain's rise now was swift, for he belonged to the trio of able but unglamorous provincial businessmen – Bonar Law, Baldwin and himself – who led the Conservative Party and served as prime minister between 1922 and 1940. He was briefly Minister of Health under Bonar Law and Chancellor of the Exchequer under Baldwin, before opting to go again to Health for the whole of

Baldwin's second term, from 1924 to 1929: 'I remain convinced,' Chamberlain said, 'that I might be a great Minister of Health, but am not likely to be more than a second-rate Chancellor.'

He amazed his Cabinet colleagues by presenting them with a list of twenty-five measures he proposed to carry through the Commons, twenty-one of which did indeed become law. His achievements included contributory pensions, sweeping improvements in health provision, a huge programme of house-building and replacing the Victorian system of local government. His capacity to get things done was unrivalled, but he also demonstrated an unattractive contempt for his opponents, as he admitted in 1927 in a letter to one of his sisters: 'Stanley [Baldwin] begged me to remember I was addressing a meeting of gentlemen. I always gave the impression I looked on the Labour Party as dirt. The fact is that intellectually, with a few exceptions, they are dirt.'

There was a growing rivalry between the two men. Chamberlain expressed his frustration that while he 'knew every flower' and loved fishing, it was Baldwin who was regarded as the countryman. In early 1931, when Baldwin was at his weakest, Chamberlain tried to bounce him into resigning. Having failed to do so, he instead accepted, later that year, the office of Chancellor of the Exchequer, and there could be no doubt he now dominated domestic policy. 'It amuses me,' he boasted in a letter to his sisters, 'to find a new policy for each of my colleagues in turn.' He imposed tariffs on imports, which he said would have pleased his father, pursued sound money and came to be seen as the inevitable successor to Baldwin.

On entering Downing Street in May 1937, Chamberlain was sixty-eight. Nye Bevan, a brilliant young Labour MP, observed from the Opposition benches the change of tone from Baldwin: 'In the funeral service of capitalism, the honeyed and soothing platitudes of the clergyman are finished, and the cortège is now under the sombre and impressive guidance of the undertaker.'

That was certainly not how Chamberlain saw himself. He was intent on a further programme of domestic reform which might have rendered the post-war creation of the National Health Service redundant. Instead he had to cope with Hitler and Mussolini. Chamberlain took an optimistic view of his ability to negotiate with them. He proposed to avert war by agreeing to their more reasonable demands: they in return would surely be reasonable enough to keep these agreements. In vain Chamberlain's brother, Austen, had warned him in a condescending tone, 'Neville, you must remember you know nothing about foreign affairs.' Austen died just before Neville took over from Baldwin.

An early difference of opinion arose over how to deal with Mussolini. Anthony Eden, the Foreign Secretary, regarded the Italian leader as 'a complete gangster and his pledged word means nothing'. Chamberlain wanted to negotiate, in order to avoid driving Italy and Germany closer together, and used his brother's widow, Ivy Chamberlain, as a channel of communication with Mussolini. In February 1938, Eden resigned, devoid of Cabinet support. The following month, Hitler marched into Austria and incorporated it into the Reich: an ominous move, and one whose success strengthened his grip on Germany.

Chamberlain's grip on the Conservative Party was at this time very strong. He accepted the need for a measure of rearmament, but did not propose to spend so much on arms that the British economy was damaged, for after all, as he had already told MPs, 'wars are not only won with arms and men: they are won with reserves of resources and credit'. He did, however, promote, partly from motives of economy, a switch from the production of bombers to fighters. Since Germany by now possessed a strong bomber force, which in 1940 would be turned against Britain, this turned out to be the right thing to do.

But Chamberlain still thought he could prevent war, and in September 1938 flew three times to Germany to negotiate with

Hitler. The Führer was now demanding the incorporation of the Sudetenland, the mountainous frontier region of Czechoslovakia, into the Reich, on the basis that it contained a minority German population. Chamberlain told his Cabinet colleagues that if Hitler were allowed to annex the Sudetenland, the very territory which rendered Czechoslovakia defensible, that would be an end of it. The Cabinet doubted this, and so did France. War seemed imminent, and Chamberlain made a famous broadcast in which he said:

> How horrible, fantastic, incredible it is that we should be digging trenches and trying on gas masks here because of a quarrel in a faraway country between people of whom we know nothing.

The prime minister went to the House of Commons, the expectation being that within hours Britain would be at war. But as he spoke, a further message arrived from Hitler, inviting him to attend a meeting in Munich the next day. The House expressed wild relief, and off the prime minister flew to Munich, where he sold the Czechs down the river, and got Hitler to sign a worthless declaration about the desire of Britain and Germany never again to go to war with each other.

Chamberlain returned to London waving a scrap of paper. He promised that, like Disraeli in 1878, he had returned home bringing 'peace with honour', and for a time his popularity soared to new heights. Churchill and a small band of Conservative rebels opposed him, and so did Labour, but the Commons approved what he had done by a large majority.

But in March 1939, Hitler seized the rest of Czechoslovakia. The policy of appeasement lay in ruins, and Chamberlain and the French now issued a guarantee to defend Poland, but were without the means to do so, unless they could make an alliance with Soviet Russia. It was instead Hitler who did a deal with Stalin, and on 1 September attacked Poland. Britain was now at war with Germany, but at first not much happened in the West. Chamberlain brought Churchill and Eden into the government and invited Labour and the Liberals to join too, but they refused to serve under him.

Still Chamberlain clung with obstinate credulity to the tatters of his policy, and was bold enough to claim as late as 5 April 1940 that 'Hitler has missed the bus'. The Führer disagreed, and invaded Norway. British forces tried and failed to stop him. In the great Commons debate of 7 and 8 May 1940, Leo Amery, from the Conservative benches, used against Chamberlain the words with which Cromwell had dismissed the Rump Parliament almost 300 years before: 'In the name of God, go!' And go Chamberlain did, having suffered a humiliating reduction in his parliamentary support.

He was disappointed to find himself replaced by Churchill rather than the altogether less bellicose Lord Halifax. But he served as a loyal member of Churchill's wartime coalition until September 1940, when advancing cancer forced him to resign. In November, he died, having written in one of his last letters, to Baldwin: 'Never for one instant have I doubted the rightness of what I did at Munich.'

His supporters say Munich gained Britain valuable time to prepare for war. But it also undermined Hitler's domestic opponents, by presenting him with a cost-free conquest. And when one reads about this abject surrender, one cannot help feeling that Chamberlain, in his arrogant naïvety, and with the full consent of public opinion, did something deeply shameful. His final service to his country was to act as scapegoat for a policy which had ended in disaster.

SIR WINSTON CHURCHILL

Lived 1874–1965; prime minister 1940–45 and 1951–55

Winston Churchill was born for war. He revelled in battle, was at his greatest in adversity, and entered Downing Street at a moment of extreme national peril. He is remembered as the greatest English war leader since Elizabeth I, a man of invigorating eloquence, indomitable courage and life-enhancing wit. But because it is conventional to praise him, it is easy to forget how unconventional Churchill himself was, and what a nuisance he made of himself for large tracts of his life. His instinct for placing himself at the centre of events made it hard to keep him out of things, but he was also, as his predecessor, Neville Chamberlain, once remarked, a 'd—d uncomfortable bedfellow'.

Most men educated, as Churchill was, at an English public school are trained in the correct way to behave, make their careers by conforming to the rules and remain inhibited in the expression of their emotions. Churchill was not like that. At Harrow, he was a failure, not from lack of ability, but because he responded badly to being told what to do. As Sebastian Haffner, a German émigré, observed in *Churchill*, a brilliant short biography, 'he never became a genuine product of the English public-school system: not a man of understatement and arrogant self-effacement, not a cricketer, not a polished "English gentleman", but rather a character from Shakespeare's England.'

His father, Lord Randolph Churchill, a younger son of the Duke of Marlborough, was a brilliant lout, magnificently rude about the Liberals and also highly disruptive to his own party, the Conservatives. He got engaged to Jennie Jerome, a beautiful American, two days after meeting her, and their elder son was born at Blenheim Palace after they had been married for only seven months. In 1886 he threw away his political career by resigning as Chancellor of the Exchequer, on the mistaken assumption that he was indispensable. Winston revered the memory of his father, who died at the age of forty-five, and lamented never having been taken seriously by him. Lord Randolph agreed that his son should go into the army, being too stupid for anything else, but this the boy only managed after taking the entrance exam three times.

On active service, Winston began to show remarkable initiative and drive. While in his early twenties, he managed, by pulling strings and flouting rules, to come under fire in Cuba, India, Sudan and South Africa. He demonstrated literary and journalistic abilities of a high order by writing about these campaigns, which infuriated the senior officers whose tactics he criticised, but earned him large sums of money. In 1898, he took part in the British army's last great cavalry charge, at the Battle of Omdurman, and the following year, while covering the Boer War as a journalist, he went forward on an armoured train which was ambushed, took command of the defence, organised the evacuation of the wounded on the engine, was taken prisoner by the Boers and then, with exceptional pluck and luck, made good his own escape.

He fought for another six months, before returning to England a hero, and gaining election in 1900 as the Conservative MP for Oldham, in Lancashire. He was now famous, and when he went on a speaking tour of America, Mark Twain introduced him to an audience in New York with the words: 'Ladies and gentlemen, I have the honour to introduce Winston Churchill: hero of five wars, author of six books, and future Prime Minister of England.'

Churchill made himself into a remarkable orator. His method was to study the works of great speakers of the past, to devote enormous pains to the composition of his own speeches and to learn them by heart. It was not an infallible method, for what he learned did not always correspond to what was required on the spur of the moment in Commons debate, and on one dreadful occasion he dried up altogether and had to sit down. But it was clear already that Churchill, who himself wept easily, had an exceptional ear for language and the ability to stir his listeners. Throughout his life he could spring what his friend Violet Bonham Carter called 'the ambush of the unexpected'. In 1904, he 'ratted' from the Conservatives, who had abandoned the cause of free trade, and joined the Liberals. His new leader, Henry Asquith, promoted him at the age of only thirty-one to the Cabinet, and as a junior partner to Lloyd George, a mercurial figure with whom he had much in common, Churchill threw himself into the creation of old-age pensions, and the great assault on the House of Lords. For many members of the upper classes, this was treachery of the most putrid kind. The Duke of Beaufort said he would like to see Churchill and Lloyd George 'in the middle of 20 couple of dog-hounds'.

But Asquith promoted him to the vital role of First Lord of the Admiralty, charged with ensuring that the Royal Navy continued to dominate the new fleet being built by imperial Germany. Churchill flung himself with gusto into the work. He even took up flying, so he could find out about aeroplanes, then the newest weapon of war. In vain his family and friends pleaded with him to refrain from this perilous pursuit, in which there was no need for a Cabinet minister to engage. Churchill was attracted by danger. When war broke out, he wanted to resign his Cabinet post and take personal command of the defence of Antwerp, which he saw at once could be a thorn in the side of the German advance. His colleagues regarded this audacious proposal as a sign of mental imbalance: a verdict they thought confirmed by the Dardanelles adventure, promoted by Churchill as a means of attacking the enemy somewhere far away from the killing fields of Flanders, but so ill executed by the admirals and generals that the Turks had ample time to prepare a lethal defence.

Churchill took the blame for this disaster, resigned from the Cabinet and, as a kind of penance, went off to fight on the Western Front. But Lloyd George had a high opinion of him, and brought him back to occupy further high ministerial posts until the collapse of the coalition government in 1922.

At the general election of November 1922, Churchill also lost his Commons seat. He looked out of it: a Liberal grandee at a time when his party was collapsing and prosaic statesmen were coming to the fore. But within a couple of years, he had rejoined the Conservatives – re-ratted, to use his own term – and had become Chancellor of the Exchequer. Yet he never lost his Liberal sympathies. In extreme old age, for he only stopped being an MP in 1964, he met a Labour MP, Bill Mallalieu, in a Commons lift, and asked: 'Who are you?' Mallalieu gave his name. 'Labour?' Churchill asked, and Mallalieu confirmed this. Churchill paused, then said: 'I'm a Liberal. *Always have been.*'

As Chancellor of the Exchequer from 1924 to 1929, Churchill delivered Budget speeches which were described even by the experts as 'extraordinarily brilliant entertainment'. He told one of his senior Treasury officials, 'I would rather see Finance less proud and Industry more content.' But he did not achieve this, for after canvassing all the arguments, he took what seemed the safe course of returning the pound to the gold standard at the pre-war rate. This was actually the more dangerous thing to do, for it meant British exports were more expensive and wages had to fall: a constraint that led directly to the General Strike of 1926, which lasted for twelve days, and to a bitter dispute in the mines which dragged on for seven months after that.

For the decade from 1929, Churchill became a prophet wandering in the political wilderness. He conducted a tremendous battle against self-government for India, dismissing Gandhi as 'a seditious Middle Temple lawyer, now posing as a fakir of a type well-known in the East, striding half-naked up the steps of the Vice-regal palace', and was comprehensively outmanoeuvred and defeated by Baldwin. He rallied to Edward VIII during the abdication crisis of 1936, and again found himself on the losing side. At times, he succumbed to depression. To many Conservative MPs, he seemed like a reactionary maverick who drank too much and could not be trusted, a gambler who must be kept far away from the levers of power, which were fortunately in the safe hands of Stanley Baldwin and Neville Chamberlain.

Churchill wrote wonderful books, of course: few politicians have composed as amusing a memoir as *My Early Life: A Roving Commission*, which appeared in 1930. *Great Contemporaries* is a collection of short and penetrating pieces about the statesmen he knew.

And then there are the far longer and more ambitious works, including his lives of his own father and of their great ancestor, John Churchill, ennobled as Duke of Marlborough, and his account of the First World War, The World Crisis, described by Arthur Balfour as 'an autobiography disguised as a history of the Universe'.

His third campaign, in the 1930s, in favour of more rapid rearmament and against appeasing Hitler, was just as unpopular and unsuccessful as the other two. The British Establishment would not see how hopeless it was to reason with Hitler. Churchill did see this, but people closed their minds to his warnings. As the general election results of 1935 came in, showing victory for the Conservatives, his friend Lord Beaverbrook told him: 'Well you're finished now. Baldwin has so good a majority that he will be able to do without you.' And so Baldwin did, claiming he wanted to keep Churchill fresh in case there was after all a war. After Munich, in 1938, when Churchill warned that the country had suffered 'a total and unmitigated defeat', efforts were even made by Conservative Central Office to get him deselected from his parliamentary seat.

In September 1939, when war broke out, Churchill had to be brought back into the government as First Lord of the Admiralty, the post he had held a quarter of a century earlier. The signal 'Winston is back' flashed round the fleet. The Royal Navy was less well prepared than in 1914, and the Norway campaign of April 1940, which was largely Churchill's idea, was a fiasco.

In the confidence debate of 7 and 8 May 1940, Churchill staunchly defended the government of which he was now a part, and was warned by Lloyd George from the backbenches that he 'must not allow himself to be converted into an air-raid shelter to keep the splinters from hitting his colleagues'. Conservative MPs, although still predominantly loyal to Chamberlain, were becoming restive, while Labour wanted to see him gone and resisted his pleas to serve in coalition under him, a man who had long treated them with contempt. Chamberlain's majority fell from 200 to only 81, and he realised he must go. He then tried to hang on, because on 10 May the Germans launched their Blitzkrieg in the West.

Churchill came through as his successor because he was a known fighter, while the other contender, Lord Halifax, was not. In 1940, a defender of lost causes was suddenly just what the country was looking for. But when Churchill entered the Commons for the first time as prime minister, the Conservatives did not cheer him. They reserved their approbation for Chamberlain, to whom many of them remained loyal. Churchill told the House, 'I have nothing to offer but blood, tears, toil and sweat', and was not applauded by his own side.

His popularity was at first much greater in the country than in the Conservative Party. He says in his war memoirs that he felt now he was 'walking with destiny', and was relieved at last to have the reins of power in his hands. But he also confessed to his personal detective that it was perhaps too late to avert defeat. Day by day, the military situation deteriorated. Disaster followed disaster. The German panzers broke through at Sedan, and then, instead of wheeling left towards Paris as expected, drove straight for the Channel. The French disintegrated and the British Expeditionary Force was in grave danger of being captured almost to the last man. Instead 198,000 British troops, and a further 140,000 French and Belgians, were rescued between 26 May and 4 June from the beaches of Dunkirk by the Royal Navy and a flotilla of small ships and pleasure craft which crossed the Channel from England.

This was a great deliverance, but they had left behind almost all their equipment and, as Churchill warned, 'wars are not won by evacuations'. The Battle of France had been a disaster, and the Battle of Britain was about to start: the struggle for the control of the skies which Hitler would need if his forces were to cross the Channel. Churchill used in these months of greatest peril an oratory which carried and lifted the nation. He admitted the magnitude of the defeats, yet persuaded people that victory would come. His honesty about the sacrifices which would be required was invigorating, and rendered him credible in a way that few politicians have ever been credible. As he told the Commons on 4 June 1940, just as Dunkirk was ending:

Even though large tracts of Europe and many old and famous States have fallen or may fall into the grip of the Gestapo and all the odious apparatus of Nazi rule, we shall not flag or fail. We shall go on to the end, we shall fight in France, we shall fight on the seas and oceans, we shall fight with growing confidence and growing strength in the air, we shall defend our island, whatever the cost may be, we shall fight on the beaches, we shall fight on the landing grounds, we shall fight in the fields and in the streets, we shall fight in the hills; we shall never surrender, and even if, which I do not for a moment believe, this island or a large part of it were subjugated and starving, then our Empire beyond the seas, armed and guarded by the British Fleet, would carry on the struggle, until in God's good time, the new world, with all its power and might, steps forth to the rescue and the liberation of the old.

Can anyone read this speech without a tear coming to the eye? No one else could have spoken in this way. Churchill shed tears, so did some of the Labour members, and even Conservatives such as Chips Channon, a rich and amusing MP who moved in gilded circles and hero-worshipped Chamberlain, were impressed. But they were also furious that 'the gangsters', as Halifax called Churchill and his band of outsiders, were now in control.

The strain on Churchill was enormous, and his wife, Clementine, to whom he was devoted and with whom he had four children, felt constrained in June 1940 to write to him:

One of the men in your entourage (a devoted friend) has been to me & told me that there is a danger of your being generally disliked by your colleagues & subordinates because of your rough sarcastic & overbearing manner ... I must confess that I have noticed a deterioration in your manner; & you are not so kind as you used to be. It is for you to give the Orders & if they are bungled – except for the King, the Archbishop of Canterbury & the Speaker you can sack anyone & everyone. Therefore with this terrific power you must combine urbanity, kindness & if possible Olympic calm ... I cannot bear that those who serve the country & yourself should not love you as well as admire and respect you. Besides you won't get the best results by irascibility and rudeness ...

Churchill was not an easy man to work for, but his staff seldom wanted him otherwise, for he was so ebullient, original, stimulating and entertaining. He was magnanimous to those he defeated: unmalicious from instinct as well as from policy. Chamberlain served loyally under Churchill, and remained leader of the Conservative Party, until dying in the autumn of 1940. Churchill, though by no means fond of the Conservatives, saw he had better become their leader himself, rather than allow some rival to build up a power base. Gradually, and as tactfully as he could, he appointed those loyal to himself, many of them recruited from outside the party, to key positions, and expelled those Chamberlainites he did not trust, such as Halifax, who in December 1940 was removed from the Foreign Office and sent as ambassador to the United States.

The Battle of Britain was won, which averted the danger of an immediate invasion. He had urged his compatriots to 'so bear ourselves that, if the British Empire and its Commonwealth last for a thousand years, men will still say, "This was their finest hour."' In the summer of 1941, Hitler committed the suicidal blunder of invading Russia, but this was a long, slow suicide, in which many millions of people perished. For Churchill, there were dismal military setbacks to bear. The fall of Singapore to the Japanese in February 1942 was one of the most ignominious surrenders in British history. He felt these disasters, but had the resilience to withstand them. And Britain no longer stood alone, as it had in the summer of 1940. Now both the Soviet Union and the United States were turned against Germany, the German army was being bled white on the Eastern Front, and eventual victory was likely. But who would win the peace? By 1942, Churchill knew real power was passing to Washington and Moscow, neither of which had any love for the British Empire, which in the event was to expire, not in a thousand years, but within his own lifetime.

While he was busy winning the war, others were charged with preparing the peace, in which wartime methods, collective solutions imposed from above, would bulk far larger than ever before. Germany surrendered in May 1945, and the Conservatives were ill prepared for the general election that, on Labour's insistence, immediately followed. Churchill had tried in vain to delay this contest, the first since 1935, until after the defeat of Japan, which had not yet occurred, though it would soon be hastened by the dropping of atomic bombs on Hiroshima and Nagasaki.

He had now to make an abrupt return to party politics. In June 1945, he launched the Conservative campaign by turning his fire on Labour, with whom he had worked in harmonious coalition for the last five years. Churchill asserted that a 'Socialist Government . . . would have to fall back on some form of Gestapo' in order to quell public criticism. This struck most people as grotesquely exaggerated, but in truth the election was already lost. The Conservatives were regarded as out-of-touch toffs, who had not cared about unemployment before the war, and Gallup polls conducted since 1943 had shown them well behind Labour.

In July 1945, Labour gained an overall majority of 146. Clementine Churchill sought to comfort her husband by telling him that this might be a blessing in disguise, to which he replied, 'At the moment it seems quite effectively disguised.' In 1942, he had nominated Anthony Eden as his successor, and had assured him that he would not repeat Lloyd George's mistake of staying on after the war. But Churchill now decided that rather than step aside, he would become leader of the Opposition, and his fame was such that nobody on his own side could force him to retire. He left domestic policy to others, and devoted himself to foreign affairs, where his name and at times prophetic insights assured him a worldwide audience. In March 1946, in a speech at Fulton, Missouri, introduced by President Truman, Churchill warned of the danger posed by Soviet Russia: 'From Stettin in the Baltic to Trieste in the Adriatic an iron curtain has descended across the Continent.' Stalin denounced this claim, and so did many newspapers in Britain and America, but the truth of it soon became evident. Yet Churchill also foresaw that Russian rule over the conquered territories in eastern Europe could not last for ever: 'After the meal comes the digestion period,' as he remarked in November 1944, while in 1953 he predicted to his private secretary that Communism would disappear from eastern Europe by the 1980s. It was actually to last until 1989.

At the general election of 1950, Labour's majority fell to only five. The force of that great reforming government was spent, and the following year, Churchill led the Tories back into power with a majority of seventeen. But he was now seventy-six years old, had suffered a number of minor strokes and was less energetic and tenacious than he used to be. He sought tranquillity.

When asked by a colleague on what terms he had settled a railway strike, he replied: 'Theirs, old cock.' In 1952, he welcomed a new monarch, Elizabeth II, onto the throne, and rejoiced to be able to say once more, as he had in his Victorian youth, 'God save the Queen'. In 1953, Stalin died, and Churchill called for a summit meeting with the Russians, but his last efforts at great power diplomacy were cut short by a stroke, which was covered up and from which his recovery was remarkable but patchy. In 1955, he at last accepted retirement, having privately expressed doubts about whether his successor, Anthony Eden, would be up to the job.

Churchill took office in darker circumstances than any other prime minister. He seized the chance to express a defiance of Hitler that will echo down the ages as long as these times are remembered. Clement Attlee, the Labour leader who served as his deputy in the wartime coalition and defeated him at the polls in 1945, remarked that Churchill was set 'the job that he was the ideal man to do', and went on: 'Winston was superbly lucky. And perhaps the most warming thing about him was that he never ceased to say so.' His funeral in 1965 afforded a valedictory glimpse of imperial pomp. A splendid and sombre procession composed of troops from all over the former empire, now the British Commonwealth, marched as his escort through London before Churchill was taken by barge and train to Bladon, within sight of his birthplace, Blenheim Palace, where he was buried next to his parents in a country churchyard.

CLEMENT ATTLEE

Lived 1883–1967; prime minister 1945–51

Clement Attlee reconciled the British people to socialism by being so evidently patriotic, decent and unselfseeking. He led the great reforming Labour government of 1945, and is regarded even by his opponents as one of the foremost peacetime prime ministers. In place of Churchillian magniloquence he offered English understatement, but it should not be supposed from this that he was weak. With laconic ruthlessness, he dropped any member of his team who was (as he once put it to a colleague who asked why he was being sacked) 'not up to it, I'm afraid'.

His father was a successful City lawyer who read family prayers each morning, instilled an ethic of public service and was prosperous enough to build a billiard room. Clement was the seventh of eight children, and as a boy became passionately fond of poetry. He hoped himself to be a poet, and throughout his life enjoyed writing verse as well as reading it. There is a vein of subdued poetry even in his spare, plain, lucid prose. His literary tastes were reassuringly old-fashioned: they included, apart from the earlier classics, Tennyson, Rossetti, Browning, Swinburne, Morris, Masefield and Kipling, but as he himself admitted, 'The moderns are absent ... I have tried but failed to appreciate them.'

He was sent to Haileybury, a boarding school for which he retained a lifelong affection, after which he read history at University College, Oxford. He was at this point an unselfconscious Conservative in politics. The story that he obtained a half-blue for taking part in the annual billiards match against Cambridge is not, unfortunately, true. But he was a good billiards player, and retained a lifelong love of cricket, for which he had no particular aptitude.

In 1906, he was called to the Bar, and he practised for a few years, but life as a lawyer did not engage his enthusiasm. He went in the evenings to the east end of London, to do voluntary work in the charitable settlements set up by Haileybury and others, and here the sight of profound poverty led him 'to reconsider the assumptions of the social class to which I belonged', and to become 'an enthusiastic convert to Socialism'. At Oxford, he had been too shy to take part in student debates. Here he began to speak to small meetings on street corners. He was to spend fourteen years living in the east end, divided by service in the First World War as an infantry officer at Gallipoli, in Mesopotamia and in France. At the start of one failed attack, he was severely wounded, which probably saved his life. He returned from the war as Major Attlee, in 1919 became Mayor of Stepney and in 1922 MP for the same area. Ministerial office followed, and in the general election of 1931, when Labour's representation collapsed from 288 to a mere 52, he kept his seat, while several other promising figures lost theirs.

Ramsay MacDonald had been expelled from Labour for agreeing to serve as prime minister of a National Government which relied mainly on Conservative support. Attlee considered this 'the greatest betrayal in the political history of this country', and became deputy leader of the shrunken party, in which capacity he had to do much of the work of the aged new leader, George Lansbury. In 1935, he succeeded Lansbury, at first on a temporary basis, for his rivals underestimated him, and were inclined to dismiss him as 'a little mouse'. He was to remain leader for the next twenty years, and in 1940 took Labour into coalition with the Conservatives under Churchill, having refused to serve under Chamberlain.

Over the next five years, Attlee and his colleagues developed into battle-hardened veterans of government. They gained valuable practice in the methods of command and control conducted for the national good, for as Churchill himself admitted, during the 1945 general election campaign, 'It is quite true that the conditions of Socialism play a great part in wartime. We all submit to being ordered about to save our country.' Churchill now wanted a return to pre-war conditions. Millions of voters did not, for they associated the 1930s with high unemployment and out-of-touch Conservative politicians.

Attlee could not be an extremist. He believed in the monarchy, made socialism sound reasonable, had done his bit in the First World War, served loyally under Churchill during the Second, and punctured the more abrasive passages in the Conservative leader's speeches. Attlee was, in fact, the moderate, so in he came, at the head of 393 Labour MPs, facing only 213 Conservatives. The British representative at the Potsdam Conference, held with the Soviet Union and the United States to discuss the administration of occupied Germany, was first Churchill and then Attlee. The latter at once proved his good sense by seeing off an attempt by Harold Laski, the chairman of the Labour Party, to dictate the new government's foreign policy, telling him that 'a period of silence on your part would be welcome'.

Attlee decided that India, in which he had long taken an interest, must become independent at the earliest possible opportunity, in 1947. But he generally left foreign affairs in the firm hands of his

friend and ally Ernest Bevin, under whom there could be no sugges-
tion that Britain had gone soft. Bevin helped set up Nato, of which
Britain was a founding member, and Labour continued to spend
more than the country could readily afford on defence. Attlee and
Bevin decided Britain must develop its own nuclear weapons.

The new government's radicalism was focused on domestic
affairs. It implemented the Beveridge Report of 1942. Beveridge
himself was a Liberal, who had declared that he wished to slay
the five giants of Want, Disease, Ignorance, Squalor and Idleness.
The measures he promoted for doing this, most famously the
introduction of the National Health Service, but also maternity
grants, unemployment and sickness benefits, old-age pensions
and a death grant, came to be indissolubly connected in the public
mind with the Labour Party. The school leaving age was raised
from fourteen to fifteen. Rationing became more severe than it
had been during the war: from 1946, it applied even to bread.

Douglas Jay, a junior minister, gave memorable expression to
the spirit in which the government intervened in people's lives:

> Housewives as a whole cannot be trusted to buy all the right
> things, where nutrition and health are concerned. This is
> really no more than an extension of the principle according
> to which the housewife herself would not trust a child of
> four to select the week's purchases. For in the case of nutri-
> tion and health, just as in the case of education, the
> gentleman from Whitehall really does know better what is
> good for people than the people know themselves.

Public ownership was thought to be the remedy, as Attlee
himself had written before the war, for 'the evils that capitalism
brings'. So the government nationalised the Bank of England,
gas, electricity, the railways, road transport, the airlines and the
iron and steel industry. All this imposed a heavy strain on a country
that was, essentially, bankrupt. Attlee took little interest in

economics. His aim was to ennoble the character of the citizenry. Stafford Cripps, who from 1947 served as Chancellor of the Exchequer, pursued a policy of austerity, saying that exports and investment must come before personal consumption.

By 1950, the government was showing signs of exhaustion. In the general election of February 1950, its majority was cut to only five. That summer, the Korean War broke out, and the government committed Britain to playing a full part in it, and to an extensive programme of rearmament. At the same time, it decided it would have to impose prescription charges. This prompted Nye Bevan, who had overseen the creation of the National Health Service, to resign, as did Harold Wilson, a future prime minister.

At a second general election, in October 1951, the Conservatives returned to power. Attlee, as usual, was driven round by his wife, Violet, who was reputed to be the worst driver in the home counties. They had four children and a happy home life. He remained Labour leader for another four years. By his personal modesty, he expanded the possibilities of political leadership, but not in a way which many of his successors have felt inclined to emulate. He made no attempt after his retirement to enrich himself. In 1955, he accepted an earldom, and the following year he was made a Knight of the Garter. This prompted him to write, for the benefit of his brother Tom, a limerick in which he refers to the other honours he has already received by becoming a Companion of Honour and a member of the Order of Merit:

Few thought he was even a starter
There were those who thought themselves smarter
But he ended P.M.
C.H. and O.M.
An earl and a knight of the garter.

SIR ANTHONY EDEN

Lived 1897–1977; prime minister 1955–57

Sir Anthony Eden's high reputation was wrecked by the Suez disaster of 1956. During Winston Churchill's post-war prime ministership, it was still possible to believe Britain was a great power, capable of independent action to safeguard a worldwide empire. That illusion was exploded by Eden's cack-handed attempt to bring an Egyptian dictator to heel, which instead precipitated his own downfall and exposed the humiliating truth that Britain was dependent on the United States. As the youngest Foreign Secretary of the twentieth century, Eden, with his film-star looks and fashionably progressive opinions, had cut a dashing figure, his fame swollen by his resignation when he fell out with Neville Chamberlain over how to deal with Mussolini. But as prime minister, his shaky judgement, excessive sensitivity to criticism, petulant treatment of colleagues and declining health sent him stumbling down the road to defeat.

His parents lived beyond their means on an 8,000-acre estate at Windlestone in County Durham, seat of the Edens since the seventeenth century. He was descended on his mother's side from Earl Grey, the Whig prime minister who put through the Reform Bill. The Edens perturbed their more conventional neighbours by buying modern art, for which Eden too had a collector's eye. In old age, he wrote a wonderful memoir called *Another World*, in which he captured the charm of life before 1914, followed by the ordeal of the Western Front, where, serving with men from his own district, he acquired a 'sense of the irrelevance and unreality of class distinction'. His younger brother, to whom he was particularly close, was killed at the age of sixteen while serving as a midshipman at the Battle of Jutland.

Eden himself came through physically unscathed, having distinguished himself as a junior officer. During the Battle of the Somme, his platoon 'in weakened numbers' was inspected by a general whom Eden much admired:

His brief inspection over, the general turned and spoke so that the riflemen could hear: 'That is the best platoon I have seen today, colonel.' 'It was Mr Eden's, sir,' came the quiet reply. The general nodded and I have never known a happier moment in my life.

Eden was to prove more content in subordinate positions, receiving the praise of older men whom he respected, than when he reached the top.

After the war, he went to Christ Church, Oxford, where he demonstrated his formidable linguistic abilities by taking a first in Persian and Arabic. Having decided to go into politics,, in 1923 he was elected an MP, and three years later he became parliamentary private secretary to the Foreign Secretary, Austen Chamberlain.

In domestic policy, he was a One Nation Conservative who greatly admired Stanley Baldwin, of whom he later said: 'No British statesman in this century has done so much to kill class hatred.' But Eden specialised in foreign affairs, where he enjoyed a meteoric rise, in 1935 becoming Foreign Secretary at the age of only thirty-eight. Baldwin, as prime minister, allowed him considerable latitude, but Chamberlain, who took over in 1937, did not. In February 1938, Eden resigned because he could not stand being overridden by the prime minister on the question of how to detach Mussolini from Hitler. Lloyd George said, 'Eden has today paid a big cheque into the bank on which he can draw in the future.' And this was true: his enduring claim to fame was that he had 'stood up to the dictators' at a time when Chamberlain was giving in.

But even in the 1930s, some observers detected flaws. Nye Bevan warned his Labour colleagues not to be taken in by the new 'juvenile lead', and went on: 'He is more pathetic than sinister. He is utterly outmatched by his international opponents. Beneath the sophistication of his appearance and manner, he has all the unplumbable stupidities and unawareness of his class and type.'

The Tory whips derided Eden and his small band of supporters as 'the glamour boys'. But when war broke out in the summer of 1939, Chamberlain had to bring him back into government, and at the end of 1940, Churchill restored him to the Foreign Office. Churchill and Eden worked closely together, almost as father and son, and in 1942 Churchill said that if anything were to happen to him, the King should ask Eden to become prime minister.

So began Eden's thirteen years as crown prince. In 1945, he suffered the dreadful blow of losing the elder of his two sons, killed on active service in Burma. His first marriage had collapsed, and he was exhausted by the strain of fighting the war. Churchill promised not to repeat Lloyd George's mistake of staying on after the end of the war, but when the time came, that is what he did.

Eden waited with every appearance of honourable good humour for Churchill to retire. In 1951, the Conservatives came back into government, and still Eden waited. He contracted a happy second marriage to Clarissa Spencer-Churchill, who was Churchill's niece, but in 1953 underwent a botched operation on his gall bladder which left his health permanently impaired. He was again Foreign Secretary, and in 1954 enjoyed perhaps his most successful year in that post, helping to defuse several crises. To outward appearances, he was still the debonair and supremely skilful master of world diplomacy, and his succession to the prime ministership could not be averted. Only much later did Churchill's remark to his private secretary in April 1955, 'I don't believe Anthony can do it', uttered late at night after giving a farewell dinner to Queen Elizabeth II in Downing Street, become public knowledge.

On taking over as prime minister, Eden enjoyed a brief honeymoon. After a few days of dithering, he called a general election, and gained an increased majority for the Conservatives. He was excellent in front of the television cameras: better than Churchill had been. Eden called for 'a property-owning democracy', a term coined in the 1920s by Noel Skelton, a Scottish Conservative and Unionist MP who originally intended it to apply to the joint ownership of industry. Now it applied more and more to housing, and it was a popular idea, for people loved the idea of owning their own home. But the economy took a turn for the worse, and Eden infuriated his Cabinet colleagues by ringing them with absurd frequency and interfering in the way they ran their departments.

He was also absurdly touchy about the way he was written about in the press. In January 1956, the usually loyal *Daily Telegraph* accused him of failing to provide 'the smack of firm government'.

This was hurtful because it was true, and Eden took the ludicrous step of issuing an official denial. The prime minister was a prima donna, too sensitive to exercise steady judgement under pressure. He flew into rages with his officials, and during the long wait for power his stamina had declined. His colleague Harold Macmillan, who was positioning himself to succeed him, observed that Eden had been trained to win the Derby of 1938, but had not been let out of the stalls until 1955.

In the summer of 1956, a very difficult problem arose. Colonel Gamal Nasser, who had recently taken power in Egypt, nationalised the Suez Canal. Eden chose to treat this as a mortal threat: he told his colleagues that Nasser could not be allowed to 'have his hand on our windpipe'. Dealing with dictators was, after all, Eden's forte, and this one was a lot weaker than Hitler and Mussolini had been in the 1930s. When a brief period of intense diplomacy failed to shift Nasser, Eden decided on the use of force. A secret plan was devised with the Israelis, who would seize the canal from the Egyptians, whereupon French and British forces would move in on the pretext of separating the combatants.

In October 1956, the plan was put into operation. From a military point of view, it proved feasible, and British public opinion supported it. But it had one fatal weakness, which was that the Americans had not consented to it. President Eisenhower had an election coming up, and was determined not to be implicated in a manoeuvre plainly designed to shore up British imperial influence at the expense of Arab nationalists striving to be free. Washington allowed a run on the pound to begin, and made it clear that no American help would be forthcoming. Eden could have responded by floating the currency and allowing it to find its natural level, but instead he backed down and left Nasser in control of the canal.

Rather than bolstering British authority by a masterful display of force, Eden had demonstrated that he and his country were pitifully weak. At the end of the Second World War, Britain had still, to outward appearances, been one of the Big Three. A decade later, she was revealed to be a mere client of the United States. Churchill said of the Suez Crisis: 'I would never have dared to do it without squaring the Americans, and once I had started I would never have dared stop.'

British self-confidence took several decades to recover from this fiasco, and Eden's prime ministership never did. He made matters worse by lying to the Commons, where in December 1956 he denied having colluded with the Israelis. His health was again terrible, a three-week holiday in Jamaica failed to get him right, and his doctors told him he must retire. So in January 1957, out he went, resigning his Commons seat on the day after he stood down as prime minister.

He was made Earl of Avon, and lived for another twenty years. His wife remarked ruefully to some Tory ladies that she'd had the Suez Canal flowing through her drawing room. He remains the most handsome leader the Conservatives have ever had, and one of only two prime ministers (the other being Wellington) who has lent his name to an item of clothing: the Anthony Eden, a black Homburg hat.

HAROLD MACMILLAN

Lived 1894–1986; prime minister 1957–63

Harold Macmillan is the most entertaining prime minister since the Second World War, and the most ambiguous. 'It's very important not to have a rigid distinction between what's flippant and what is serious,' he remarked in old age. One of his most famous jokes was made in September 1960, in a speech on nuclear arms control to the General Assembly of the United Nations. The Soviet leader, Nikita Khrushchev, interrupted by banging the table with his shoe and emitting disruptive cries, to which Macmillan responded in an unflustered aside: 'Well I'd like it translated, if you would.'

He faced the task of putting as good a face as he could on the Suez debacle, and this he did with panache for several years, during which he led the Conservatives to a tremendous general election victory. But in the satire boom of the early 1960s, the joke was suddenly on him. Having defeated Labour by showing how progressive he was, he now seemed old-fashioned and out of touch.

In class terms, Macmillan had long enjoyed playing things both ways, as the great-grandson of a crofter but also the son-in-law of a duke. On his desk at 10 Downing Street, he kept a photograph of the croft on the Isle of Arran where his grandfather, Daniel Macmillan, had been born. Daniel founded the Macmillan publishing house, which developed into the major business for which Harold worked. He had an acute feeling both for literature and for commerce. His family were rising in the world, and he was sent to the establishments where he could become a member of the ruling class: Eton followed by Balliol College, Oxford. His mother, who was American, was ambitious for him, and he had the brains to go far.

But first he went into the First World War as a subaltern in the Grenadier Guards. He served with bravery on the Western Front, where he was severely wounded, and added another persona to his collection: the officer with an unquenchable loyalty to the lion-hearted men with whom he had been under fire and a lifelong duty to ensure their welfare. Not long after the war, he met and married Lady Dorothy Cavendish, daughter of the Duke of Devonshire, and in 1924, he entered Parliament as MP for Stockton.

For the next fifteen years he got nowhere much. He was deeply distressed by the unemployment he witnessed in Stockton, and wanted to do something about it. John Maynard Keynes was one of his authors, and Macmillan promoted Keynesian economics before they became orthodox. He was deeply in earnest, and people thought he could be a bit of a bore. His wife, with whom he had four children, who all grew up to become alcoholics, began a lifelong affair with another Tory MP, and Macmillan had a nervous breakdown. He stayed married and kept going, but was so out of sympathy with the Conservatives that at one point he resigned the party whip. He insisted that 'Toryism has always been a form of paternal socialism', and some close observers assumed he would join the Labour Party. Towards the end of the 1930s, he opposed appeasement, and got to know and admire Churchill.

The Second World War transformed his prospects. As Macmillan wrote ten years later in his diary, 'I reminded Winston ... that it took Hitler to make him PM and me an under-secretary. The Tory Party would do neither.' Churchill spotted latent qualities in Macmillan, and after giving him a brief spell at the Ministry of Supply, in 1942 sent him to run the politics of the huge British military effort in the Mediterranean: a viceregal post where he proved he could play the part of leader. His task was to maximise British influence over the Americans, who in the person of General Eisenhower held the supreme command. Richard Crossman, who was later to become a Labour Cabinet minister, has left this brilliant account of the briefing he received from Macmillan on arriving at Allied Forces HQ in Algiers as Director of Psychological Warfare:

> Macmillan sent for me straight away. No doubt the speech he made to me was made to every other arrival, but it impressed itself indelibly on my memory. 'Remember,' he said, 'when you go to the Hotel St George, you will regularly enter a room and see an American colonel, his cigar in his mouth and his feet on the table. When your eyes get used to the darkness, you will see in a corner an English captain, his feet down, his shoulders hunched, writing like mad, with a full in-tray and a full out-tray, and no cigar.

'Mr Crossman, you will never call attention to this discrepancy. When you install a similar arrangement in your own office, you will always permit your American colleague not only to have a superior rank to yourself and much higher pay, but also the feeling that he is running the show. This will enable you to run it yourself.

'We, my dear Crossman, are Greeks in this American empire. You will find the Americans much as the Greeks found the Romans – great big, vulgar, bustling people, more vigorous than we are and also more idle, with more unspoiled virtues but also more corrupt. We must run AFHQ as the Greek slaves ran the operations of the Emperor Claudius.'

Comic gifts of a high order are placed at the service of ambition. By the time Macmillan reached the top of British politics, his old wartime friend, Eisenhower, was installed as American President. The new prime minister was to make a good thing out of his ability to get on with the Americans: something at which Eden had proved culpably inept. And perhaps the classical analogy – the pose of intellectual superiority – helped reconcile him to a special relationship in which the balance of power so clearly favoured Washington.

In the Labour landslide of 1945, Macmillan lost Stockton, a seat which had meant much to him. But he soon got back in at a by-election in Bromley, a suburban constituency on the southern fringes of London for which he never felt much affection. In 1951, Churchill returned as prime minister, and gave Macmillan the daunting task of fulfilling the Tory pledge to build 300,000 houses a year.

Macmillan was by now fifty-seven years old. To get the job done, he used the techniques he had seen the ruthless, energetic, self-publicising and unscrupulous Lord Beaverbrook employ in wartime at the Ministry of Supply. Macmillan reached his target, and made his name, by agreeing to every single housebuilding proposal put up by local councils, and by freeing up the private market too.

He was suddenly in contention for the top job. Churchill warned Eden that Macmillan was 'very ambitious', but Eden did not see this. He made Macmillan Foreign Secretary and then Chancellor of the Exchequer. While in the latter post, Macmillan demonstrated his flair for publicity by launching premium bonds. He encouraged the Suez adventure, then abandoned it: 'first in, first out', as Harold Wilson said for Labour. Yet addressing Conservative backbenchers at the end of November 1956 as the news of the retreat started to sink in, Macmillan managed to give the impression that some kind of a victory had occurred, and offered hope that the party could win the next general election. He outshone his rival for the succession, Rab Butler, whom the press expected to win.

Eden stood down on health grounds in January 1957, and Lord Salisbury, descended from the prime minister of that name and unable to pronounce the letter 'r', asked each member of the Cabinet: 'Well which is it, Wab or Hawold?' The answer, overwhelmingly, was Hawold.

And yet when Macmillan took over as prime minister, he warned the Queen, 'half in joke, half in earnest', that he might only last six weeks. He had hinted to the party that he could serve as a caretaker, who would soon make way for a younger man. Yet he lasted for almost seven years, and at first did very well. Tory MPs of an imperialist outlook wanted to believe Suez had not been a fatal blow to British prestige, and Macmillan's manner was sufficiently Churchillian to deceive them. At a dinner in 1957, Harold Wilson, who within six years would become Labour leader, told a journalist: 'Macmillan is a genius. He is holding up the banner of Suez for the party to follow and is leading the party away from Suez. That's what I'd like to do with the Labour party.'

Macmillan mended fences with the Americans and engaged in summit diplomacy, casting himself as the honest broker between the United States and the Soviet Union. The cartoonist Vicky tried to mock him as Supermac, a concept borrowed from the writer Stephen Potter, who had just published an amusing volume called Supermanship. To Vicky's dismay, the term Supermac was taken as a compliment.

A new prosperity was evident, households were acquiring undreamt-of luxuries such as washing machines, and Macmillan observed, in a famous phrase delivered at Bedford in July 1957, that 'most of our people have never had it so good', though he added the less memorable words: 'What is beginning to worry some of us is, "Is it too good to be true?" or perhaps I should say "Is it too good to last?"'

It lasted long enough for Macmillan to lead his party in the summer of 1959 to their third general election victory in a row, fought under the slogan: 'Life's better with the Conservatives. Don't let Labour ruin it.' On the ascent to this high point he had dismissed, with characteristic sangfroid, the resignation of the Chancellor of the Exchequer and two junior Treasury ministers as 'little local difficulties', and managed somehow to be at the same time a moderniser and a reassuringly traditional figure.

But from the early 1960s, he started to lose his touch. He was so anxious to be seen as progressive that he began to dismay traditionalists. His decision in 1961, in defiance of appeals from John Betjeman and many others, to sanction the destruction of the Euston Arch, the great portico at the entrance to Euston Station in London, epitomised the ruthless philistinism with which he treated architectural questions. Some of the housing built in the Macmillan era was so shoddy that for many years it made people deeply suspicious of any proposals for redevelopment.

In 1960, the Americans elected a glamorous young President, John F. Kennedy, with whom Macmillan established a good relationship, assisted by the fact that Kennedy's elder sister had married Lady Dorothy Macmillan's nephew. But the satirists who then burst on the scene saw in the prime minister an irresistible target. In a sketch for *Beyond the Fringe*, which took London by storm in 1961, Peter Cook performed a monologue in which Macmillan reported on a visit to Kennedy: 'We talked of many things, including Great Britain's position in the world as some kind of honest broker. I agreed with him when he said no nation could be more honest, and he agreed with me when I said no nation could be broker.' On the night Macmillan himself attended the show, Cook added an extra line: 'When I've got a spare evening there's nothing I like better than to wander over to a theatre and sit there listening to a group of sappy, urgent, vibrant young satirists, with a stupid great grin spread all over my silly old face.'

In 1962 Macmillan tried to show he was in charge by conducting a wholesale reshuffle of his Cabinet which included the sacking of seven ministers. The Night of the Long Knives, as it became known, instead suggested panic. And the British economy looked undynamic, even feeble, compared to various countries, including Germany and Japan, which less than twenty years before had lain in ruins.

Macmillan pressed ahead with granting independence to various colonies in Africa. He decided Britain should join the European Economic Community, and somehow convinced himself that the French President, General de Gaulle, whom he had got to know during the Second World War, would agree to this. In January 1963, the general shocked the prime minister by vetoing British membership, leading Macmillan to confide to his diary: 'All our policies at home and abroad are in ruins.' De Gaulle added insult to injury by quoting a line from Edith Piaf: '*Ne pleurez pas, milord.*'

The Profumo scandal, which broke upon an astonished world in the spring of 1963, was a farce involving a blonde, a brunette, a peer, a physiotherapist, a country-house swimming pool, a Cabinet minister, the Soviet defence attaché and a supposed threat to national security. The minister, Jack Profumo, was foolish enough to deny in the Commons that he had slept with the brunette, Christine Keeler, who had also been enjoying the attentions of the attaché. The blonde, Mandy Rice-Davis, when told in court that the peer denied having slept with her, uttered the immortal words, 'He would, wouldn't he?' The press revelled in the story, Profumo had to resign and Macmillan was assailed in the subsequent confidence debate by Nigel Birch, one of the three ministers who had resigned from the Treasury in 1958, who quoted with deadly effect from Browning's poem *The Lost Leader*:

> ... let him never come back to us!
> There would be doubt, hesitation and pain,
> Forced praise on our part – the glimmer of twilight,
> Never glad confident morning again!

But Macmillan's actual resignation occurred on health grounds in October. He had prostate trouble, which for a brief period seemed more serious than it really was. At this moment of crisis, he did all he could to prevent Rab Butler from succeeding him, and in this he succeeded.

Macmillan enjoyed a prolonged swansong, and in old age accepted, as Earl of Stockton, a hereditary peerage. In his maiden speech in the Lords, delivered in 1984 at the age of ninety, he deplored the miners' strike, then being fought by Margaret Thatcher, for whom he felt little affection: 'It breaks my heart to see – and I cannot interfere – what is happening in our country today. This terrible strike, by the best men in the world, who beat the Kaiser's and Hitler's armies and never gave in.' To the end, he remained, among other qualities, loyal to the men with whom he had served in Flanders seventy years before.

SIR ALEC DOUGLAS-HOME
Lived 1903–95; prime minister 1963–64

Sir Alec Douglas-Home was the best-mannered and most unexpected of all Tory prime ministers. No one foresaw he would win the leadership race of October 1963, in which he did not appear to be a runner. The idea that instead of choosing one of their 363 MPs, the Conservatives would turn to the 14th Earl of Home, as he was when Macmillan resigned, was frankly unbelievable. Home, as he was known to the Tories and will be known here, was a Scottish landowner of ancient lineage and wide estates. He loved shooting and fishing, was a considerable amateur naturalist, and at moments of tension would calm himself by arranging a large bowl of flowers.

He had left the Commons in 1951 on inheriting his peerage, and although in 1960 he had ascended, somewhat unexpectedly, to the foreign secretaryship, that looked the upper limit of what he could achieve in politics. Home himself thought so: he made no attempt to learn about economics, and when asked in 1962 by an interviewer if he could be prime minister, he replied: 'No, because I do my sums with matchsticks.' After all, no peer had become prime minister since Lord Salisbury at the end of the nineteenth century, and Home did not seem the right kind of person to take on Harold Wilson, the Labour leader, who was never slow to condemn the Tories as out-of-touch, grouse-moor toffs. Home's favourite game bird was the red grouse.

But as the American ambassador in London, David Bruce, reported to Washington in the summer 1963, after the shock of the Profumo scandal, the Conservative party felt the need for 'morally impeccable leadership'. And Home was a figure of unquestioned honour. His judgement was not warped by ambition, he played no tricks, he had no enemies except for Iain Macleod, a ministerial colleague who wanted to proceed faster with decolonisation in Africa than Home thought wise.

And by a curious chance, from 31 July 1963 it became possible to disclaim a hereditary peerage: a measure passed after a campaign by a Labour MP, Antony Wedgwood Benn, who had become Viscount Stansgate on the death of his father but wanted to stay in the Commons. So if a compromise candidate were to be required, Home would now be feasible.

In an earlier age, he would have been not just feasible but probable. Cyril Connolly, who was his exact contemporary at Eton, wrote of him in *Enemies of Promise*:

He was a votary of the esoteric Eton religion, the kind of graceful, tolerant, sleepy boy who is showered with favours and admired by the boys without any apparent exertion on his part, without experiencing the ill-effects of success himself or arousing the pangs of envy in others. In the eighteenth century he would have become Prime Minister before he was thirty; as it was he appeared honourably ineligible for the struggle of life.

Home read history at Christ Church, Oxford, narrowly missed getting a cricket blue, played some first-class cricket (the only prime minister to have done so) and decided to enter the struggle of life by way of politics. He entered the Commons in 1931 as MP for Lanark, and in that decade received much abuse from angry voters in industrial areas of Scotland. But his evident friendliness and lack of side did sometimes disarm criticism. James Maxton, a famously extreme left-wing Glasgow MP, once said to him in the Commons tea room: 'Alec, I had been thinking that, come the revolution, I'll have you strung up on a lamp post, but I think instead I'll offer you a cup of tea.'

In 1936, Home began his happy, fifty-four-year marriage to Elizabeth Alington, a woman as steadfast and welcoming as himself, the daughter of Dr Cyril Alington, who had been his headmaster at Eton and was now Dean of Durham. He also became parliamentary private secretary to Neville Chamberlain, who the following year took over as prime minister. Home flew to Munich with him for the meeting in 1938 with Hitler, after which he invited Chamberlain to recuperate at The Hirsel, seat of the Earls of Home at Coldstream, on the Tweed, a visit which was not entirely successful: 'He shot some partridges and fished occasionally, but he was off-colour and preoccupied.'

In May 1940, when Chamberlain was forced out and replaced by Churchill, the MP and diarist Chips Channon recorded the dark mood among Chamberlain loyalists:

We were all sad, angry and felt cheated and out-witted. Alec [Home] who, more than any other, has been with the Prime Minister these past few weeks, and knows his words and actions by heart, let himself go. I opened a bottle of Champagne and we four loyal adherents of Mr Chamberlain drank 'To the King over the water'.

A fortnight after Churchill came in, Home said that since then the Commons 'stunk in the nostrils of decent people' and described those round the new prime minister as 'scum'. Having been just too young to fight in the First World War, he tried to join the army, but his medical revealed he was suffering from tuberculosis of the spine, a very dangerous condition which required the grafting of flakes of bone from his shin onto his vertebrae, followed by two years of total immobility. During this period, he often felt he would be better dead, though he afterwards remarked to an audience of nurses that his surgeons had 'achieved what had hitherto been thought to be impossible – namely to put backbone into a politician'.

In 1943, he was well enough to return to the Commons, where he was soon protesting that the Soviet Union must not be given a free hand in Eastern Europe, but at the 1945 general election he lost his seat. He was narrowly re-elected in 1950, in part by exposing his Labour opponent's Communist sympathies, but the next year his father, the 13th Earl of Home, died and he was obliged to go to the House of Lords: 'I was resigned to the ending of my political career.'

James Stuart, Secretary of State for Scotland, instead requested that Home become Minister of State for Scotland, operating mainly north of the border. To this, Churchill agreed: 'All right – have your Home sweet Home.' In the mid 1950s, Antony Eden brought Home into the Cabinet as Commonwealth Secretary, and in 1960 Harold Macmillan made him Foreign Secretary, where he demonstrated a calm preparedness to take decisions and an unwavering determination to stand up to the Soviet Union.

In October 1963, the leading candidates to succeed Macmillan were Rab Butler, Lord Hailsham and Reginald Maudling, but all had grave defects. Macmillan was determined not to have Butler, a very able minister who was expected by the press to win, but who lacked the killer instinct and delivered a dull speech to the party conference in Blackpool. Hailsham, by contrast, did himself fatal damage in that seaside resort by looking too eager to grasp the crown, engaging in such vulgar stunts as feeding his baby child from a bottle and announcing at a rally that he would renounce his peerage. Maudling gave a dull speech, which prevented him from building up any kind of momentum.

Home's conference speech began with the words, 'I am offering a prize to any newspaperman this morning who can find a clue in my speech that this is Lord Home's bid to take over the leadership of the Conservative Party.' He got a very good reception, for the Conservatives trusted him, and approved of his old-fashioned reticence. The 'customary soundings' undertaken within the party went in his favour, his doctors assured him he could cope with the physical strain of being prime minister, and Macmillan advised the Queen to send for him. Home agreed to form a government once he had established that his rivals, including Butler and Hailsham, would serve in it. Only two ministers, Iain Macleod and Enoch Powell, both of whom had pleaded with Butler to make a fight of it, refused to do so.

Wilson, as leader of the Opposition, remarked that 'after half a century of democratic advance ... the whole process has ground to a halt with a 14th Earl.' Home parried this thrust by retorting: 'As far as the 14th Earl is concerned, I suppose Mr Wilson, when you come to think of it, is the 14th Mr Wilson.'

He disclaimed his peerage, became known as Sir Alec Douglas-Home and in November 1963 was returned to the Commons at a by-election held in Kinross and West Perthshire. He regretted his lack of preparation in two vital areas: he had not informed himself about domestic policy, where he was not allowed to forget his 'matchsticks' remark about economics, and he had not learned how to perform on television. In his memoir, *The Way the Wind Blows*, he quoted a conversation he had after becoming prime minister with 'the young lady who was applying the powder and tab':

Q. Can you not make me look better than I do on television?
A. No.
Q. Why not?
A. Because you have a head like a skull.
Q. Does not everyone have a head like a skull?
A. No.

Wilson excelled at adversarial politics of a frankly abusive type, for which Home had no relish. His courtesy concealed his toughness and put him at a disadvantage. Macmillan reached an unkind judgement on the man he had chosen to succeed him: 'Home didn't have enough fire in his belly – he wouldn't say "Bugger Off".' The television satirists presented the Home–Wilson contest as 'Dull Alec versus Smart Alec'. But not everyone in the early 1960s thought it was clever to be rude. Millions of respectable voters were perturbed by the new tendency to hurl abuse at those in authority, and liked having a prime minister who knew how to behave.

In January 1964, Macleod wrote a celebrated piece for *The Spectator* in which he claimed the new prime minister had been chosen the previous October by a 'magic circle', and pointed out that, with one exception, the men involved were Old Etonians. This was a declaration of class war, and Home was convinced it helped to lose him the election of October 1964. 'Had those two pulled their weight,' he later wrote of Macleod and Powell, 'I have no doubt at all that our short-head defeat would have been converted into a narrow victory.'

For Wilson only gained a majority of four in the Commons. Home, on the day he stepped down as prime minister, could be found pacing up and down the flat of his supporter, Selwyn Lloyd, 'blaming the defeat on Macleod in language those who were present had not heard him use before'. But most people thought Home had done well, after thirteen years of Conservative rule and three successive general election victories, to come so close to winning. It is possible that victory only slipped away from him because he got so badly barracked in his final rally, at the Rag Market in Birmingham, by Labour supporters who had arrived in very large numbers. Home did not realise there was no need to shout over them to make himself heard to the viewers watching at home. This produced, as he later said, 'An appearance of strain … I looked rather hunted.'

He carried on as Conservative leader after the election, and introduced a new way of selecting the leader, by ballot of the parliamentary party, so that no successor could be declared illegitimate in the way he had been by Macleod. In July 1965, Home himself stepped down. But there was a surprising coda to his leadership. He became, under Edward Heath, spokesman on foreign affairs, and served again as Foreign Secretary from 1970 to 1974. In a demonstration of his underlying toughness, he expelled 105 Soviet diplomats from London who were suspected of being KGB agents. On retiring from the Commons, he accepted, as Lord Home of the Hirsel, a life peerage.

In his old age, two middle-aged ladies engaged him in conversation on the train from London to Berwick, and told him, 'We always say it was a great tragedy for this country that you were never prime minister.'

'As a matter of fact, I was,' Home replied with a smile, 'but only for a very short time.'

HAROLD WILSON

Lived 1916–95; prime minister 1964–70 and 1974–76

Harold Wilson was a clever, quick-witted man whose instinct was to manoeuvre rather than decide. He kept Britain out of the Vietnam War and inside the European Economic Community, but even his admirers admitted he was a slippery character, much given to tactical ruses and without any clear attachment to principle. They said this was the only way to keep the Labour Party together, and cited that as his greatest achievement.

Wilson became famous for saying to some journalists in 1964, 'A week is a long time in politics', but led the party for thirteen years and was prime minister for a total of almost eight years, in a period when the country suffered from such grave economic problems – strikes, inflation, the collapse of whole industries – that it became known as the sick man of Europe. Neither he nor his Conservative rival, Edward Heath, could avert a growing national sense of inferiority, prompted by the superior performance of countries such as West Germany. British Leyland – a state-owned amalgam of various once-proud motor manufacturers – was no match for Mercedes-Benz.

But Wilson also offered hope by showing how an able boy from a modest home could rise to the top. The last three prime ministers had all been to Eton. Wilson's parents were lower-middle-class Nonconformists, who lived near Huddersfield and played a leading role in their local Baptist Church and the Boy Scouts. His father, an industrial chemist, was unemployed for a time and had to move several times to get work. Harold went to two different grammar schools. He won an exhibition to Jesus College, Oxford, where he worked extremely hard and in 1937 took a First in philosophy, politics and economics: a new course with a strong appeal to aspiring politicians.

But for a few years he pursued an academic career as a statistician. In 1940, he married Gladys Mary Baldwin, the daughter of a Congregationalist minister. They had two sons, and Mary Wilson, as she became known, made a name for herself as a poet. She disliked political life and said: 'All I have ever wanted is a nice little house in North Oxford and a don for a husband.'

After a cursory attempt to join the armed forces, Wilson instead entered the wartime civil service, where he worked on the problems of the coal industry. As a student, he had joined the Liberal Club, but in 1945 he gained election as a Labour MP and was at once given a junior ministerial post, since he was one of the few members of that intake with an inside knowledge of government. In 1947, Attlee made him President of the Board of Trade, and Wilson, at the age of thirty-one, became the youngest Cabinet minister since Lord Henry Petty in 1806. Brilliant vistas opened before him, but not everyone in the Labour Party took to him. Another rising star, Hugh Gaitskell, wrote of him in 1950:

> What is depressing really is not so much that he is swollen headed but that he is such a very impersonal person. You don't feel that really you could ever be close friends with him, or in fact that he would ever have any close friends.

A year later, Wilson resigned in protest at increased defence spending and the introduction of prescription charges. He was presenting himself as a leader of the left: a manoeuvre which brought charges of opportunism. But his gifts were such that in 1956, Gaitskell, who had just succeeded Attlee as party leader, made him shadow Chancellor. In 1960, Wilson tried to overthrow Gaitskell, and failed. But in January 1963, Gaitskell unexpectedly died, at the age of only fifty-six, and the subsequent leadership battle was between Wilson and George Brown. As Tony Crosland, an intellectual Labour MP who had made his name as the author of *The Future of Socialism*, complained, 'It's a choice between a crook [Wilson] and a drunk [Brown].'

Wilson won, for he was a more skilful campaigner than Brown, and had successfully profiled himself as an outsider who was not just longing to become an insider:

> The Right-wing Establishment has never tried to embrace me or buy me off. That's probably a compliment. Lady Whatsit or Lord So-and-So haven't plied me with invitations. I don't do much socialising and my tastes are simple. If I had the choice between smoked salmon and tinned salmon I'd have it tinned. With vinegar. I prefer beer to champagne and if I get the chance to go home I have a North Country high tea – without wine.

His cronies knew he preferred brandy to beer, and cigars to the pipe which figured so conspicuously in his public appearances. But Wilson did express the spirit of the age by displaying no desire whatever to be taken for a gentleman. In this respect, he was an authentically modern figure.

While the Tories were convulsed by the battle to succeed Macmillan, Wilson at the Labour Party conference presented himself as a leader who could forge a new Britain in the 'white heat' of a 'scientific revolution', which would see the sweeping away of 'restrictive practices' and 'outdated methods' on both sides of industry. By offering this progressive vision, he managed to scrape a bare majority of four seats in the 1964 general election.

The new prime minister was faced on his first day with a crucial decision. The pound was in a parlous state: would he devalue it? This was the moment at which he could have freed the government from the battle to defend an overvalued currency, while blaming his predecessors for having launched an unsustainable pre-election boom. But Wilson, along with two ministerial colleagues who knew less about economics than he did, baulked at taking so daring a step. He instead opted for temporary import surcharges: a palliative measure that did not deal with the underlying problem. Like most members of the British political class, Wilson hoped he could manage his way out of trouble. He installed a gifted team of ministers, launched a National Plan, which was supposed to lead to much higher growth, enjoyed a honeymoon with the press and at a second general election, held in March 1966, increased his Commons majority to ninety-eight.

Then it all went wrong. The pound again came under pressure, and some of his more astute colleagues, including Crosland, wanted to devalue. Wilson opted instead for spending cuts and the abandonment of the National Plan. These 'July measures' destroyed the credibility of his managerial version of socialism, for they did not work and, although he kept going, the press and the public were never again inclined to place much trust in him. Just over a year later, there was another run on sterling, and devaluation followed. Wilson went on television, where he claimed the pound 'in your pocket' had not been devalued. This assertion made him a laughing stock. He also came under attack because of his 'Kitchen Cabinet', a somewhat ropey collection of intimates who helped him to run things.

And yet he did not go. Why not? In part because he kept his ministerial colleagues on the hop by conducting very frequent reshuffles. They were a talented bunch, including as they did James Callaghan, who in 1976 would succeed him as prime minister; Roy Jenkins, who helped liberalise the laws on divorce, abortion and homosexuality; Denis Healey, who was a formidable Defence Secretary; Barbara Castle, who tried and failed to reform the trade unions; and Tony Crosland, who was busy bringing in comprehensive schools, by which means he hoped to attain greater social equality.

Wilson under pressure could still perform very well. Richard Crossman, another Labour heavyweight, paid tribute in his diary to the prime minister's performance when taking questions in the Commons in 1969: 'It was a most deft and brilliant exhibition of parliamentary lightweight boxing.' Wilson was usually more nimble than Heath.

Even after he lost the 1970 election to the Conservatives, he did not go. He grew increasingly paranoid about criticism, detecting plots even where these did not exist, and some of his enemies grew increasingly paranoid about him. But he had a sort of India rubber quality. He bounced back from episodes which would have sunk a less resilient person. And Heath, who had beaten him in 1970, was soon making serious mistakes, culminating in a botched election campaign at the start of 1974.

In February, Wilson was back at the head of a minority government, for which at the second election of 1974, held in October, he gained a majority of three. He coped with Labour's deep divisions on Europe by holding a referendum, in which ministers were free to campaign on either side, with Wilson himself remaining somewhat above the battle. In the summer of 1975, the British people voted by a margin of two to one to stay in the European Economic Union: a verdict that settled the matter for the next forty years.

Wilson in his second term behaved more and more oddly. After George Bush, a future American president who was at this time director of the Central Intelligence Agency, visited him in Downing Street, he asked: 'Is that man crazy? He thinks there's a bug behind all the pictures.' In March 1976, Wilson surprised people by announcing that he was stepping down as prime minister. For once in his life, he seemed to have done something disinterested. But he wrecked this good impression by publishing a list of resignation honours, said to have been written out on lavender paper by Marcia Falkender, who since 1956 had worked very closely with him as his political secretary. The lavender list, as it became known, inflicted lasting damage on Wilson's reputation, for he rewarded a number of his associates who were regarded as unworthy of honours.

At a moment of vexation with his colleagues in the early 1970s, Wilson complained: 'I've been wading in shit for three months to allow others to indulge their conscience.' His strength, but also his weakness, as a politician was that he did not seem to have much of a conscience of his own.

EDWARD HEATH

Lived 1916–2005; prime minister 1970–74

Ted Heath presented himself as the man who would rescue the country from Harold Wilson, but turned out to be not the kind of person one would wish to be rescued by. He won a great personal victory in the general election of 1970, which everyone expected him to lose, but within two years lost credibility by conducting a clumsy U-turn in economic policy, and by the start of 1974 was so unpopular that the voters actually decided, by a narrow margin, to let Wilson back in. Heath alienated many of his own MPs by treating them with extreme rudeness, and in 1975 they replaced him with Margaret Thatcher, after which he descended into a thirty-year sulk.

His tragedy was to be a thin-skinned man, who strove as a form of self-protection to become completely insensitive and ended up finding normal human relations, in which one has to show some consideration for other people's feelings, more or less impossible. The journalist Simon Hoggart, who had a delightful time with him in a pub during the second election of 1974, was soon afterwards treated by him with sour disdain, and concluded: 'There were two Ted Heaths, the good Ted and the bad Ted. It was pure chance which you got.'

Heath's proudest achievement was to have got Britain into the European Economic Community, for which he was admired far beyond the ranks of the Conservatives. Roy Jenkins, leader of the Labour MPs who voted with him in 1972 in order to get this through the Commons, later said of him: 'For me, he is a great lighthouse which, indifferent to the storms and to the spray, shines out a wholly dependable beam.'

That dependability was one reason why Heath rose so far and so fast. His father was a carpenter, who later set up a small building firm, and his mother had been a lady's maid. He was born and brought up at Broadstairs, on the coast of Kent, and by hard work and ability got to Balliol College, Oxford. When asked by the admissions tutor what he wanted to become, he was the only candidate ever to say 'professional politician'. He became organ scholar, for music was already an essential part of his life, and like Wilson he read philosophy, politics and economics. But Heath also flung himself into politics, becoming president of both the Union debating society and the Oxford University Conservative Association, and a notable undergraduate opponent of Neville Chamberlain's appeasement policy.

He served as a gunner during the Second World War, seeing action in north-western Europe in 1944–45 and rising to the rank of acting colonel. Like many of his generation, he resolved that such a horrific conflict must never happen again and decided the way to prevent it was through a united Europe. His approach to political problems was always rather military: proper staff work was indispensable. In the late 1940s, he passed out top of the civil service exams, served somewhat incongruously as news editor of the *Church Times* and started work with a merchant bank.

But his main aim was to find a parliamentary seat. 'The road to Westminster,' he later said, 'was not so much a long march as an interminable dinner dance.' He got adopted at Bexley, on the Kentish border of London, a seat in Labour hands which he fought with superhuman industry and managed to win in 1950, and hold for the next fifty-one years.

Soon after this victory, a Tory whip of the old school, Sir Walter Bromley-Davenport, who had served in the Grenadier Guards and was a boxing enthusiast, spotted a well-dressed man leaving the Palace of Westminster just before a vote, and ordered him to stop, on the assumption that he was a Conservative MP. He refused, so Sir Walter kicked him downstairs. The man turned out to be the Belgian ambassador, Sir Walter was sacked and Heath was appointed in his place.

Whipping suited him. He had a kind of genius for the organisation and discipline that it required. Soon he was Chief Whip, and through the disaster of Suez he held the party together for Anthony Eden, and then for Eden's successor, Macmillan, who dined with him on oysters and champagne on the night he took over, and valued his advice. Heath had swiftly become, as befitted an able and loyal servant of the party leader, an insider.

Macmillan gave him the vital task of conducting the negotiations for Britain's entry to the European Economic Union. Through no fault of Heath, these failed. General de Gaulle said

'Non', but everyone knew the General was an appallingly difficult character. Heath deserved promotion, and got it under Sir Alec Douglas-Home, who gave him the important job of Industry Secretary, where he proved his toughness by pushing through the abolition of Resale Price Maintenance, a measure unpopular with small shopkeepers.

Sir Alec lost the 1964 general election, after which he made Heath shadow Chancellor of the Exchequer, giving him the chance to distinguish himself by harrying the incumbent, James Callaghan, as the Finance Bill went through Parliament. In the 1965 leadership contest, the first in which Tory MPs had a vote, they opted for Heath rather than his more laid-back rival, Reginald Maudling, who had entered the race well ahead in the opinion polls.

Despite the advantage of having started life nowhere near a grouse moor, Heath proceeded to lose, resoundingly, to Wilson the following year, and was seldom able to worst him in debate. But it would be unfair to drop the new leader so soon after he had taken over, and at least he seemed to know his own mind. He was a serious figure, who had instituted an unprecedentedly extensive programme of policy development, though with the benefit of hindsight one cannot help noticing it omitted any policy to curb inflation. In 1968, Heath had no hesitation in sacking Enoch Powell from the shadow Cabinet for delivering the notorious 'Rivers of Blood' speech against immigration. Heath also demonstrated his competitiveness by winning the Sydney-to-Hobart race in 1969, despite having only just taken up ocean racing. His was the first British boat to win since 1945.

When Wilson called the 1970 general election, Heath went for him in the introduction to the Conservative manifesto:

During the last six years we have suffered not only from bad policies, but from a cheap and trivial style of government.

Decisions have been dictated simply by the desire to catch tomorrow's headlines ... government by gimmick has become the order of the day ... once a decision is made, once a policy is established, the prime minister and his colleagues should have the courage to stick to it.

Douglas Hurd, who worked for Heath and would later become Foreign Secretary, pointed out what a key document this was:

There runs through it a note of genuine puritan protest, which is familiar in British history, sometimes in one party, sometimes in the other. It is the note struck by Pym against the court of Charles I, by Pitt against the Fox–North coalition, by Gladstone against Disraeli, by the Conservatives in 1922 against Lloyd George. It is the outraged assertion of a strict view of what public life is about, after a period in which its rules have been perverted and its atmosphere corrupted.

Like many puritans, Heath suffered from a blinkered and naïve self-righteousness. He won the election, which put him in an unassailable position within his party, but meant he was committed to a set of free-market reforms, including tax cuts and a refusal to prop up 'lame duck' industries. What therefore was he to do in January 1972, when unemployment burst through the barrier of one million, which at that time was regarded, in the words of *The Times*, as 'morally, economically, socially and politically intolerable'? Heath himself agreed with this: he was a child of the 1930s, who despised his Tory predecessors for having failed to bring unemployment down. In an attempt to do so, he started to prop up every failed firm he could find. Indeed, he had started to do this the previous year, when Rolls-Royce, the great producer of aero engines, went bankrupt, and was bailed out with taxpayers' money. Heath, it turned out, was at heart another managerialist, who believed the problems of the British economy could be cured by pulling levers in Whitehall. Despite having promised not to do so, he instituted prices and incomes controls.

He tried to do far too much. Some dreadful problems were forced upon him: the troubles in Northern Ireland reached their height in 1972, when 476 people were killed. As usual, Heath thought the answer lay in taking personal charge: he instituted direct rule from London, then tried and failed to make the two sides reach a reasonable compromise. This was an age of rationalism in politics: plans conceived before Heath entered Downing Street were ruthlessly implemented by him. Britain's handsome old coinage was decimalised, a process which gave an extra spur to runaway inflation, and the ancient counties were rationalised, with some, such as Rutland, being abolished. John Biffen, one of an as yet very small group of dissident Conservative backbenchers, described the prime minister as 'a glorified management consultant'.

Heath brought in an ambitious reform of trade union law, but like Wilson before him, his efforts ended in failure. People began to ask, 'Which is worse, Heath or Wilson?' Few contended either prime minister was better. In 1972, more days were lost to strikes than in any year since the General Strike in 1926. Heath fought the National Union of Mineworkers, and lost to them in 1972, when Arthur Scargill leapt to fame as a union leader by deploying flying pickets to shut Saltley Coke Depot. At the end of 1973, when a second strike began, Heath instituted a three-day week, in order to save fuel. There were frequent power cuts, which intensified the sense of national crisis. The prime minister now held an election on the question 'Who governs Britain?' The voters replied: 'Not you.'

For he had obtained slightly fewer seats than Labour under the specious, gimmicky, untrustworthy Wilson. In vain Heath tried to stay in power by doing a deal with the Liberals. He failed, and out he went. That was the end of him, though he refused, as usual, to recognise the fact. He fought a second election, which he lost more conclusively than the first. If at this point he had resubmitted himself for re-election by his own MPs, he would probably have received their support, but he instead denied anything was wrong.

His troops muttered, for they knew he had made a hash of things. Margaret Thatcher had the courage to stand against him, and knocked him out in the first round. This was a dreadful blow, and he did not accept its finality. To his credit, he stayed in the Commons, but to his discredit, he was persistently disloyal to his successor. He became the outstanding curmudgeon in parliamentary history, a man incapable of showing the slightest generosity of spirit. When in 1990 she was forced to resign, a reporter asked him if it was true he had said, 'Rejoice, rejoice!' – words echoing what Thatcher had said after South Georgia was recaptured from the Argentines.

'No,' Heath replied gravely, 'what I said was, "Rejoice, rejoice, rejoice!"'

He died in 2005. Ten years later, horrible accusations were raised against him. He was said to have been a paedophile, charges the police for a time took seriously. It is difficult to prove a negative, but I am convinced these accusations are false. Heath's shyness with women prevented him from marrying, even though a marriage might have been to his political advantage, and could also have made him better at understanding other people. But he was a dutiful public servant, and the fact that in the difficult circumstances of the early 1970s he failed to put the British economy right does not mean he deserves to be denounced as a sex offender.

JAMES CALLAGHAN

Lived 1912–2005; prime minister 1976–79

James Callaghan was the first prime minister since Winston Churchill who had not gone to university. Labour MPs chose him as their leader in preference to five Oxford graduates, all of them considerable figures: Michael Foot, Roy Jenkins, Tony Benn, Denis Healey and Tony Crosland. Sunny Jim, as Callaghan was often known, commanded wide acceptance as prime minister, for he had an air of authority and a gift for making what he said sound like common sense. He was shrewd, genial and experienced, and for the three years of his prime ministership remained more popular than his Tory challenger, Margaret Thatcher.

Like Wilson and Heath, he failed to surmount the severe economic problems which beset Britain, but unlike them, he told people soon after becoming prime minister that the assumptions on which economic policy was based were no longer tenable. At the start of 1979, he was sunk by the trade unions, in what became known as the Winter of Discontent. His own side destroyed him, and here too it had become clear that things could not go on as they had before.

His father served as a chief petty officer in the Royal Navy, was wounded at the Battle of Jutland and died in 1921, leaving his mother with no pension. She and her 9-year-old son lived in straitened circumstances in lodgings in Portsmouth. She was a strict Baptist, who believed in the second coming of the Lord. One day, when James came home from school and she was not there, he imagined, wrongly, that she had been taken up into heaven and he had been left behind. In 1924, the first Labour government, led by Ramsay MacDonald, got her a pension of ten shillings a week – 50 pence in modern money – and she became a Labour supporter.

Callaghan left Portsmouth Northern Secondary School at the age of seventeen and got a job as a clerk in the Inland Revenue in Maidstone, where he was paid a pound a week. His mother was delighted, for at the age of sixty he would be entitled to a pension. The Baptists helped look after him in Maidstone, where he taught in their Sunday School and met a 16-year-old girl called Audrey. Her first words to him were: 'Mrs Boorman is expecting you to tea this afternoon.'

He joined the Inland Revenue trade union, and was recognised as a young man of exceptional ability. In 1936 he defeated many other candidates to become assistant secretary of the Inland Revenue Staff Federation on a salary of £350 a year, whereupon he married Audrey. During the Second World War he served in the Royal Navy, which he joined as a seaman and left as a junior officer, and in 1945 he stood and won for Labour in Cardiff South. He was regarded at this time as a left-winger. In 1947, Attlee gave him his first ministerial job, at the Department of Transport, but it was in opposition that Callaghan blossomed. He proved himself an entirely unselfconscious television performer, very good at showing that he understood the other chap's point of view without actually sharing it, and from 1961 he was shadow Chancellor of the Exchequer.

In the Labour government of 1964, Wilson made him Chancellor, and they at once committed themselves to the defence of the overvalued pound. Callaghan did not question this misguided policy, and showed enormous resilience as he strove to uphold it. He felt horribly discredited in November 1967 when devaluation came, handed in his resignation and was made Home Secretary instead, where he gradually recovered his spirits, and in 1969 took the decision to send troops into Northern Ireland. He also helped crush Wilson's attempt, with Barbara Castle, to reform the trade unions. For Callaghan had come out of the unions, and thought they should be allowed to run their own affairs.

In the second Wilson government, from 1974, he served as Foreign Secretary and was seen as the heir apparent. In April 1976, he saw off strong competition and became prime minister. The position was dire. The government's parliamentary majority was evaporating, the public finances were collapsing and the Cabinet was split. Callaghan feared this could be another 1931, with himself cast as Ramsay MacDonald, the traitor to the Labour cause who sold out to the bankers. While restoring stability, he had to carry the party with him. In the autumn of 1976, he delivered a fighting speech to the Labour conference, in which he renounced the post-war orthodoxy:

We used to think that you could just spend your way out of a recession and increase employment by cutting taxes and boosting government spending. I tell you, in all candour, that this option no longer exists, and that in so far as it ever did exist it only worked by injecting bigger doses of inflation into the economy followed by higher levels of unemployment as the next step.

By means of an exhausting series of nine full Cabinet meetings, in which the arguments of all the different factions were aired, Callaghan got everyone to unite behind a programme of deep spending cuts, in order to obtain a loan from the International Monetary Fund.

Labour's Commons majority was whittled away by a series of by-election defeats, but Callaghan shored up his position by doing a deal with the Liberals and prevailed on the unions to observe a degree of pay restraint. By the autumn of 1978, things were going better. Labour had regained its lead in the opinion polls, and the prime minister was expected to call a general election. Instead he went to the annual conference of the Trades Union Congress and performed a music-hall song, about a woman waiting to get married:

> There was I, waiting at the church,
> Waiting at the church,
> Waiting at the church …
> All at once, he sent me round a note
> Here's the very note
> This is what he wrote:
> 'Can't get away
> To marry you today
> My wife won't let me.'

It is hard to imagine another prime minister performing this song half so enjoyably. But the actual message was disastrous. For Callaghan, rendered over-confident by success, was telling the trade unions he had decided to defer the general election until after the winter pay round, in which he had already said he expected them to limit their demands to 5 per cent. They regarded this attempt to tell them what to do as an insult. In December 1978, after a three-week strike, the Ford Motor Company conceded a rise of 17 per cent to its workers, and in the public sector, the unions launched impossible demands of up to 40 per cent, and went on strike when these were not met. In the first months of 1979, rubbish accumulated in the streets, hospitals stopped admitting all but emergencies, and in some places the dead went unburied.

As the Winter of Discontent began, Callaghan attended an international conference on the island of Guadeloupe, in the West Indies, where he was photographed having a swim. On his return, he was unwise enough to give a news conference at the airport, before he had adjusted to the grimmer atmosphere at home. Asked if he intended to do anything about the 'mounting chaos', the prime minister replied: 'Well, that is a judgement that you are making and I promise if you look at it from outside – and perhaps you are taking a rather parochial view at the moment – I don't think that other people in the world would share the view that there is mounting chaos.' The Sun translated this into the headline 'Crisis – What Crisis?'

The deeper the actual crisis got, the worse those words sounded. In the Commons, where public opinion quickly makes itself felt, the government's position was desperate. The Labour whips strove night after night to get even their sickest MPs through the division lobbies, but on the night of 28 March 1979, Callaghan was defeated by a single vote on a motion of no confidence. He called a general election: the first time a prime minister had been forced into this by losing a confidence vote since the fall of the first Labour government in 1924.

During the election campaign, an adviser pointed out to him that the opinion polls had improved and 'we might just squeeze through'. Callaghan replied:

> I should not be too sure. There are times, perhaps once every 30 years, when there is a sea-change in politics. It then does not matter what you say or what you do. There is a shift in what the public wants and what it approves of. I suspect there is now such a change – and it is for Mrs Thatcher.

Callaghan lost the election, but did not stand down as Labour leader until October 1980, by which time Michael Foot, the candidate of the Left, was strong enough to defeat Denis Healey. A year later, the Labour party split, with a substantial contingent of MPs marching off to form the Social Democratic Party, led by Roy Jenkins. The forces which Callaghan had held together were now so weak and divided they would not win another general election until 1997. But he himself lived on, a respected elder statesman, until 2005. He had raised the tone of public life, and is remembered with affection.

MARGARET THATCHER

Lived 1925–2013; prime minister 1979–90

Margaret Thatcher inspired greater extremes of adoration and loathing than any other prime minister, imposed her personality more deeply on the country than any leader since Churchill, and like him, but unlike most of her contemporaries, was no defeatist. She was the first woman to become prime minister, won three general elections in a row, dominated politics for almost twelve years, was denounced by 364 economists, defeated General Galtieri and Arthur Scargill, survived an assassination attempt by the IRA, stood shoulder to shoulder with Ronald Reagan to win the Cold War and was soon afterwards ditched by her own MPs.

Her aversion to consensus politics made her a threat to the Establishment. She liked to confront problems rather than evade them. But neither her admirers, who often reduced Thatcherism to an economic doctrine, nor her critics, who were blinded by hatred, identified the morality of what she was doing. Shirley Letwin, author of *The Anatomy of Thatcherism*, pointed out that Thatcher was reasserting the 'vigorous virtues', which entailed a preference for the individual who is 'upright, self-sufficient, energetic, adventurous, independent-minded, loyal to friends and robust against enemies'.

She herself was a strange mixture: very brave yet also very cautious; a serious woman who flung herself with brio into election stunts; a puritan who enjoyed the company of raffish men; a conventional Tory who wrong-footed her opponents by breaking the polite conventions which ease communication between ambitious men, who at least make some pretence of seeing the other chap's point of view. She didn't. Her conversation rendered the standard English methods of evasion – jokes, paradoxes, understatement, any number of ironical devices which enable one to avoid commitment – unusable. All this is described by Ferdinand Mount in his very funny account, at the end of his memoir *Cold Cream*, of working for her in Downing Street as head of her policy unit.

Thatcher was born in Grantham, where her father, Alfred Roberts, ran his own grocery shop, served as a local councillor and was a Methodist lay preacher of sternly pious outlook. He was unremittingly industrious, and taught his younger daughter the value of hard work, not only to support oneself, but 'in the formation of character'. Her mother, who helped run the shop, insisted on the need always to be respectably dressed: 'Never leave the house looking untidy.'

Their daughter remained true to that rule. From the local girls' grammar school, she won a place to read chemistry at Somerville College, Oxford, where she got involved in the Oxford University Conservative Association. Her first job was as a research chemist at a plastics company in Essex. Here a farmer fell in love with her, but she arranged for him to transfer his affections to her elder sister, whom he married. Charles Moore, in his magisterial life of her, casts much new light on her early life and loves, when she was an unknown woman in provincial England.

Thatcher was selected in January 1949, at the age of twenty-five, as the Conservative parliamentary candidate for Dartford, a seat held by Labour with a majority of 20,000. The local Tory party had 2,300 members, a number which by 1951 she had increased to the still more extraordinary figure of 3,160. She fought and lost the general elections of 1950 and 1951, and met Denis Thatcher, whom she married at the end of that year. He had fought in the war, during which he contracted a first marriage which did not work, and now owned and ran a paint company near Dartford, where he had been asked if he himself was interested in standing. He said no, for he did not want a political career. When his wife became prime minister, the Dear Bill letters in *Private Eye* presented him as a man constantly incurring his wife's annoyance by drinking too much and expressing inconveniently reactionary opinions. But he was in many ways an ideal political spouse, for he was content not to compete with his wife, and supported her rather than trying to hold her back.

The new Mrs Thatcher soon gave birth to twins, a boy and a girl. With superhuman industry, she qualified at almost the same time as a barrister, and a few years later, in 1959, was elected as the MP for Finchley, in north London. Her rise within the Conservative party was swift, for she was by far the most capable of the very small number of women MPs, well able to master the intricacies of any subject – pensions, tax law, comprehensive schools – which was put before her. Edward Heath made her Education Secretary, in which capacity she served from 1970 to 1974, approving more applications for comprehensive schools than any other holder of that office, though also becoming known as Milk-Snatcher, because of a spending cut the Treasury forced her to make on school milk. She was loyal to Heath, but certainly not close to him. At this stage in her career, she looked like a token – albeit highly competent – woman, with highly conventional opinions. Almost no one realised she was a future prime minister.

Heath lost the two elections of 1974. He had never been a master of the soft word that turneth away wrath, but now he seemed to go out of his way to antagonise his backbenchers. They in turn felt badly let down, and cast around for someone who was not Heath. At first it seemed this might be Sir Keith Joseph, an intellectual who saw the need for a complete rethink of Conservative policy, but although he had a sweet disposition, he also had a tendency to give tactless speeches, including one in which he suggested the lower orders were having too many children. While several well-known men who felt themselves under a duty of loyalty to the leader hung back, reckoning they could enter the contest once he had been wounded by some lesser figure, Thatcher, with Joseph's backing, had the courage to raise the standard of rebellion and, to general astonishment, beat Heath in the first round.

She had now to proceed with care, for not being Heath was an inadequate basis for retaining the allegiance of the great majority of former Cabinet ministers who really just wanted a less clumsy version of Heath. Thatcher did not think that would suffice to deal with Britain's problems, which in 1975 included inflation of 24 per cent and trade unions neither Labour nor the Conservatives were able to bring under control. She and her supporters set up the Centre for Policy Studies, a think tank which built on the long-disregarded work done by the Institute of Economic Affairs. Soon after taking over, she gave a fierce speech about the threat posed by the Soviet Union, and the Red Army newspaper dubbed her the Iron Lady, a nickname she embraced as a compliment.

From the first, she aroused deep contempt among avant-garde artistic figures in London, who saw in her a philistine who set their teeth on edge. They hated her patriotism, which was somehow too obvious; her voice, which sounded highly artificial; her clothes, which to bohemian eyes seemed to consist of an interminable series of dreary blue suits; and her whole air of suburban gentility. Many of them hated having a woman in charge, though few admitted this even to themselves. Jonathan Miller, who had first come to public attention in the *Beyond the Fringe* revue which mocked Harold Macmillan, called her 'loathsome, repulsive in almost every way', and added that she had 'the diction of a perfumed fart'. The novelist Ian McEwen said after her death, 'It was never enough to dislike her. We *liked* disliking her.'

But in many non-metropolitan circles, her indefatigable respectability was an asset. So too was the policy of selling council houses, long mooted by the Conservatives but only now adopted with gusto. The unions demonstrated during the Winter of Discontent that they were as out of control as ever, and in April 1979 she was elected as Britain's first woman prime minister.

We now know that she would remain in office for eleven years and 209 days, a longer period of continuous service than anyone since Lord Liverpool, though Gladstone and Lord Salisbury had in total done longer. But neither Thatcher nor her opponents knew this in 1979. To her, and indeed to them, her position seemed highly precarious.

Within her Cabinet, she was outnumbered by the Wets, the name given to the grand traditional Conservatives with a grand, traditional tendency to buy off trouble by loosening the purse strings. They did not share the monetarist view, adopted by the

Thatcherites, that inflation, running at about 15 per cent, was caused by incontinent public spending and could be cured by bringing spending under control. They believed that, like Heath before her, Thatcher would become so unpopular she would be forced in her second year to conduct a U-turn. She knew they were expecting this, and in the autumn of 1980 she told the Conservative Party conference: 'You turn if you want to. The lady's not for turning.' Six months later, the Chancellor, Geoffrey Howe, introduced the famous 1981 Budget in which, although unemployment had risen by a million in the last year, he tightened policy by raising taxes. This impelled 364 economists to sign a letter to *The Times* saying there was 'no basis in economic theory' for his action. Large swathes of British industry collapsed, and unemployment rose to 3 million.

The following year, a quite different threat arose, when the Argentine junta, led by General Galtieri, invaded the Falkland Islands. Thatcher resolved that this British territory must be recaptured, and a task force was dispatched within days to achieve this. Had it been sunk, Thatcher would have had to go. Instead, it recaptured the islands, at a cost of 258 British and 649 Argentinian lives. Even Thatcher's detractors could scarce forbear to cheer, and the economy was also showing signs of recovery. In 1983, she won the second of her general election victories, in which the Conservatives benefited from an opposition split between Labour and the Social Democratic Party.

In her second term, Thatcher pressed ahead with the privatisation of large parts of the economy. She had sacked most of the Wets from her Cabinet, but revealed an unfortunate tendency to fall out even with those ministers who agreed with her. In 1984, the IRA blew up the Grand Hotel in Brighton while she was staying in it for the party conference, but although they murdered five people and maimed several others, she was not among them. In the same year, Arthur Scargill took the National Union of

Mineworkers out on strike without a ballot. Ten years before, the miners had brought down Heath. Now Thatcher and her colleagues, who had prepared with care for this trial of strength, defeated the NUM, whom she referred to as 'the enemy within'. This bitter conflict left a residue of hatred, but the crushing of Scargill set the seal on a step-by-step programme of union reform which, along with the heavy burden of unemployment and the decline of many old industries, destroyed the power of the trade union barons to bring the country to a juddering halt.

The greatest threat Thatcher faced was from her own colleagues. In 1986, one of these, Michael Heseltine, sought to precipitate her downfall by resigning from the Cabinet during a complicated row about the future of the Westland helicopter company. He narrowly failed, and in 1987 she told the BBC, 'I hope to go on and on and on', and proceeded to win by a handsome margin her third general election in a row, though not without a bad wobble behind the scenes when one minister screamed at another, 'We're going to lose this fucking election.' Thatcher was now at the height of her international fame, the best-known British prime minister since Churchill. With Reagan, she faced down the Soviet Union, and sooner than others she identified the new leader in Moscow, Mikhail Gorbachev, as someone she could do business with. In March 1987, she gave an uncensored broadcast to the Soviet bloc in which she denounced the Soviet system. Across Eastern Europe, this plain-spoken champion of liberty had millions of admirers. Where others took refuge in diplomatic inanities, she could be relied on to speak her mind, as when she told Le Monde, on the day before she arrived in Paris in 1989 for the celebrations marking the 200th anniversary of the French Revolution:

> Human rights did not begin with the French Revolution ... [they] really stem from a mixture of Judaism and Christianity

... [we English] had 1688, our quiet revolution, where Parliament exerted its will over the King ... it was not the sort of Revolution that France's was ... 'Liberty, equality, fraternity' – they forgot obligations and duties I think. And then of course the fraternity went missing for a long time.

Her treatment of colleagues was worse than ever. Even her warmest admirers said they had never seen anyone be so rude for so long as she was to Geoffrey Howe, the hero of the 1981 Budget. The economy had recovered to such an extent that the term 'yuppy' was coined to describe the rich young thrusters with more money than manners who were becoming so distressingly visible in the City of London. Sir Peregrine Worsthorne, editor of the *Sunday Telegraph*, deprecated this 'bourgeois triumphalism'.

It is surprising that Thatcher had not blown herself up before this time, for few people can stand the strain of life at the top for more than about eight years. She turned out to be remarkably good at crisis management, but now she created a quite unnecessary and unmanageable crisis, by resolving to replace the domestic rates, which were levied on property, with the poll tax, which was levied on people, and was meant to be fairer, because everyone paid the same. That is not how it struck the public, who could not see the justice in levying the new tax at the same rate on a millionaire and a pauper.

At the same time, Thatcher resisted moves in the European Union towards a single currency. This was a dangerous issue for her, because it split her own party. She grew intransigent: she would trust her own instincts, which had so often proved correct in the past. Howe resigned, and said in his resignation speech that she had let down both the Chancellor of the Exchequer and the governor of the Bank of England by dismissing in public their compromise proposal on the single currency issue:

It is rather like sending your opening batsmen to the crease only for them to find, the moment the first balls are bowled, that their bats have been broken before the game by the team captain.

This denunciation of her for being disloyal to her own team was devastating, and opened the way for a leadership challenge by Heseltine. The Conservatives are not always good at running the country, but every twenty or thirty years – in 1922, 1940, 1963, 1990 and 2016 – they produce tremendously exciting leadership contests. Thatcher resolved to stand and fight, but could not quite defeat Heseltine on the first ballot, after which she was forced to realise that unless she stepped down, she would make it impossible for anyone else to stop him. John Major duly emerged as the 'stop Heseltine' candidate, which was enough to ensure victory. Thatcher was, however, very soon disappointed in her protégé's conduct, and could not conceal her disappointment.

Her overthrow cast a long shadow. She had inspired many people to enter the Conservative Party, and they wanted whoever led it to be a Thatcherite. But nobody who came after Thatcher was anything like as convincing as she seemed at least in retrospect to have been, and it was in any case very difficult, as a Thatcherite, to win a general election, for the mere thought of her still set many people's teeth on edge. Her last years were clouded by declining mental powers, but she was given a grand funeral at St Paul's, during which the crowds who lined the route treated her with greater respect than the BBC had expected. For most people by now accepted that even if you detested her, she was one of the great peacetime prime ministers.

JOHN MAJOR

Lived 1943–; prime minister 1990–97

John Major began his prime ministership with the great advantage of not being Margaret Thatcher. He said he wanted a nation 'at ease with itself'. His own manners were certainly easier than hers, and he confounded the pollsters by getting on his soapbox and winning the 1992 general election. But a few months later the Conservatives acquired, on Black Wednesday, a reputation for economic incompetence from which Major was unable to recover, and at the 1997 general election he led his party to one of its worst-ever defeats.

His parents were music-hall performers who fell on hard times. On retiring from the stage, his father, who was sixty-three when Major was born, had set up a business, Major's Garden Ornaments, which made gnomes and other concrete figures. After a period of prosperity, it got into severe difficulties and in 1955, when John was twelve, the five-strong Major family had to sell their bungalow in Worcester Park, in south London, and rent two rooms in Coldharbour Lane, Brixton, with a gas cooker on the landing and a bathroom shared with two other tenants.

Major did not do himself justice at Rutlish Grammar School, which he left at the age of sixteen. His ambition was to become an MP. He spoke well for the local Young Conservatives from a soapbox and began a long affair with a Brixton Conservative, an attractive and self-confident divorcee thirteen years his senior, called Jean Kierans. He resolved to become a banker, got a job at Standard Chartered and was posted to Nigeria, but after seven months was involved in a car accident in which his kneecap was shattered. He returned home for treatment and in 1968 was elected to Lambeth Council at the age of twenty-five. Here he made his name as chairman of the Housing Committee, and fell in love with an opera enthusiast and Conservative activist, Norma Johnson, whom he married despite having fallen asleep when she took him to hear Joan Sutherland.

He fought and lost the London seat of St Pancras North in the two elections of 1974, and in 1979 was returned for the safe seat of Huntingdonshire. He worked very hard, demonstrated competence in junior ministerial posts and in 1987 was promoted to the Cabinet as Chief Secretary to the Treasury. The prime minister, Margaret Thatcher, was by now running out of allies, for she had contrived to fall out even with those ministers who had originally been on her side. In May 1988, she insulted them all by giving an interview in which she said: 'I shall hang on until I believe there are people who can take the banner forward with the same commitment, belief, vision, strength and single-ness of purpose.'

It began to seem to her that Major was at least somewhat less defective than the rest of her colleagues. He had a gift for convincing people that he was on their side, without actually saying so, and became the latest in a long line of favourites, none of whom had lasted long. In July 1989, she removed Geoffrey Howe from the Foreign Office and put Major there instead: a remarkable promotion for so inexperienced a figure. But he spent only 94 days in his new post, for in October, the Chancellor of the Exchequer, Nigel Lawson, who with Howe had been trying to force Thatcher to take the pound into the European exchange rate mechanism, resigned in protest at her intransigent support for floating exchange rates, and she decided she must plug the gap at the Treasury with Major.

The new Chancellor, along with the new Foreign Secretary, Douglas Hurd, now forced her to accept British membership of the exchange rate mechanism, which the pound joined at what was soon found to be too high a rate against the German mark. But she continued to goad her colleagues by denouncing European moves towards a single currency, and in November 1990 Howe resigned from the government, setting in motion a leadership challenge by Michael Heseltine, who had resigned some years earlier. With her back to the wall, Thatcher looked around for someone who was not Heseltine.

Major possessed that negative virtue, and was on friendly terms with almost everyone in the parliamentary party. He had no side about him, and his modest start in life gave him the edge over Hurd, who also entered the race, but had been educated at Eton and had no idea how to deal with the inverted snobbery which that school evoked. Thatcher anointed Major as her rightful successor, and he got 185 votes on the first ballot, with 131 for Heseltine and 56 for Hurd. Major thus became, at the age of forty-seven, the youngest prime minister since Lord Rosebery.

The charm of simplicity of manners worked as well with the general public as it had with Tory MPs. Major came as a breath of fresh air. He got rid of the poll tax and, in the negotiations in December 1991 at Maastricht on a new European treaty, reckoned he had obtained a wonderful deal for Britain, including an opt-out from the single currency. But his use of language was extraordinarily limited, and by the time of the general election, held in April 1992, the pollsters and pundits expected him to lose. In this moment of crisis, he reverted to the simple campaigning methods he had used in his youth in Brixton and took to addressing often hostile audiences through a loud hailer while standing on a wooden crate and having eggs thrown at him. Two members of his team, Jonathan Hill and Sarah Hogg, described the effect on Major:

> He had come out of the crowd positively crackling with electricity. He was a different person. No more Treasury-speak and whirring sub-clauses. Instead, a tough street-fighter who drew his strength from direct contact with the crowd and knew how to speak their language – simple, uncomplicated English spoken straight from the heart.

Major had discovered a way of being authentic, and beat the Labour leader, Neil Kinnock, who made the vainglorious error of seeming to think victory was in the bag. But although the Conservatives gained 14 million votes, and an eight-point lead, that translated into a Commons majority of only 21.

Within months, Major's authority was shot to pieces on Black Wednesday, 16 September 1992, when after a vain attempt to defend the pound by raising interest rates to 15 per cent, Britain was forced out of the exchange rate mechanism. Billions of pounds had been wasted on this exercise, but Major, perhaps because he had fully supported it, did not get round to removing the Chancellor of the Exchequer, Norman Lamont, until eight months later. Lamont observed in his resignation statement that the government was 'in office but not in power'.

In 1993, while the Commons ratified the Maastricht Treaty, and indeed for the rest of his prime ministership, Major was run ragged by the Eurosceptics in his own party. He was heard referring to them as 'bastards', but had no way of bringing them into line. His friend Chris Patten said of him:

John was one of the most decent people ever to lead the Conservative party ... He actually listened to other opinions ... But its senior members had got used to being roughed up, and seemed to find it difficult to summon the grace to behave well when they were themselves treated like grown-ups.

In the autumn of 1993, Major tried to recover by launching a 'back to basics' campaign, which was taken by the press to mean a return to implausibly strict standards of sexual morality. From now on, any deviation from those standards by any Tory MP, and also any evidence of financial wrongdoing, was fitted into a narrative of 'Tory sleaze'. And there seemed to be an unending supply of deviations of one kind or another.

In 1995, Major became so fed up with the attacks on him from his own side that he resigned the Conservative leadership, invited his detractors to 'put up or shut up' and defeated the clever but cranky John Redwood by the far from resounding margin of 218 votes to 89.

Throughout his time in office, Major made matters worse for himself by reading the newspapers and taking to heart what they said. In vain his friends pleaded with him to stop doing this. He was the most thin-skinned prime minister in British history, always ready to believe he was being patronised because of his humble origins, and once the media realised how touchy he was, they bullied him even more. He lived with the fear that news would break of his affair during the 1980s with another Tory MP, Edwina Currie. In the event, the story did not come out until 2002, when, with her usual self-seeking vulgarity, she published it in her diaries. Major said it was the thing in his political career of which he was 'most ashamed'.

In the general election of 1997, Labour under Tony Blair triumphed over the Conservatives, who had been in office for eighteen years. On the morning of his defeat, Major resigned the leadership of his generally ungrateful party and went off to watch cricket at the Oval. The economy was recovering well, but Blair would reap the benefit of this. The peace process in Northern Ireland was far advanced, but again Blair would take most of the credit. Major's task, on taking over almost by accident from one of the most dominant leaders of modern times, was well-nigh impossible, and it is hard to avoid the thought that this sensitive man might have been happier if he had never become prime minister.

TONY BLAIR

Lived 1953–; prime minister 1997–2007

Tony Blair had an unnaturally long honeymoon as prime minister, followed by an even longer period in which few people could bear the sound of his voice. On entering office, he was forty-three years old, which made him the youngest prime minister since Lord Liverpool in 1812. From an electoral point of view, he was the most successful leader in Labour history, winning three general elections in a row. But he had the good fortune to be the only Labour prime minister to take over a flourishing economy, and gained the trust of middle England by making attacks on his own party.

That is one reason why such a wave of accumulated resentment burst over him in 2003, after he had successfully insisted on British participation in the American-led invasion of Iraq and it became clear the occupation of that country was going wrong. In earlier years, Blair would have made some concessions to his critics, or at least made rueful, self-deprecating jokes which showed he understood why they were so angry with him. But towards the end of his decade in Downing Street, and for many years afterwards, he instead used his remarkable powers of advocacy to try to force everyone to agree he had always been in the right, or at least that he had invariably acted in good faith. His moral vanity became unbearable.

In his early years, he was charm personified, and knew how to strike the right note with everyone from a duchess to a cleaning lady. His father, Leo Blair, the illegitimate child of two actors, was adopted and raised by a working-class couple in Glasgow, started out in life as a communist, rose to the rank of major in the army, qualified as a lawyer, taught law at Durham, practised as a barrister in Newcastle upon Tyne and was well on his way to becoming a Conservative MP when he suffered a stroke, which disabled him without actually killing him. Tony was eleven years old, and at Durham Choristers School, when this blow befell the family. He nevertheless went on, like his elder brother, to Fettes College, on the edge of Edinburgh, conventionally described as the Eton of Scotland, where he perfected his persona of quick-witted, good-natured and essentially unthreatening rebel: the kind of person the Establishment loves, for he upholds the status quo while making life less dull.

He was a good actor, playing Mark Antony in *Julius Caesar*, and was at ease performing, not very well, in a rock band called Ugly Rumours, which he set up with some friends after leaving school. While reading law at St John's College, Oxford, he came under the influence of an Australian priest called Peter Thomson, and was confirmed into the Church of England. In London, Blair joined his local Labour Party, made his way as a barrister and married a fellow lawyer, Cherie Booth, whose father, an actor called Tony Booth, had not been around much. Blair was fond of saying that his wife was a better lawyer than he was, while she could not help indicating that being married to a well-known politician was something of a strain. They had four children, of whom the youngest, Leo, became the first child born to a serving prime minister since 1849, in which year Lord John Russell's wife gave birth to her third child: an event which barely figured in the newspapers.

To gain political experience, Blair stood as the Labour candidate in the Beaconsfield by-election in 1982 and lost his deposit. This was the last election he lost, for just before the 1983 general election, he managed to persuade the selectors in Sedgefield, a safe Labour seat in County Durham, that he was their man. At Westminster, he shared a windowless office with another newly elected Labour MP, Gordon Brown. They formed a partnership in which Brown, who had arrived from Edinburgh with a reputation as a heavyweight, was the senior figure, while Blair was the apprentice.

After Labour's fourth general election defeat in a row, in 1992, John Smith became party leader and made Brown shadow Chancellor of the Exchequer, while Blair became shadow Home Secretary. Blair gained rave reviews and reversed Labour's reputation for being soft on crime, by repeating an impregnable soundbite which had been devised for him by Brown: 'tough on crime, and tough on the causes of crime'.

In 1994, Smith suddenly died. Who would succeed him as leader? Brown hesitated. Blair went for it and got it. He had shown he was a better communicator than Brown. He was not, however, very good at communicating with Brown, who felt horribly betrayed but believed Blair had at least agreed, at a meeting in the Granita restaurant in Islington, to hand over to him during the second term of a Labour government. Blair saw no need to make himself clear on that point.

For Blair was now in charge, and with the same ruthless audacity that had enabled him to see off his friend, he set about ensuring a Labour victory at the next election. He decided to dramatise the change in the party by ditching Clause IV, the traditional socialist commitment, adopted in 1918, to 'the common ownership of the means of production, distribution and exchange'. One of his closest advisers, Philip Gould, has described a 'brainstorming' session with Blair and other senior figures shortly before this manoeuvre was sprung on the Labour conference in the autumn of 1994:

> For me the day is memorable for one defining moment: in the queue with Tony, waiting for the buffet, we talked about the need for rapid change and Blair turned to me and made one of the most compelling political statements I have ever heard: 'Conference must build New Labour. It is time we gave the party some electric shock treatment.'

The language is that of a torturer, and many members of the Labour Party did indeed feel tortured, once they understood what Blair was doing to them, for as usual he briefed the media and did not immediately make his intentions plain to his comrades. Their screams of pain convinced middle England that he must be a sound, small-c conservative. Labour was indeed no longer committed to repealing what Margaret Thatcher had done. Even her trade union reforms would remain in place.

In 1997, Blair won a landslide victory with a Commons majority of 179; in 2001, he still had a majority of 165 and in 2005 he managed to hang on and get a majority of 67. It was not entirely clear what he was going to do with these victories. He wished to take Britain into the single European currency, but Brown blocked him. He wished to reform the public sector, but after two years said, 'I bear the scars on my back' from the fierce opposition he encountered.

Blair's first government did devolve power to Scotland and Wales, and in 1998 he and his chief of staff, Jonathan Powell, brought the peace process in Northern Ireland to a successful conclusion with the Good Friday Agreement. Blair told the cameras: 'A day like today is not a day for soundbites, we can leave those at home, but I feel the hand of history upon our shoulder.' Such moments of self-parody encouraged the accusation that his government was all about spin. Alistair Campbell, his conspicuously powerful and aggressive communications director, also prompted that thought. So too did a third member of Blair's inner circle, Peter Mandelson, who was by now an MP and a minister, but had become known as 'the Prince of Darkness' while acting as a witty, feline and threatening spin doctor to an earlier Labour leader, Neil Kinnock.

Before his first victory, Blair remarked that 'my project will be complete when the Labour Party learns to love Peter Mandelson'. But in 1998, the slim chances of that happening were further reduced by Mandelson himself when he told a group of computer executives in California, 'We are intensely relaxed about people getting filthy rich, as long as they pay their taxes.' The 'filthy rich' bit stuck in people's minds, and contributed to the idea that the Blairites were promoting an *enrichissez-vous* mentality, especially as Blair himself had a marked taste for going on holiday as the guest of various plutocrats. Mandelson's own morality seemed a bit elastic, for on two occasions, one of them involving an undeclared loan from another Labour MP, he was forced to resign his ministerial posts.

Blair's remarkably prolonged electoral success was underpinned by an economic boom that continued throughout his time in power. He also remained to the end of his prime ministership a brilliant debater and speaker, with a genius for detecting the vulnerabilities of the five Conservative leaders whom he faced, as he explained in his memoir, *A Journey*:

> I defined Major as weak; Hague as better at jokes than judgement; Howard as an opportunist; Cameron as a flip-flop, not knowing where he wanted to go. (The Tories did my work for me in undermining Iain Duncan Smith.) Expressed like that, these attacks seem flat, rather mundane almost, and not exactly inspiring – but that's their appeal. Any one of those charges, if it comes to be believed, is actually fatal. Yes, it's not like calling your opponent a liar, or a fraud, or a villain or a hypocrite, but the middle-ground floating voter kind of shrugs their shoulders at those claims. They don't chime. They're too over the top, too heavy, and they represent an insult, not an argument. Whereas the lesser charge, because it's more accurate and precisely because it's more low-key, can stick.

But Blair did not want to be remembered merely as a master of disparaging understatement. He wanted solid achievements to his name, and in part because these were so hard to come by at home, he grew more and more interested in foreign policy, which appealed strongly to the messianic streak in his nature. Successful interventions in Kosovo in 1999 and Sierra Leone in 2000 led him on towards the Iraq War. On 11 September 2001, almost 3,000 people were killed in the attack on the Twin Towers in New York, and Blair immediately seized on this as a pretext for American-led global intervention to ensure the triumph of good over evil. As he told the Labour conference the following month: 'The kaleidoscope has been shaken. The pieces are in flux. Soon they will settle again. Before they do, let us reorder this world around us.'

The Americans set out to reorder the world by intervening in Afghanistan and then, in March 2003, by overthrowing Saddam Hussein, the ruler of Iraq, even though, as it happened, that thoroughly unpleasant man had nothing to do with the attack on the Twin Towers. Blair's chief of staff, Jonathan Powell, had already told the British ambassador to Washington, 'Basically, Christopher, what we want you to do is get up the arse of the White House and stay there.' Blair himself managed, with exceptional energy and adaptability, to present himself as the foremost guide, philosopher and friend both to President Bill Clinton and to his ideologically opposed successor, George W. Bush, who took over in 2001. The British prime minister duly persuaded the Commons to vote for British troops to join the American-led invasion of Iraq. A huge protest march in London and a rebellion by 139 Labour MPs did not deter Blair, who knew he could rely on the support of the Conservatives.

The invasion went fine, but the occupation did not and soon descended into a bloody civil war, with huge civilian casualties. British forces lost 179 dead and many more were wounded as they strove in vain to keep the peace in Basra, in southern Iraq. Blair, the great advocate of war, had given excessive credence to reports that Saddam Hussein possessed weapons of mass destruction.

His reputation has not recovered from this disaster. Large parts of the Labour Party and of the wider public were confirmed in their view that he was an American lackey with blood on his hands. In the spring of 2006, he was forced by his opponents within the party to promise he would stand down a year later. Like Thatcher, it was his own side who brought him down.

Brown was at last prime minister, and in 2009 yielded to pressure to set up an inquiry into the Iraq War. In 2017, the Chilcot report appeared, and Chilcot said in an interview with the BBC:

I think any prime minister taking a country into war has got to be straight with the nation and carry it, so far as possible, with him or her. I don't believe that was the case in the Iraq instance.

In 1997, Blair had shrugged off a minor scandal by remarking: 'I think most people who have dealt with me think I am a pretty straight sort of guy, and I am.' Few people thought this any longer. His rare public appearances became painful to watch, for he was rent by an unbearable conflict between his self-righteousness and the public's contempt. After leaving office, he served as a peace envoy in the Middle East, but found its problems just as intractable. He also joined the Roman Catholic Church, in which confession plays a bigger role than it does in Anglicanism, but would make no public confession of guilt. Robert Harris, a close friend of Mandelson, wrote a novel, *The Ghost*, in which the character based on Blair turns out to be married to an American agent, which explains why he always does what the Americans want. To many people on the left, Blair had become a traitor and a war criminal, who just wanted to make money and consort with the super-rich. Not since Ramsay MacDonald had a Labour prime minister come to be so scorned by the party for which he had done so much.

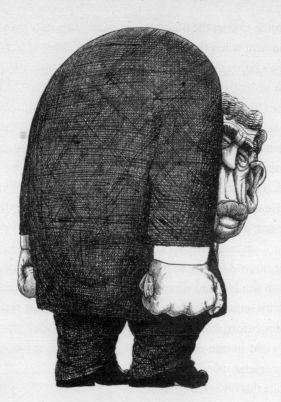

GORDON BROWN

Lived 1951–; prime minister 2007–10

ordon Brown became prime minister a decade too late to enjoy it. He had expected he would lead Labour back into power in 1997, in the full flood of youthful hope and energy. But Brown's fatal hesitancy, his inability in the first part of that decade to grasp the crown when it was within his reach, allowed the swifter and more decisive Tony Blair to take the Labour leadership from under his nose. Brown was condemned to spend year after year pretending to feel fulfilled as Chancellor of the Exchequer. Behind the scenes, he and his henchmen waged a bitter battle to evict the Blairites, something they only managed at the moment when the economic boom was about to burst.

Brown's father, for whom he expressed great admiration, was a Church of Scotland minister in Kirkcaldy, on the coast of Fife, and Brown himself felt obliged to thunder in a Calvinist manner on serious economic and political questions, and to hide the shy and sensitive side of his nature. On becoming prime minister, he quoted the motto of Kirkcaldy High School, which he had attended: 'I will try my utmost'. No one doubted he had lived up to this. He was a gifted pupil, good at both academic work and sport. As part of an educational experiment he got pushed through the school at excessive speed, and so arrived at Edinburgh University to read history at the age of only sixteen. His eyes were giving him trouble, and when he went to the doctor, he learned that both his retinas were detached, the result of an injury suffered six months before while playing rugby against an adult side. He lost the sight in one eye and was for six months in danger of going completely blind.

Despite this ordeal, he became the most celebrated student of his time at Edinburgh, being elected rector of the university, in which role he caused the authorities much grief by championing constructive reform. He took a first-class degree, and for five years his girlfriend was Princess Margarita of Romania, a cousin of the Queen. Their friends imagined they would get married, but the Red Princess, as she was known, at length wearied of the inordinate amount of time he devoted to politics. He had other long-term relationships, but was not the sort of man to rush into the commitment of marriage.

After spending a few years as an academic and a journalist, he was in 1983 elected MP for Dunfermline East, and at once started making his mark at Westminster. He shared an office with his fellow newcomer, Tony Blair, became close friends with him and taught him a lot about politics. The Conservatives were riding high under Margaret Thatcher, but Peter Mandelson, who was Labour's director of communications, often deployed Brown and Blair on television, for they were better than most of the old guard.

In 1992, Blair and others urged Brown to enter the Labour leadership race, which was triggered by the party's unexpected defeat at the general election. But Brown's innate streak of caution held him back, and he used his intelligence to devise good reasons for inaction. John Smith, who won, made him shadow Chancellor, in which capacity Brown got rid of Labour's traditional 'tax and spend' policies. This accommodation to reality made him less popular among Labour MPs.

He nevertheless assumed, when Smith suddenly died, that he would succeed him. Blair instead nipped in and claimed the top job while the funeral baked meats were still being consumed. And Brown accepted this. With the benefit of hindsight, it is easy to see he should have stood and fought. At least then the question would have been decided in open battle, rather than in a deal confirmed in an Islington restaurant, with Brown believing Blair had promised to hand over to him during Labour's second term.

Brown became Chancellor of the Exchequer: an office which to most politicians would represent success. And he began with a *coup de théâtre*: he set the Bank of England free to determine interest rates. Politicians could no longer try to fix these to suit themselves. This was a big step, and Brown also kept his promise to stick to the Tories' spending limits for the first two years. He spoke of 'prudence with a purpose', and acted as a kind of brake on Blair, preventing him from taking Britain into the euro. In 2000, at the age of forty-nine, Brown at last got married, to Sarah Macaulay, a partner in a public relations firm. They attracted deep sympathy when their baby daughter died after only ten days, and went on to have two sons.

During Labour's second term, Blair did not keep his supposed promise to hand over power. Behind closed doors, Brown raged against Blair. But he would not push things to an open rupture, and Blair hung on. Brown loosened the purse strings, the economy continued to grow and, although property prices were rising at an unsustainable rate, he was unwise enough to go on promising 'no return to boom and bust'.

Only after the disaster of the Iraq War and a third, much narrower, victory, did Brown and his gang feel strong enough to move in for the kill. In September 2006, Blair was forced to announce he would be gone within a year, and in May 2007, out he went.

In came Brown, and at first he did very well. He enjoyed a honeymoon, during which he handled various minor crises – an attack on Glasgow airport, some floods, an outbreak of foot-and-mouth disease – with aplomb. Labour's opinion poll ratings improved and his advisers urged him to go for an early election. Brown neither agreed with them nor discouraged them. During the Labour Party conference, the expectation grew that he would go for it.

The Conservatives were deeply alarmed, but did not lose their nerve. Their shadow Chancellor, George Osborne, announced a proposal to cut inheritance tax, and somehow that was enough to puncture the Labour bubble. Brown drew back in fear, and was ridiculed for doing so. Like the Grand Old Duke of York, he marched his troops to the top of the hill, and marched them down again.

At about the same time, there was a run on the Northern Rock bank, which heralded a much more general collapse. Though caught by surprise, and at first in denial about how bad the news was, Brown coped manfully with the crisis. He helped save not just Britain's but the world's banks. Despite this tremendous achievement, it was impossible for him to escape some blame for the crash. He had, after all, been Chancellor of the Exchequer since 1997.

When his friend and successor as Chancellor, Alistair Darling, suggested in the summer of 2008 that things were as bad as they had been for sixty years, Brown's attack dogs went for him. Darling said it was like having 'the forces of hell' unleashed on him, and added in his memoirs: 'systematic anonymous briefing from people you have known for years, and who are supposed to be on your side, is deeply unpleasant'. This perfidious attempt to blame the present Chancellor for his own errors did not make people think any better of Brown.

At this low point in his fortunes, he did an extraordinary thing. In October 2008, he brought back Mandelson, who in 1994 had incurred his profound enmity by backing Blair for the leadership, and had later gone off to Brussels to become an EU commissioner. Mandelson, who became the second most powerful man in the government, steadied the ship when other ministers were deserting it. During one mutiny, he rang round the other potential rebels and almost certainly saved Brown from being toppled by his own side.

Brown looked exhausted. He worked harder and harder, but became no better at taking decisions. In 2009, he produced a weak and vacillating response to the MPs' expenses scandal, for it had long been clear that he had no ear for the concerns of middle England. The sight in his remaining eye worsened, and he suffered the terrible though in the event mistaken fear that he was about to go blind. During the 2010 general election campaign, he suffered a dreadful encounter with an elderly woman in Rochdale, who said she normally voted Labour, but accused him of being unduly tolerant of immigration. Brown got back in his car with his microphone still switched on, and asked who 'that bigot' was and whose fault it was that he had been made to talk to her. This episode illustrated, with humiliating clarity, his lack of sympathy with traditional Labour supporters and his tendency in a tight spot to look for someone else to blame.

In such adverse circumstances, it could be said he did well to deny his Conservative opponents an overall majority. But Labour, with 258 seats to the Conservatives' 306, had certainly been defeated, and Brown was by now too discredited a figure to have any serious chance of clinging on by doing a deal with the Liberal Democrats, who had 57 seats. He stepped down not just from the prime ministership but from the Labour leadership, though he lingered as a mostly silent backbencher until 2015. Blair had won three elections in a row, and Brown had not managed to win one. Harold Wilson's defenders say his great achievement was to keep Britain out of Vietnam. Brown's defenders say his was to keep Britain out of the euro.

DAVID CAMERON

Lived 1966–; prime minster 2010–16

David Cameron announced, on the morning of 24 June 2016, a few hours after losing the EU referendum, that he would be stepping down as prime minister. Distraught supporters of remaining in the EU bitterly reproached him for ever having called the vote, which for them became the defining catastrophe of his premiership, comparable in ignominy to Suez for Anthony Eden. Cameron's earlier successes, which included returning the Conservatives to power in 2010 and running the country well enough to win an overall majority in 2015, were blotted out by the referendum.

Cameron was descended on his father's side from a long line of successful stockbrokers, while his mother was a Mount, a county family in Berkshire with a tradition of public service. According to one of the most literary members of the family, Ferdinand Mount, 'a high moral tone came naturally to them'. Cameron was brought up in a handsome old rectory in Berkshire and educated at Heatherdown, a posh prep school which no longer exists, followed by Eton, where he was slightly younger than Boris Johnson and much less well known. He went on to Brasenose College, Oxford, where he took a first in philosophy, politics and economics, and was again less well known than Johnson.

When Cameron started at last to emerge into public consciousness, which did not happen until he unexpectedly became Conservative leader at the end of 2005, the press noticed he had been educated at Eton and Oxford, and that while at the latter, he had been a member of the Bullingdon Club. This background made him the most upper-class Tory leader since Sir Alec Douglas-Home, prime minister in 1963–64, and was taken to mean he must suffer the drawback of being an out-of-touch toff: a walking anachronism, who would be useless at getting on with ordinary people. For members of the Bullingdon dress up in special tailcoats, get disgustingly drunk, vandalise restaurants and are described, by one of Evelyn Waugh's characters, as looking 'like a lot of most disorderly footmen'.

Cameron himself seemed a bit embarrassed by his background. Either he or one of his supporters arranged for the official group photographs of the Bullingdon to be withdrawn from circulation, and Cameron also resigned his membership of White's, the grand London club of which his father was chairman. But the media's obsession with the Bullingdon, though tiresome, also helped Cameron, for it led his opponents to underestimate him. His professionalism was ignored. This was developed after

Oxford, in the less glamorous setting of the Conservative Research Department, where Cameron worked in his twenties for senior ministers, including Margaret Thatcher and John Major. On Black Wednesday, in September 1992, he was special adviser to Norman Lamont, the Chancellor of the Exchequer, and drafted the immortal words used by his master as the pound crashed out of the European exchange rate mechanism: 'Today has been an extremely difficult and turbulent day.'

Cameron acquired such a thorough grounding in politics, and such a gifted gang of friends, soon dubbed the Notting Hill set or the Cameroons, that at the age of only thirty-nine, he was able to win the Conservative leadership and avoid falling flat on his face once he had done so. In the autumn of 2005, when the contest took place, Cameron delivered an uplifting speech without notes and was able to show himself richer in potential than his rival, David Davis, whom most observers had expected to win. He was by now married to Samantha Sheffield, a well-connected art student. They had four children, of whom the first, Ivan, was very severely handicapped and died when he was only six. The youngest, Florence, was born while Cameron was prime minister: another respect in which he emulated Blair, whose example was much admired by the Cameroons.

As leader, Cameron set out to modernise the party, notably by increasing the number of women and ethnic minority candidates, and stressing subjects like the environment, an interest he dramatised by being photographed in the far north with a sledge and some husky dogs. Commentators of an ideological cast of mind found most of what he did unsatisfying, for he refused to define himself in their terms. As an Anglican, Cameron set high store by good behaviour, but was free from dogma and amenable to compromise, so felt no need to characterise himself as a Thatcherite or an anti-Thatcherite. On the great question of the European Union, he tried to pursue a *via media*, or middle course, where the dogmatists were unable to detect one, but mostly he just asked his backbenchers to shut up.

In the general election of 2010, the first with Cameron in charge, the Conservatives gained over a hundred seats, but fell short of an overall majority. In this hour of crisis, Cameron at once offered such generous terms to the Liberal Democrats, who had 57 seats, that they felt compelled to form a coalition with him. Their manifesto had been subjected to searching analysis by Oliver Letwin, Cameron's head of policy, in preparation for just such an eventuality. The Liberal Democrat leader, Nick Clegg, held a joint press conference with Cameron in the garden of 10 Downing Street, and looked indecently pleased to have become deputy prime minister. The new government declared that Labour had left the public finances in a desperate state, and made austerity its guiding purpose. It also passed the Fixed Term Parliaments Act, so neither party could let the other down by precipitating a snap election.

On coming into office, Cameron was a few months younger than Tony Blair, so replaced him as the youngest prime minister since Lord Liverpool. One of Cameron's contemporaries observed: 'He always knew what you could say and what you couldn't.' He could almost always find the right words, though like Blair, he sometimes set out to annoy his own party, in order to show the public how progressive he was. Three years into his prime minis-tership, he enraged many Conservatives by legalising same-sex marriage.

It cannot be said Cameron ever managed to form a close emotional connection with the British people. He seldom if ever sounded convincing when he tried to be passionate, for he would not give enough of himself away. He took the probably unavoid-able risk of conceding a referendum on Scottish independence, and in 2014, after a bitterly divisive campaign, the Scots voted by 55 to 45 per cent to stay in the United Kingdom.

Like John Major in the 1990s, Cameron faced the danger that his prime ministership would be ruined by civil war within the Conservative Party over Europe. He dealt with this by promising, in his Bloomberg speech in January 2013, that if re-elected in 2015, he would within two years hold a referendum on Britain's membership of the European Union. Essentially, he was saying to his Eurosceptic wing, and also to the UK Independence Party, which at this period was gaining an alarming number of votes and activists, and one or two MPs, from the Conservatives: 'You can have your referendum, but I'm going to win it.'

Before the referendum could take place, Cameron had to win the 2015 general election. The pundits and pollsters were convinced he would fail to do this: another instance of their inability to read him, for he astonished them by gaining another 25 seats, and thus a narrow overall majority in the Commons. His Liberal Democrat allies lost almost all their seats. Cameron had killed them with kindness.

Control and competence are seen as dreary virtues, and few people spotted the methodical shamelessness with which Cameron used his powers of patronage to strengthen his grip on power. In the creation of privy councillors and life peers, he was profligate on an eighteenth-century scale. This does not mean he handed out, like a latter-day Walpole, offices of enormous profit to their holders, or that he gave most of the best places to members of his own family.

In twenty-first-century politics, people can be bought for so much less than in the eighteenth century: most often, just by some soothing of their vanity. One has only to read Alan Clark's diaries about politics in the 1980s to see how an intelligent person can be consumed by the desire for a footling ministerial post. And no one in recent times had a greater genius than Cameron for distributing those footling ministerial posts to the combination of people best calculated to keep him in power. He gave hope to everyone, young and old, male and female, left and right, bright and dim, that their time would come.

But once he had won the 2015 general election, he had to fulfil his promise to hold the EU referendum. And here, he became too obviously a representative of the pro-European Establishment. His renegotiation of British membership was carried out with such lack of conviction that he acquired nothing very much, and certainly no limits on immigration from the EU, which worried many voters a great deal. During the campaign, he tried to frighten people into voting for the status quo, by insisting that voting to leave would precipitate economic disaster. His side contradicted itself by saying that leaving the EU would be a leap in the dark, yet also specifying how much it would cost each man, woman and child. Meanwhile his brilliant but mercurial contemporary, Boris Johnson, whom he had always kept at a safe distance, decided to become the frontman for the Leave campaign, and proved again his superior ability to connect with the wider public.

Cameron lost the referendum, by the slim margin of 52 to 48 per cent, and with characteristic swiftness and decency stepped down. The man who had tried, by passing the Fixed Term Parliaments Act, to make British politics more predictable fell victim to the sudden-death tradition operating in a different form introduced by himself. Cameron also retired as an MP, and went off to write his memoirs. His reputation will depend on whether or not Brexit is the disaster his opponents expect. He could turn out to be the man who by accident wrecked his country, or the man who by accident liberated it.

THERESA MAY

Lived 1956–; prime minister 2016–

Theresa May aspired from an early age to become the first woman prime minister. There was not, however, much expectation among her colleagues that she would rise above the level of Home Secretary, the office she held in David Cameron's government. Then Cameron exploded himself by holding the referendum. May at once decided to run for the leadership, but faced a formidable rival in Boris Johnson, the most prominent figure in the campaign to leave the EU. But he in turn was exploded by his close ally, Michael Gove, who astonished everyone by declaring Johnson unfit to be prime minister.

May now looked like the only grown-up in the race. Indeed, she was ten years older than the outgoing prime minister. At the launch of her campaign, she was able, with her modest background and solitary habits, to make herself sound like a refreshing change from Cameron and Johnson, the ostentatious and convivial sons of privilege:

If you're from an ordinary, working-class family, life is just much harder than many people in politics realise ... You can just about manage, but you worry about the cost of living and the quality of the local school, because there's no other choice for you ... I know I'm not a showy politician. I don't tour the television studios. I don't gossip about people over lunch. I don't go drinking in Parliament's bars. I don't often wear my heart on my sleeve. I just get on with the job in front of me.

How soothing this sounded. The referendum and its aftermath had afforded more than enough excitement. Now May could calm everything down, and with quiet pragmatism steer the country through the complicated business of leaving the EU. On 13 July 2016, she became the second woman, after Margaret Thatcher, to reach 10 Downing Street.

Her background was indeed markedly less moneyed than Cameron's, and helped explain the affinity she felt with the 'just about managings'. May was the only child of a clergyman who was himself the son of a regimental sergeant major. Both her grandmothers had worked as maids. Her father belonged to the Anglo-Catholic wing of the Church of England, trained at Mirfield in Yorkshire and became vicar of Wheatley, in Oxfordshire. She too is a devout Anglo-Catholic.

From the local girls' grammar school, which became, not very happily, a comprehensive in her last year, she went to read geography at St Hugh's College, Oxford. She was introduced by Benazir Bhutto (a future prime minister of Pakistan, assassinated in 2007) to her future husband, Philip May: 'I hate to say this, but it was at an Oxford University Conservative Association disco ... this is wild stuff. He was a good debater and Benazir had got to know him through that.'

Philip was at this stage seen as more of a star than she was. But she was the one who pursued a career as a Conservative politician, first as a local councillor in Merton, in south London, and from 1997 as MP for Maidenhead. At Westminster, she was soon identified as the most gifted of the embarrassingly small number of Conservative women, who faced a huge contingent of Labour women MPs elected under Tony Blair's leadership.

May proved her competence in various shadow ministerial posts before becoming Conservative chairman, where she leapt to prominence by telling the annual conference, a year after the party had again been trounced by Labour: 'You know what some people call us – the nasty party.' Many Tories deeply resented this statement, which put her clearly on the modernising side of the party. But from 2005, it was David Cameron who carried forward as leader the cause of rendering the Conservative Party more electable. May had taken soundings, and discovered that if she were to stand for leader, she would get virtually no support. She instead threw her energies into creating, with Anne Jenkin, Women2Win, which recruited and trained far more women to become Conservative candidates. But May was best known for wearing exotic shoes: a way of getting a lot of press coverage, without having to talk about ideas. The media's obsession with what women wear allowed her to keep what was going on inside her head very much to herself.

In 2010, Cameron asked her to become Home Secretary. In this department she displayed remarkable grip, exercised partly through her special advisers, and dealt with various very tricky extradition cases. She had the courage to take on the Police Federation, and to defend herself against Cabinet colleagues. From 2013, she began to stray beyond her brief, in an evident attempt to prepare herself for a leadership bid.

But most Conservatives were still surprised when the cards fell so well for her in the summer of 2016. She was on the Remain side of the EU argument, but indicated that she would not be distraught if the referendum went the other way, and enraged Cameron's people by refusing to campaign for the result that would have saved him. So she was now in the right position to reunite the party: a Remainer who got the message and was going to implement Brexit. She delighted the Leavers by saying 'Brexit means Brexit'.

The party was now so united that she decided she could afford to sack the Cameroons. She chucked out almost everyone who had been at all close to her predecessor, while bringing in prominent Leavers, including David Davis as Brexit secretary and Boris Johnson as Foreign Secretary, as a guarantee that she could be trusted to see the project through. During her honeymoon, she also delighted many people by being extremely rude to parts of the media, though not to the *Daily Mail*, which backed her to the hilt. Her special advisers, Nick Timothy and Fiona Hill, whom she had brought with her from the Home Office, were now in full cry, bringing the smack of firm government to 10 Downing Street. The Labour Party had elected a new leader, Jeremy Corbyn, who mouthed the left-wing verities of the late 1970s and looked completely unworthy to be prime minister. Meanwhile, UKIP was in collapse – by holding the referendum, Cameron had shot its fox – and the Liberal Democrats were a shadow of their former strength.

May bestrode the scene. In the autumn of 2016, she wowed the Eurosceptics at the Tory conference by assuring them she was pressing ahead for a full and complete Brexit. Meanwhile, the Remainers had nowhere to go: they were dragged along in her slipstream.

She called a general election, to be held in June 2017. This news burst like a thunderbolt on Westminster: she had achieved complete surprise. Her aim was to get a much larger majority, so a small number of her own backbenchers could not torment her once she presented them with a Brexit deal, as John Major had been tormented in the 1990s during the ratification of the Maastricht Treaty.

The general assumption, fortified by the opinion pollsters, was that she would win an enormous victory. But she was by now overconfident, and produced a highly objectionable manifesto which alarmed the old, notably by proposing what the press dubbed a 'dementia tax', without including anything to enthuse the young. And during a highly personalised campaign, she sounded like a conscientious but not very imaginative schoolchild, drearily repeating her promise of 'strong and stable government'.

She got 13 fewer seats than Cameron had won in 2015. The electorate recoiled at the thought of giving her an unfettered mandate. Far from winning an increased majority, she now had no majority at all, and was forced to cobble up a deal with the ten Democratic Unionists from Northern Ireland. Meanwhile Corbyn, the despised Labour leader, gained 30 seats. May had won an increased share of the vote, but here too Corbyn had gained more.

This was a heavy blow to May's authority over her own party. Her imperious manner began to seem like the self-defence mechanism of a limited woman, and Cabinet ministers started to squabble openly between themselves. Since the party was far from agreed on who to replace her with, and afraid of having to fight another general election, and each faction feared it might end up with someone less amenable to pressure than May, it decided she should nevertheless be given the chance to struggle on, and to try to cope with the complexities of Brexit.

At the party conference held in Manchester in the autumn of 2017, she tried to regain the initiative, but instead advertised her vulnerability by grinding repeatedly to a halt during her own speech, overcome by fits of coughing. She evoked pity rather than respect, and it seemed unlikely she could continue for long to sustain the burden of high office. Even sooner than most of her 53 predecessors, May had demonstrated the precarious and transitory nature of a tenancy at 10 Downing Street.

AFTERWORD

We abuse our prime ministers. Our tradition of liberty includes the right to be rude about all politicians, and especially about anyone who tells us what to do. On social media, we insult anyone who so much as disagrees with us.

When I started this book, I thought I might follow in this tradition, which at its best was adorned by the eighteenth-century caricaturists. And I hope I have quite often managed to insult the five prime ministers – Major, Blair, Brown, Cameron and May – who at the time of writing are still alive. As for the dead, I thought I would mock them for their folly and impotence.

While reading Victor Sebestyen's recent life of Lenin, I was reminded of Karl Marx's observation in *The Eighteenth Brumaire of Louis Napoleon*, published in 1852:

> Men make their own history, but they do not make it just as they please; they do not make it under circumstances chosen by themselves, but under circumstances directly found, and given and transmitted from the past. The tradition of all the dead generations weighs like a nightmare on the living.

The first part of this is true, but the longer I worked on the lives of the prime ministers, the more absurd I found the second part – the idea that tradition weighed like a nightmare on them.

Tradition constrained them, but it also enabled them to flourish, and to be themselves. They are so different from each other that it does not occur to historians to describe one of them as being the same as another. If anything, their individuality flowers under pressure. They are liberated by tradition, and at their best attain a kind of candour about what the nation needs. The greatest of them – a list which includes Walpole, the two Pitts, Grey, Peel, Gladstone, Disraeli, Salisbury, Lloyd George, Churchill, Attlee and Thatcher – defined their times.

We have confused a decline in Britain's relative power in the world – a decline which from the end of the nineteenth century was inevitable – with a decline in our political tradition. There are always things wrong with our politics. Our leaders have glaring defects, for they are human beings. Grievances cry out for redress, and decades or centuries may elapse before the necessary action is taken. The need for the most notable reforms of the last three centuries – the abolition of slavery, say, or the extension to all adults of the franchise, or the introduction of universal health care – was proclaimed well before anything much happened.

Prime ministers have often failed. They have gone down in sorrow to the grave. But this does not mean parliamentary government has failed. For it is a system well adapted to human weakness. The feeblest prime ministers are soon removed, and even the strongest before long have to give way to new leaders capable of coping with changed circumstances.

Tradition, Michael Oakeshott observes in his great essay *Rationalism in Politics*, 'is pre-eminently fluid'. The traditions of behaviour and constitutional practice which enabled the prime ministers in this volume to be chosen, and also to be sacked, undergo constant modification. In 1924, the illegitimate son of a Scottish ploughman became prime minister. In 1979, the daughter of a grocer from Grantham entered 10 Downing Street, where she remained for almost twelve years. The story is never over, and one never knows what will happen next. As I lay down my pen, I cannot even be sure who will be prime minister when this book appears in March 2018, let alone at any later date.

But we can be sure that whoever is in Downing Street can somehow scrape together a majority in the House of Commons. That is a cardinal point which all concerned take for granted. In France, which Marx had in mind when he wrote the brilliant account quoted above, it could not be taken for granted. To Marx's malicious amusement, French parliamentarians had been routed by Louis Napoleon, the nephew of the great Napoleon, who seized power in the coup d'état of 2 December 1851. Nothing remotely comparable has taken place at Westminster since the seventeenth century, for we do not have, or want to have, a revolutionary politics, with the dictators it usually throws up. For us, the leap-to-glory style of politics is a threat not just to peace but to liberty.

In British politics there is usually a vast amount of talk about who ought to be the next prime minister, or who would be the least objectionable holder of that office. High-minded columnists sometimes lament this obsessive discussion of personalities rather than policies. The answer to their complaint is given by Canning on page 71 of this book: 'Away with the cant of "measures not men", the idle supposition that it is the harness and not the horses that draw the chariot along.'

Bringing the great manoeuvre known as Brexit to a successful conclusion will require in whoever is prime minister all the qualities (especially courage and luck) enumerated at the start of this volume. The settlement (if there is one) will be reached under pressure, and will be coloured by the temperament of whoever negotiates it. Europe has split the Conservative party as deeply and dangerously as the forgotten issue of tariff reform under Arthur Balfour, prime minister from 1902–05. The European question became so difficult for the politicians that they asked the people to answer it on their behalf. In the referendum of 2016, a bitterly divisive contest, the people voted to leave the EU, and hand control back to the Westminster Parliament.

So Brexit makes this book more timely, for the referendum outcome can be described as a declaration of confidence in our own way of doing things, or at least a declaration that we find it marginally less tiresome than having our affairs run from Brussels. Our own governments may not be much good, but at least we can get rid of them. The British constitution is imperfect, but not contemptible. The prime ministers who have guided our affairs over the last three centuries are likewise imperfect, but not, with a few exceptions, contemptible. At the same time as we decry our politicians, we can be proud of our parliamentary tradition, which entails never giving power to any individual for very long, and seldom in such measure that he or she is tempted to acts of heroism. The business of being prime minister is for the most part unglamorous, and instead of being disappointed to find it so, we should be delighted.

PRIME
GREA

FOR SALE

27. Earl of ABERDEEN
1852–5
28. Lord PALMERSTON
1855–8; 1859–65
29. Benjamin DISRAELI
1868; 1874–80
30. William GLADSTONE
1868–74; 1880–5
1886; 1892–4

31. Marquess of SALISBURY
1885–6; 1886–92; 1895–1902
32. Earl of ROSEBERY 1894–5
33. Arthur BALFOUR 1902–5
34. Sir Henry CAMPBELL-
BANNERMAN 1905–8
35. H.H. ASQUITH 1908–16
36. David LLOYD GEORGE
1916–22

37. Andre
19
38. Stanle
1923–4; 192
39. Ramsay
1924;
40. Neville (
41. Sir Wins
1940–5;